Steel Rail Educational Publishing
Copyright 1979 E.K. Shaw

Shaw, E.K.
There Never Was An Arrow
ISBN 0-88791-020-3 (paper) 0-88791-022-X (cloth)

This book is published with the assistance of the Ontario Arts Council.

THERE NEVER WAS AN ARROW

E.K. Shaw

Steel Rail Educational Publishing

Steel Rail Educational Publishing is incorporated without share capital and is run by the Steel Rail Collective.

The main thrust of Steel Rail is to search for and publish books written by Canadians, about Canada and the Canadian people's struggles throughout their history. The Press also publishes international titles of interest and value. Steel Rail is a house through which people can exchange ideas and publish materials that might not otherwise be published.

Steel Rail Educational Publishing
Toronto, Canada
1979

Printed and Bound in Canada
Charters Publishing Company Limited
Brampton, Ontario

 40

THERE NEVER WAS AN ARROW

WAS
AN ARROW

E.K. Shaw

Contents

Preface

February 20th, 1979 marks the twentieth anniversary of a unique Canadian event. At about 4 p.m. on the afternoon of February 20th, 1959, the author was one of 14,000 skilled workmen, technicians, engineers and supporting staff who learned over the public address system of the A.V. Roe Company that their services would no longer be required. The background of this absurd and unbelievable event was so unusual and the forces involved were so complex that the author began a search for information in an attempt to explain how and why it could happen.

The resulting study was undertaken under considerable difficulty and within a very limited time span. It was completed on April 30, 1959. It was never published but was privately distributed. In the almost twenty years since that study was produced there have been, from time to time, requests that it be revised and up-dated. Several current issues make this study relevant again. The fundamental Canadian conditions which contributed to setting the stage for this event and the wide-spread political and psychological effects resulting from it have greatly affected the rate and direction of our development since, as well as our role on the international stage. These conditions and these effects are very relevant to three issues now facing the Canadian people and their government:

Designer Jim Floyd with model of C-102, the first jetliner in North America and second in the world, which flew two weeks after the British Comet and nine years before the first U.S. Jetliner the Boeing 707.

Courtesy D. Rogers

the current search for a suitable foreign plane to re-equip the Canadian armed forces, the downward slide of the Canadian economy, and the search for national unity. These issues are not as unrelated as they may appear.

This book is based on the original study - an attempt to describe and explain an extraordinary episode in the history of Canadian industrial development. The episode was so bizarre and the behaviour of the government, the media and the Canadian people so unprecedented that it has no parallel in the economic or political history of any other country. This was the deliberate destruction of a large and technologically-advanced segment of Canadian industry, the dispersal of one of the most outstanding design and engineering teams on the continent, and the reduction to scrap of all its large research and development facilities, records and data, its complex equipment, and all of its finished and partly finished products, worth hundreds of millions of dollars.

Further delving into records revealed that there had been in Canada over a considerable period of time, many smaller but similar episodes. This particular episode was unique only in the size of the project and the manner of its destruction. In order to further explore the economic and political background in Canada which makes such behaviour possible, the author returned to university to study political science and economics, with emphasis on problems of economic development. The theories of past and present economists as taught at the University of Toronto shed little light on the real-life act-ualities of present-day industrial development and internation-al relationships and, even more specifically, on the reasons for Canada's continuing state of under-development. Too many of the accepted 'myths' remained unquestioned and vital factors which should have entered into the equations were ignored, either because they were 'unquantifiable' or because they were 'unmentionable' — in Canada.

After graduation, therefore, the author spent three years working in a newly-independent, developing former colony in Africa, where it was possible to see at first hand the problems faced by third world countries as they attempted to raise their level of development to meet the demands of the twentieth cen-tury. However, these countries were attempting to industrialize in the mid-twentieth century era of the multi-national enterprise, with no indigenous base of general skills, literacy, technology or specialized education; with the most minimum of infrastructure and of capital accumulation. The barriers they faced were different both in nature and severity from those faced by Canada in over one hundred years as a 'developing' nation. The contrast merely served to underscore the 'uniqueness' of the Canadian situation.

In the 1960s, Eric Kierans, Walter Gordon, Herbert Gray, Kari Levitt and others saw very clearly the direction in which Canada was heading and tried to persuade the government to take some small but positive steps towards a degree of political and economic independence. They lost out to the 'establishment' and to the apathy of the Canadian public. Since 1970, a number of studies have been made and books published by writers who were appalled at the degree to which Canada has lost her economic and political independence and the ease with which we have been conned into letting it be taken over. The neglect or hostility which their works have received indicates very clearly the extent of the takeover not only of our political and economic life but also of our attitudes and those of the opinion-makers who mould them; it demonstrates the extent to which Canadians have sub-consciously absorbed the many myths we have been sold concerning Canada's dependent position and why we must remain in that position. Outside of war, no other country has ever been taken over so completely by a foreign country; and she has been a 'consenting adult' to the take-over.

The author worked in the aviation industry for nineteen years, first at Noorduyn Aviation in Montreal, then at Victory Aircraft and at A.V. Roe in Malton and is therefore able to contribute first-hand knowledge and experience of the events described. This episode, because of the magnitude of its impact on Canadian economic development, then and since, and because of the curious manner in which it was carried out, illustrates in a most extraordinary way the findings of many of these studies.

Many of these authors have attempted to analyze the process through which this dependence has occurred, the indigenous Canadian interests which have facilitated it, the forces which have orchestrated it and have reaped the benefits. Their research has reinforced the author's own analyses. The author has drawn heavily on the mass of evidence and data which has been accumulated by these writers and acknowledges her debt to Philippe J. Brossard, author of *Sold American!*, to J.J. Brown, author of *Ideas in Exile*, to D.W. Carr, author of *Recovering Canada's Nationhood*, to Wallace Clement, author of *The Canadian Corporate Elite* and *Continental Corporate Power: Economic Linkages between Canada and the United States*, to Brian Cuthbertson, author of *Canadian Military Independence in the age of Superpowers*, to Kari Levitt, author of *Silent Surrender: the Multinational Corporation in Canada*, to Jon B. McLin, of Alabama University, author of *Canada's Changing Defence Policy, 1957-1963*, and to the Government of Canada for its very useful publication *Foreign Direct Investment in Canada*, one of the few informative studies on this subject made available by the government. Particular mention must also be made of magazines such as *Canadian Aviation*, *Wings* magazine, and the American publication *Aviation Week*, with special reference to articles published by the first two magazines in their special issues of 1978, which give detailed histories of the aviation industry in Canada and an analysis of Canadian procurement policies with respect to military aircraft since 1958. None of the above authors or publishers has had any part in the writing of this book and may or may not share the views expressed herein.

The author appreciates the assistance of the staff at the National Library and National Archives and of the Ottawa and Metropolitan Toronto Public Libraries for their help in locating records and papers, of Statistics Canada and the Conference Council in Canada for statistical information and wishes to thank the many former colleagues and interested friends who have assisted with documents, data and other information and who have helped to trace former colleagues who are now scattered throughout Canada, the United States and elsewhere. Their support and assistance is gratefully acknowledged, with special thanks to Bill Fitzakerley, Irv Liss, Dick Littleboy, John Marshall, Ross Richardson, Gerald Saunders, Bryan Wood, Stan Curtiss, Don Rogers and Ivan

Schlegel.

Susan Crean of CBC, Al Rankin of Canadair, Les Wilkinson, curator of the Aviation Historical Society, E.G. Salmond, formerly of *Aircraft* magazine, John Painter of Hawker-Siddeley, and Greg Stewart, writer, provided pictures, information and other assistance. Ciarla Decker provided technical assistance and Gail Dexter helped the author through the editing and publishing process.

Wayne Ralph, editor, *Wings* magazine, and Irving Liss, formerly with A.V. Roe, provided information and comments on certain technical matters of design and electronics.

The author acknowledges the assistance of the Ontario Arts Council. The author owes a debt of gratitude to those mentioned as well as to the general assistance of many others. The author alone is, of course, wholly responsible for opinions and errors contained in the book.

E.K. Shaw, Ottawa.
November, 1978.

Introduction: The Myth-Makers

In order to understand the events which are the main subject of this book, it is necessary to understand Canada's situation with respect to the political and economic power structures that have developed on the North American continent. It is also necessary to inquire into the indigenous institutional factors which made possible over the past one hundred years a pattern of development in Canada which was not in any sense inevitable, contrary to the myths which we have so skilfully been persuaded to accept without really questioning their validity. These myths have been carefully fostered by a complex of groups and institutions who have profited immensely by rationalizing our situation and persuading us that it is inevitable.

There is the myth, one of our earliest economic myths, that Canada derives a comparative advantage from relying on a 'staple economy'.[1] Use of a country's staple natural products is usually regarded elsewhere as being merely the first stage of development on which to base a more developed economy. But the myth tells us that Canada does not have the ability or capacity to move on to the second stage of industrial development, in spite of her wealth of resources and skills, while other countries move past her into first the industrial and then the technological stages.

The second myth, propounded by historian A.R.M. Lower, contends that Canada is a 'geographical absurdity', attempting to develop along east-west lines over great, thinly-populated distances, instead of along the lines of 'natural north-south flow'.[2] There is no economic logic in the argument that development must follow certain directions of the compass. In Canada's case, it would simply represent, as elsewhere in the world, the pull of an economic metropolis exerted on a less developed hinterland, and would serve to accentuate Canada's condition as a source of raw materials for the southern economy.   John Deutsch, our eminent Canadian economist carries the theme even further. He has described Canada as "a large empty land, empty of people, capital and skills."[3] Immured in their ivory towers, perhaps these good Canadian scholars are not yet aware that modern transportation and technology in Canada as elsewhere have largely overcome the problems of distance and that, in any case, the pull of trade with much of the world is in an east-west direction. The impressions of empty space are derived, not from the actual geographical dimensions of Canada, but from the thin concentration of population along the southern border which creates its own problems. However, that concentration was not necessarily inevitable either, and may be a result rather than a cause; so also may be the lack of growth in population.

The third myth contends that we lack the technological and managerial skills necessary for indigenous development and entrepreneurship, implying that these are capacities which Canada is not capable of developing, as other nations have done, by a process of experience and growth, but which must be there, full-blown, from the very beginning or not at all.[4] No one asks why Canada, alone, of all the modern countries in the world should not have been able to develop these skills. Belief in such a myth would have provided little hope for recently-developed or developing countries which have faced much greater difficulties than Canada, without her resources, educational background or opportunities. Yet the Wahn Committee Report, commissioned by the government, stated that: "The levels of Canadian technological, management and entrepreneurial skills are inferior to foreign capabilities."[5] There is much evidence that this is not necessarily true, other things being equal. Other things not being equal, the suspicion exists that this is an end result, not the cause of our situation.

A fourth and dangerously pervasive myth is that Canada is too small and too poor to develop her own resources and industries, a theory which leads to the conviction that the only alternative to creating and directing our own sources of capital is the complete sell-out of the country to foreign ownership. This myth has been rejected by countries smaller either in size or in population or both, and with almost no resources of their own except a willingness to work and faith in their ability to succeeed, supported by their own government and financial institutions. Perhaps these are the resources most lacking in Canada. The constantly reiterated need for foreign capital will be considered later.

Then there is the myth of the overpowering neighbour, fostered by the intense penetration of Canada by U.S. culture and media, which has led to an adulation of American achievements and contempt for our own. This myth is constantly reinforced even by our Canadian media, our academics and government. It is maintained by the almost total lack of any general public knowledge of a long series of outstanding Canadian achievements. There would appear to be a conspiracy to suppress all mention of any Canadian developments or breakthroughs, except, recently, in the fields of the arts and literature. As a result of the general ignorance concerning a long list of outstanding Canadian achievements, the myth becomes credible in the minds of Canadians.[6]

This is closely related to the myth that Canadian nationalism is absurd and naive. It would be difficult to find any other nation in the world which would accept this peculiar proposition, least of all the United States. In studying history, we applaud the courage of the Spartans in resisting the power of neighbouring Athens, or of the countries in Eastern Europe who fought against the power of the Holy Roman Empire. We honour the Czechs who resisted the takeover of their country by their powerful neighbour, Germany. We admire the Polish people who have resisted the influence and coercion of their mighty neighbour to the East and who have struggled to maintain their independence. But in Canada, to suggest that one is a Canadian nationalist, to even whisper that one believes that

Canada should be an independent country is to be dismissed as not quite sane, or even to be some kind of 'kook'. Is it because the conquest has been so subtle, so insidious, achieved gradually and over a long period of time, that we have not noticed, or have become used to it; or is it because we have been conned, not from outside, but from within our country?

In examining the validity of these myths, it would be well to ask first whether they arose out of our actual situation, or whether, in fact, our present situation is the result of the skilful propagation of these myths so that among other things, they have made us acquiesce in the almost total control of our economy, along with our political decision-making, by a foreign power. According to Mitchell Sharpe, former Minister of External Affairs: "The Canada-U.S. relationship affects virtually every aspect of Canadian national interest, and thus, of Canadian domestic concerns."[7] Canada is in the midst of a growing economic crisis, with a mushrooming national debt, a rapidly deteriorating balance-of-payments deficit, inflation, unemployment, and a loss of world confidence in our economic management as expressed in our declining dollar. It is therefore important to examine this relationship, since without understanding where we are, and, above all, why, it is futile to attempt an analysis of any event of either national interest or domestic concern. In the process, we may also shed some light on the origin of the myths.

---

1   *cf.* Carr, D.W., *Recovering Canada's Nationhood*, Canada Publishing, Ottawa, 1971

2   Carr, *op. cit.*, p. 23; *cf.* Lower, A.R.M., *Colony to Nation,* Longmans, Toronto, 1964

3   Carr, *loc. cit.*, citing John Deutsch's Brief to the Wahn Committee

4   Wahn Committee, *Eleventh Report of Standing Committee on External Affairs and National Defence, respecting Canada-United States Relations*, Second Session, 28th Parliament, Ottawa, July, 1970

5   Carr, *op. cit.*, pp. 26-7

6   Brown, J.J., *Ideas in Exile*, McClelland & Stewart, Toronto, 1967

7   Sharpe, Mitchell, "Canada-U.S. Relations: Options for the Future," *International Perspectives*, Vol. 1, No. 4, Autumn, 1972.   Mitchell Sharpe is former Minister of External Affairs.

Chapter I
Canadian Politico-Economic Development

Canada's chief role as a colony, was to act as a source of primary resources and raw materials. Her financial institutions served as go-betweens for the extraction and export of Canadian resources and the markets for these resources in Britain and the continent. These financial institutions were centralized and closely integrated with the small, closely-knit groups — the Family Compact, the Chateau Clique and the Maritime Establishment, who governed Canada.

Even when Canada's ties of trade with Britain began to weaken, the interests of these groups remained fixed on commerce. They did not assume the more active and positive role of developing the new country, supporting Canadian entrepreneurs or financing Canadian enterprises. They channeled Canada's considerable capital into a narrow area of traditional development: transportation, utilities, mining and newsprint development, investments which were closely related to the extraction and export of raw materials. Surplus capital was largely directed into established American corporations to the south. Their criteria were safety of investment and security of profits.

Canadian governments adopted the attitudes of the financial community. They failed to develop new economic policies to direct Canada's new trade patterns in such a way as to provide opportunity for indigenous growth and development. Manufacturing enterprises, to serve either domestic or export markets, received little support, although these undertakings lead to the greatest development and provide the highest employment. It was easier to continue to strip off the country's natural resources and export them without even preliminary processing.

The U.S., by contrast, had already developed as a diversified economy. Supplementing a small group of eastern commercial banks at the turn of the century were over nine thousand autonomous local banks that collected available capital and savings and used them to support regional growth and the development of local manufacturing enterprise. By 1910, there were twenty-five thousand banks spread across the U.S. but only eleven in Canada, all with head offices located in the east. The rest of the country was served only by branches that had little discretion in matters of loans or financing for local industries. Such requests were usually vetoed by the remote eastern head office. Canadian savings, which were relatively high, were not channeled into Canadian growth industries, which continued to be starved for development capital. This, along with Canadian government apathy, created a vacuum into which U.S. capital began to move.

American demands for raw materials for its rapidly growing industries, the need for markets not inhibited by tariff barriers, and the new theory of a continental market all stimulated the movement of U.S. capital into Canada. It was, at first, directed mainly into extractive industries to feed U.S. factories with raw materials, but was gradually moved into certain sectors of manufacturing such as automobiles, electrical and rubber goods, chemicals and related fields. Geographically, it was concentrated largely in southern Ontario and southwest Quebec, close to American parent companies, at the expense of more northerly, more rationally distributed development.

Canada opened the doors very wide. As early as 1900, at least 95 municipalities were offering incentives and bonuses to U.S. firms to move in; Canadian manufacturers, unable to find domestic capital for development or expansion, invited them in to undertake joint ventures or to go into partnerships.

American capital flowed in, but with a very big string at-
tached, the string of equity ownership and control. The U.S.
firm, supported and financed by the parent company, by U.S.
financial investors and, in many cases, by Canadian financial
houses as well, usually ended up by owning the business.
Development and ownership of patents and technology were
often a means of obtaining controlling ownership of a
Canadian business.

For instance, the McLaughlin Motor Car Company was
established in Oshawa in 1907 by Col. R.S. McLaughlin who
had acquired the Canadian rights to manufacture the Buick
car. By 1914, General Motors and McLaughlin shared ownership in the company, with McLaughlin owning the slightly
larger share. By 1918, General Motors of Canada, wholly-
owned by the U.S. parent, owned both companies. Earlier, in
1904, Gordon M. McGregor, carriage-maker, had suggested to
Henry Ford that Ford cars be manufactured in Canada.
McGregor raised the necessary capital in Canada and the
United States. Ford and stockholders in the U.S. Ford Motor
Co. were given a controlling interest of 51 percent *in return for
patents, drawings, and Henry Ford's services.*[1] For many
Canadian firms who could not find capital in Canada, it
became a choice between selling out to a U.S. firm or going
bankrupt. By 1913, Canadian bankruptcies reached a rate of
75 percent, twice the American rate. Much of the increase in
U.S. ownership therefore represented, not new enterprises but
merely the take-over of existing Canadian ones, starved for
lack of access to Canadian capital.

Successive Canadian governments, tailoring their policies to
suit those of the financial sector, also aided the growth of
foreign ownership. Incentives, bonuses, tax and other benefits
favoured foreign, largely U.S.-controlled industries in
preference to Canadian entreprises. Provincial governments
competed with each other to attract additional branch plants.
Seventy-five years later, this pattern has not changed; it has
accelerated. Indigenous enterprise and entrepreneurship is still
being forced to give up and sell out to American buyers who
always appear able to obtain financing from the same
Canadian banks which refuse to finance the Canadian company, even when they can point to growing markets or export

development, both signs of successful enterprises. In other cases, Canadian firms are forced to sell out because of punitive Canadian tax laws and succession duties.[2]

One of the most widely-accepted Canadian myths is how lucky we are to have a friendly neighbour along our four-thousand-mile undefended border. After the war of 1812, the Americans largely gave up the idea of taking over Canada by force. By 1912, they knew they didn't have to.* Why break down the door when it is wide open and you are invited in to take over? That 'undefended border' has been no bar to economic invasion. The U.S. has been much luckier than we have in the choice of neighbours: they have one who is good-natured and stupid. Like Gulliver, we have been bound, gagged and tied hand and foot, while the myth lulled us to sleep.

The most disastrous concept has been the universally accepted and unquestioned myth that Canada must have 'foreign capital' in order to develop industrially. This conflicts somewhat with the 'staple economy' concept, but no matter; we have accepted both. Our governments, our financial houses, our American corporations, all tell us that this takeover is good for Canada since we are 'too poor' to develop our own industries and resources. They point out that even the United States used large amounts of foreign capital when they were building up their utilities, transportation and infrastructure, and opening up the west. True! But before applying it to Canada, one must look behind the argument. In the first place, the argument refers to an early stage of development when costs of putting the infrastructure in place were enormous, and development had not yet begun to generate its own internal capital. Canada as well as the U.S. should have long since passed that stage. Secondly, one must ask what *kind* of foreign capital has been used to develop the United States and Canada, and why the results have been so disastrously different. Proponents of this myth are well aware that there are two kinds of foreign investment. The effects of

---

* After the signing of the Anglo-Japanese Treaty, plans were drawn up by the United States for a possible war against Britain, with Canada as the main target. Although the Treaty lapsed in 1921, these plans were not destroyed until six months before Munich.[3]

the differences between the use of 'loan capital' and 'equity investment' are so great that they should be given quite different and distinctive names so that no one could become confused by a general reference to 'foreign investment'.

Early North American development made use of huge amounts of 'loan capital', obtained from Europe, chiefly Britain. In effect, the United States and Canada borrowed the money, used it to construct the railways, canals, power generating systems, and utilities needed to open up the countries and to support secondary development. The loans were paid back over time, out of increased profits from prosperity and trade. The lenders got back the loan with interest, while Canada and the United States retained ownership and the right to all future profits.*

However, when American capital began to move into Canada, first into the extraction industries and then into manufacturing, its owners were not satisfied with the interest on 'loan capital', except on such guaranteed investments as government bonds and utilities. They could obtain much larger profits and, more important, the *control* to be derived from 'equity investment', that is, the ownership of part or all of an industry in return for their capital investment. In the case of equity investment, the enterprise becomes theirs, not ours; the control as well as the profits acrue to the investor.

We cannot pay back the original investment out of profits and use future profits for our further development or expansion, because the foreign investors own the business and all future profits are theirs. They control the location of the enterprise, the nature of production, the use of resources and the extent of Canadian processing, the development or restriction of exports, the extent of research and development, the decision whether to import from the parent company all component parts, technology and management, or to develop a network of sources in Canada which would open the door to indigenous enterprise and employment, and the option whether to expand the enterprise or to shut down the branch plant and transfer its activities to the United States or elsewhere as International

---

* An exception was certain small eastern railways, including the Grand Trunk Railway, which were partly financed by 'equity capital'. The shares were held in London. Everyone who knows the history of the CNR debt knows what it has cost us to buy back the equity in *that* decrepit railway.

Nickel of Sudbury is now doing, assisted by Canadian government funds. In other words, 'equity' or 'direct' investment, gives the foreign investor control over the direction of Canadian development, production and trade, among other things.

There is no modern western country except Canada which does not impose restrictions over the extent of direct foreign investment, and limitations on the way it may operate. No other country has anything approaching the degree of foreign ownership and control to be found in Canada — not even the eastern satellite countries, and they at least put up a fight.

By the end of the First World War, the type of foreign investment as well as the source had changed radically. In 1914, foreign investment in Canada amounted to just under four billion dollars, but two-thirds of this was in the form of loan capital, largely debt securities from London markets. But even then, Canada "had more U.S.-controlled manufacturing plants than any other foreign nation."[4] By the end of the war, five years later, the U.S. had replaced the U.K. as the major supplier of capital. U.S. *direct* investment in Canada had increased by 32 percent. By 1935, there were 1,350 U.S.-controlled companies. These included 200 of the largest firms, capitalized at over $1 million each. Over half were engaged in manufacturing and the balance in merchandising, pulp and paper, mining and smelting. President Wilson reportedly said : "There is nothing in which I am more interested than the fullest development of the trade of this country and its righteous conquest of foreign markets."[5] But between 1926 and 1929, the five leading U.S. aircraft companies set up branches in Canada as "part of the industry's *domestic* expansion."[6] Clearly, by 1935, "U.S. businessmen regarded Canada as part of the domestic (U.S.) market."

The Second World War put great demands on Canada's industrial development. With Britain and Europe being heavily bombed, some sectors of production were moved to Canada. Among these was the production of the huge four-engine Lancaster bomber. During the war, production in Canada rose by over 140 percent. From 1939 to 1945, Canada's average annual growth rate was 23 percent. The government spent $15 billion on war supplies and invested $900 million in Crown

Corporations, usually to fill gaps which the private sector would not undertake.*

C.D. Howe, then Minister of Munitions and Supply, stated during the war, that "foreign investors are treated the same as domestic investors."[8] The Foreign Exchange Control Board even issued special licences to U.S. subsidiaries to facilitate transfers of funds between themselves and their parent companies in the United States. Over 4,200 companies were allowed accelerated amortization on their capital investments (as U.S. oil and gas companies now are). Alcan alone, on just one project, realized $164 million from this source. Of all those employees engaged in manufacturing, 60 percent were engaged in defence production.[9] By the end of the war, Canada's work force had achieved a high level of technological and production skills. Markets for consumer products were large and growing. Conditions were ripe for an indigenous industrial take-off, if we had the national will to mobilize our resources and take advantage of it.

In the U.S., plants built during the war under contract for 31 major corporations alone, at a cost of $7 billion, were sold back to the companies at a fraction of their cost and efforts were made to convert wartime production to consumer goods.

Canada also was left with empty plants and rising unemployment but, by 1947, had been able to sell or lease $107 million worth of plants to private industry, generally at about one-- third of their original construction costs. Many were taken over by U.S. firms, as was the plant of the former Canadian Vickers, renamed Canadair, in Montreal.

By 1950, the outbreak of the Korean war created shortages of raw materials in the U.S. and their world-wide search for these materials was accelerated, especially in Canada. The post-war U.S. Paley Report *Resources for Freedom* identified 29 key

---

* An example is the Polymer Corporation set up in Sarnia to produce butane, a synthetic rubber. Private industry would not risk their assured wartime profits on a high risk project, especially one not based in the U.S. When Polymer later became highly successful, earning large returns through export markets developed as a result of its active research and development teams, the private sector clamored for its sale to private enterprise. Apparently it is all right for government to invest taxpayers' funds in a risk venture but highly improper for it to pay a profit on the venture. Polymer was eventually sold to the Canadian Development Corporation which was established by the government primarily as a means of divesting itself of Polymer.[7]

commodities essential to U.S. industrial and defence requirements. Canada was mentioned as a major source of twelve of them.[10] From 1946 to 1955, 70 percent of all U.S. direct capital investment in Canada went into petroleum products, mining, and pulp and paper. Canada replaced Latin America as the major centre of investment, since Canada offered a "more suitable investment climate."[11] From 1945 to 1957, foreign control of manufacturing in Canada increased from 35 percent to 56 percent, and of mining and smelting, from 35 percent to 70 percent. Clement states that "Nowhere and at no time (except by military conquest) has the increase in control from outside been so rapid as it was in Canada following the war."[12] Canada opened the door to foreign takeovers and offered incentives to U.S.-owned corporations which gave them considerable advantages over Canadian enterprises. Canada offered the advantage of stability and accessibility in every sense.

As one American executive stated in 1946, U.S. foreign investments had not, in general, been very profitable "except for those in Canada, which I do not regard as a foreign country".[13] Canadian political and financial managers apparently agreed. By letting the U.S. take over and control our industries Canadian indigenous capital investment could again be limited to demands of the traditional corporations, or directed into investments in U.S. securities. However, as far as Canada is concerned, this is a static role; it provides little growth, relatively low profits and few jobs for the capital involved. It leaves Canada far behind in modern technological developments and innovations. Canadian demand for high-technology products had vastly increased since the days when the export of unprocessed raw materials or wheat could pay for the relatively simple and limited manufactured goods we imported. This system, however, complemented U.S. industrial development, their employment and profit needs, and allowed them to fill our markets with their manufactured goods. In spite of the obvious lack of control over our choice of manufacturing industries, or over the direction of our production into competitive or distinctive export goods, and in spite of the huge cost of imported parts, components, technology, management and other fees paid by our branch plants to their parent plants, no one mentioned the balance-of-payments problems we were storing up for the future.*

According to Pierre Bourgault, "Our pride in being a trading nation must be tempered by the realization that we excel [only] in the sale of those products which most developed countries want, on which they impose no tariffs and which they use to make products for sales abroad, thus creating jobs for their citizens." So do Ghana, Zaire and Zambia; but even these very young countries are trying to produce at least some of their domestic needs, in order to reduce the cost of their imports. But Canada imports back, "in more science-intensive forms" the same raw materials that it exports, and at much higher costs.[14] Exports of raw materials and of jobs are a poor exchange.

The *Toronto Star* in 1976 pointed out that "We import more manufactured goods per person than any other major nation: twice the European average and four times the American [average]." In 1975, Canada imported $10 billion more manufactured end-products than it exported".[15] By 1977, the deficit had risen to over $11 billion.

Since 1957, U.S. direct investment has steadily increased. In the two years 1971 and 1972, it increased by 6 percent per year and, in 1973, by 11 percent, or a whopping $3.3 billion. However, this no longer represented a flow of foreign capital into Canada. From 1946 to 1967, only 22 percent ($725 million) represented foreign capital; it fell to 19 percent by 1967. According to Kari Levitt, the percentage was steadily decreasing. She states that "over the years 1957 to 1965, 85 percent of the funds used to expand U.S.-controlled industry in Canada was provided from Canadian domestic savings, ... 73 percent from retained earnings and depreciation [allowances]**, a further 12 percent from other Canadian

---

* Purchases made in the U.S. by American branch plants in Canada account for 75 percent of Canada's cross-border trade with the U.S. Even a partial reduction in this outflow would help to correct our balance-of-payments deficit. But, with rare exceptions, these corporations do not purchase components, supplies or support services from Canadian suppliers. The effects of this policy are evident in the fate of the Canadian auto parts industry under the Auto Pact agreements. The U.S.-owned auto manufacturers in Canada now simply buy in bulk from the U.S. suppliers who supply the parent companies in the U.S.

**From 1946 to 1964, retained profits alone of U.S. subsidiaries, totalled $5.2 billion.

sources, and only 15 percent from the United States.''[16] Data released by the U.S. Department of Commerce put the amount even lower, showing new funds from the U.S. to have been only $127 million, or less than 5 percent of a total of $2,611 million in 1968, down from 10 percent in 1963. The balance was obtained from funds generated in Canada.[17] Using Canadian savings to supply from 85 to 95 percent of the capital, in the six years from 1963 to 1969, over 606 Canadian businesses were taken over by U.S. firms or about 100 per year. These included such large and important Canadian enterprises as Canadian Breweries, City Service Oil, Royalite, Pure Oil and Jefferson Lake Oil companies, as well as Bick's Pickles, Black Diamond Cheese, Clark Foods, Canterbury Foods, Versafood Services, Stedman Clothes, Holt-Renfrew, Simpson's mail-order division and hundreds of smaller companies. They also included Copp-Clark Textbook Publishers and Ryerson Press, including its Gage Textbook division.[18] Most of these firms were forced to sell out and were taken over because they had to buy their technology or patents abroad or because they could not find capital available in Canada. The U.S. takeover companies could find it here very easily.

In the mid-1960s, a Toronto firm, Morrison Brass, tried to raise funds for expansion from its Canadian bank, but failed. It was then sold to an American firm, Lukenheimer, U.S.A. The same Canadian bank immediately made capital available to the U.S. takeover firm. This situation has been repeated over and over in Canada. In some cases, after having refused funding to a successful Canadian company, the same branch of the same bank has tipped off a U.S. customer to the fact that the company might soon be up for sale and has sent the U.S. firm's representative over to offer to buy it out. The bank has then made available to the U.S. firm the Canadian funds needed for the U.S. takeover. A manager of a large U.S. publishing subsidiary, Van Nostrand, owned by Litton Industries, stated that he had no need to import capital from his parent corporation in the United States. The Canadian banks provide him with all he needs.[19] At the same time, it was announced that McClelland and Stewart, the last major remaining Canadian book publisher, was up for sale, as it had been unable to raise the capital it required in Canada. The firm was saved only by a grant from the Ontario government.

Brossard recounts many such cases, including the story of Bill Stroud, an inventor confined to a wheel-chair in McKellar, Ontario:

> Stroud developed a genuine 'breakthrough' kind of printing press. For a dozen years his company has been kept going with the greatest of difficulty but, because of the unavailability of development money, it has never grown as it should have. Unable to find the funds to build presses for sale in the U.S., and elsewhere, the Canadian company has had to license an American company to use its patents. The press is now being built and sold in the U.S., and it is the talk of the printing trade. Although in Canada the machine is known, appropriately and correctly, as the Stroud press, in the U.S., it is becoming famous as the Cameron Press, so named after the American company that is exploiting Bill Stroud's patents.[20]

According to Brossard, "Canadian financial institutions... compete eagerly to provide Canadian funds for the branch plant subsidiaries of American corporations, but the cash-box closes with a snap when a Canadian entrepreneur needs capital."[21] Brossard quotes example after example of Canadian entrepreneurs unable to obtain capital from Canadian sources for existing companies, for new inventions or for patentable products; but funds are made easily available to U.S. corporations to buy them out and, thereafter, unlimited funds are again available for production and marketing — under an American name, of course. Often the project in Canada is closed down and moved to the U.S. It would destroy the myth if Canadians ever found out that we really do not lack entrepreneurs, technological capacity or successful management. All we lack is a financial establishment which does not actively promote the U.S. takeover of Canadian firms, and which would reserve at least some small proportion of our large stores of Canadian capital for Canadian ventures; and a government that would make this possible.

At the same time as they were investing *Canadian* funds in Canada, U.S. firms took out of Canada, in 1968, $487 million *net;* in 1969, $611 million *net;* from 1969 to 1971, over $1 billion more than they brought in. At about the same time, from 1961 to 1967, $1,337 million was invested by Canadians to purchase U.S. securities or foreign-held Canadian securities. Altogether, over $3 billion of Canadian-generated capital was lost to Canada in the one year, 1968, or was used by foreigners to buy up more of our economy. Few countries need or would tolerate this kind of *foreign* investment.

For some time now, U.S. investment has represented, not an inflow of foreign capital, but an increasing net outflow, as well as the use of funds generated in Canada itself to buy out our country. Further, the takeover of existing and important Canadian enterprises at the rate of 100 per year represents no net gain or expansion, but considerable loss to Canada, except to the investment dealers who handle these takeovers. The percentage of firms entering Canada by buying up existing Canadian firms rose between 1958 and 1967 from 45 to 58 percent, "much higher than in all other countries entered by U.S. firms. The tendency was to take over existing Canadian firms rather than to open new ones."[23]

The government finally made a show of regulating these takeovers by passing the Foreign Investment Review Act. The U.S. was upset at this show of tentative control. According to *Weekend Magazine*, William Porter, former U.S. ambassador to Ottawa, "gave the world to understand that people in the United States were growing restless, even a trifle resentful, over Canadian handling of American economic interests. He was referring to such matters as the Foreign Investment Review Act and the purchase of foreign-owned potash holdings by the government of Saskatchewan!" With respect to the FIRA, Barron's *Financial Weekly* of New York commented that "It is difficult to imagine a legitimate business venture which would be impeded by the Foreign Investment Review Act...The only U.S. business which wouldn't be cordially welcomed to Canada is Murder, Inc."[24] Most people believe that the Canadian government exists to protect *Canadian* economic interests, but perhaps Ambassador Porter is more aware of the real situation than are most Canadians. Even a token gesture at control of our own economy calls for a reprimand from our foreign owner. But then, they "do not regard Canada as a foreign country." Canada is called on to give priority *to U.S. economic interests*, not to Canadian economic interests. A strange concept to come from the U.S., one of the most fiercely protective countries in the world where its own interests, and those of its corporations, are concerned.

The media control information and help to mould public opinion, the public opinion which makes possible this takeover and the control of Canadian decision-making. We are deluged by American radio, TV, magazines and news. No modern country except Canada reads more foreign magazines than domestic ones. But are our domestic ones any better? The best-known one, *Maclean's*, is published by Maclean-Hunter which depends for its profits on its specialized publications aimed at business and industry, most of which is foreign -owned. In order to do business, it must maintain the goodwill of this business community. Is *Maclean's* really independent? (We shall return to *Maclean's* magazine later, and the role it played in the Arrow debacle twenty years ago.) The daily press is largely owned and controlled by the U.S.-oriented financial community. Even our text-books are now published mainly in the U.S.; many of our university professors come from U.S. universities. We learn of our history and our society filtered through the American experience.

We are now generating enough net savings to meet our own development capital requirements; we are a net exporter of capital, but we are still wooing foreign capital as hard as ever, in spite of the fact that, *as a result* of foreign ownership, "the profits of our enterprise flow away from us in torrents".[25] It is largely Canadian-generated capital that is being used to buy us out. It is our unprocessed resources that are sent south to feed U.S. industry and to provide jobs in the U.S. It is our potential exports of manufactured products for world markets that are being curtailed through the refusal of U.S.-owned branch plants to compete with parent companies or to invest in research and development to develop innovative export products, rather than mere copies of American manufactured goods. If we owned and supported our own industries we could produce manufactured goods which would better meet not only our own specific domestic requirements but also the demands of foreign markets; products which often enough have been designed in Canada but have been stifled by Canadian suppliers of capital, since they might compete with U.S. exports or trading patterns. U.S. firms contribute little to our flow of exports, except through sales to parent companies. These are more than compensated for by purchases made by the branch plants from the parent companies.

It is our financial houses that refuse to make Canadian savings available to existing Canadian enterprises, or to provide venture capital for new ones, but will finance any takeover bid by an American. And it is our government that is so afraid of the big neighbour to the south that it has given up even a pretense of independence or control and is reduced to asking for 'special favours' when things get too bad. With leaders such as this it is no wonder that the separate regions are opting to go it alone - that the country is disintegrating. In its expensive promotion of 'national unity' the government has missed the point.

Canadian-U.S. relations have been examined here at length because it is important in the understanding of what happened to the Arrow 20 years ago to understand the full extent of U.S. control over Canadian resources, industries and institutions, up to and including government and finance. It is important to understand the extent to which the U.S. takes Canada's role for granted and attempts to prevent any change in a profitable pattern. It is important to understand where and through what Canadian agencies and institutions that control is effected and maintained. It is important to understand that U.S. investment in Canada did not occur to serve Canada's development; but to ensure that Canadian development serves U.S. needs, and does not threaten to compete in areas which the U.S. has staked out as its own monopoly.

In Cuba, under U.S.-supported Battista, only small unimportant service industries and the construction industry were left to the Cubans. When Cuba tried to use some of the large vacant estates owned by absentee land owners to develop a market garden industry to replace the expensive fruits and vegetables imported from the States, mid-Western U.S. farmers lobbied to prevent it.* Eventually, even the con-

---

* It is interesting to note that the Ontario Minister of Agriculture was recently reported as saying that preservation of the unique Niagara fruitlands was of little concern to him. We could always import our fruits and vegetables from

struction industry was taken over by American speculators and gambling interests, the sugar profits never left the New York banks, and there was no money left in Cuba for schools, hospitals or services of any kind to its own people. If anyone dared to protest, he could be found dead in the streets in the morning with his tongue cut out. Canada is a bit larger and has more articulate friends, but U.S. corporations and government treat Canadian interests with only slightly less contempt. We really can't blame the Americans; it is difficult for the Americans or anyone else to respect people who are afraid to stand up and who lack the courage to believe in themselves.

In the process of restricting and controlling Canadian development, the media, the economists, the academics, American corporate personnel in Canada, and Canadian financial institutions have done a massive job of mental persuasion. It is important that Canadians continue to believe the old myths: that we don't have the capital, the technological or management skills or the entrepreneurship to develop our own country. Again and again, individual Canadians and companies have proved them wrong, in spite of the institutional odds against them. Again and again, Canadian financial institutions or governments have been able to frustrate or destroy their achievements, or to force their sale to Americans. In most instances, news of their achievements is so completely ignored that most Canadians remain unaware of them. When the achievement—as with the Arrow—is too big to be suppressed, the captive Canadian media, dependent on the Canadian-U.S. financial/industrial establishment, steps in and does a hatchet job. Because it is so apathetic, so misinformed, so convinced that we can do nothing for ourselves competently, the Canadian public believes what it is told and helps to complete the job.

It is interesting to note that, while the Canadian academic world has sold out to U.S. dominance in everything from primary school text-books to university department heads, the media have fought hard to protect themselves from American

---

the United States more cheaply. Unlike Cuba we already have an unusually valuable and productive fruit-growing region in the Niagara peninsula. Unlike Cuba, it was not an American lobby which threatened to kill it, but the policies of our own provincial government. With protectors such as these, who can blame the Americans?

competition. Authors like Pierre Berton complain bitterly when their income is affected by the right of American publishers to dispose of residuals in Canada and call for government action. *Time* magazine was eventually deprived of its special privileges to protect Canadian magazines, chiefly *Maclean's*. Radio and television are protected from foreign takeovers, but, in spite of that protection, rely on an inordinate amount of American programming, rather than develop competitive excellence at home. Banks and financial institutions are also well protected, for what purpose it is difficult to understand, since they serve American investment needs both here and in the United States better than they serve Canadian capital requirements.

It is unfortunate that those who are so protected apparently do not realize that a country cannot survive on culture or on service industries alone. There must be a solid and prosperous industrial base to support that culture and those services; and some degree of respect for and pride in one's country. Otherwise why bother to promote Canadian literature or to support the national arts — or national unity? What is essential about a country's survival as a quaint culture if its technology, its economic development, its ability to control its national policy and direction have been taken over by a foreign country? Conquered countries have seldom been able to preserve their culture or their institutions unless they cared about their country more strongly than many Canadians do.

---

1 Clement, Wallace, *Continental Corporate Power*, McClelland & Stewart, Toronto, 1977, p. 60

2 Brossard, Philippe J., *Sold American!*, Peter Martin, Toronto, 1971. Brossard cites numerous examples of such forced sell-outs; the author knows of still more.

3 Cuthbertson, Brian, *Canadian Military Independence in the age of the Super-Powers*, Fitzhenry & Whiteside, Don Mills, Ont., 1978, p. 8

4 Clement, *op. cit.*, p. 64

5 *ibid.*, p. 66

6 *ibid.*, p. 70

7 Polysar Ltd., "The Polysar Story," *Annual Report*, 1972. Polysar is the former Polymer Corporation.

8 Clement, *op. cit.*, p. 85

9 *ibid.*, p. 82

10 *ibid.*, p. 84
11 Wilkins, Mira, *The Maturing of Multinational Enterprise*: *American Business Abroad from 1914 to 1970,* Harvard, Cambridge, Mass., 1974, p. 392
12 Clement, *op. cit.*, p. 83
13 Wilkins, *op. cit.*, p. 311
14 Bourgault, Pierre, *Innovation and the Structure of Canadian Industry*, Science Council of Canada, Information Canada, Ottawa, 1972, pp. 82-3
15 Clement, *op. cit.*, p. 86
16 Brossard, *op. cit.,* p. 28; *cf.* Levitt, Kari, *Silent Surrender*, Macmillan, Toronto, 1970
17 U.S. Dept. of Commerce, *Survey of Current Business*, Washington, Nov., 1970; cf. Brossard, *op. cit.*, pp.59, 146
18 Brossard, *op. cit.*, pp. 28-9
19 Interview with the author, and personal affidavit from former employee
20 Brossard, *op. cit.*, p. 58; *cf.* Brown, J.J., *Ideas in Exile*, McClelland & Stewart, Toronto, 1967, p. 148
21 Brossard, *op. cit.*, p. 95
22 *ibid.*, pp. 59-60
23 Clement, *op. cit.*, p. 88
24 *Weekend*, Mar. 12, 1977
25 Brossard, *op. cit.*, p. 111

Chapter 2
A New Kind of Development
I   The Jetliner

During the Second World War, Britain asked Canada to take on the production of the Lancaster bomber. This was one of the most successful designs of the war years. Weighing almost 20 tons, it flew faster than the Hurricane fighter. It was produced in a matter of months, rather than the usual four years. It was the brain child of designer Sir Roy Dobson, managing director of A.V. Roe Limited, in Manchester, England. From 1919 to 1945, he was responsible for 180 aircraft projects in England. In response to the British request, the Canadian government took over the National Steel Car facilities at Malton, renamed it Victory Aircraft and began production of Lancasters, eventually employing 10,000 workers, few of whom had ever worked on aircraft production before. They achieved a production rate of one Lancaster per day, producing a total of 422 Lancasters and some Lincolns in Canada, plus two almost-completed York transports, by the time the war ended. The one completed York and the remaining Lancasters were then mothballed. Employment dropped to about three hundred, working on small contracts for domestic products. All over the country, the government had idle plants on its hands and, as the troops came home, unemployment was rising.

The Hon. C.D. Howe, Minister of Munitions and Supply

Aerial view of Avro plant at Malton, Ontario.

Courtesy W. Fitzakerley

and of Reconstruction, was responsible for the disposal of war assets. Some plants were taken over by U.S. firms at a fraction of their construction costs. During the war, Dobson had visited Malton and had been much impressed by the way in which Lancasters were being produced. In the summer of 1945, he expressed an interest in purchasing or renting the Victory Aircraft plant. Because of currency restrictions, no money could be brought from England, but he suggested that half of any profits could be paid as rental. C.D. Howe was interested in the establishment in Canada of integrated facilities for the aeronautical research, design and development of civil and military aircraft, including the design and development of turbojet engines.* When the war ended in the Pacific, an agreement was reached and Avro Canada opened on December 1, 1945, as a subsidiary of Hawker-Siddeley of England, with Dobson as President, J.P. Bickell as Chairman of the Board and Walter Deisher, former head of Fleet Aircraft Ltd. of Canada, as Vice-President and General Manager. A young Canadian engineer, Fred Smye, became Assistant Vice-President and, later, succeeded to the position of President and General Manager. In order to open the plant, J.P. Bickell, former President of Victory Aircraft, guaranteed a loan for Dobson, of $2½ million. Until the mid-1950's, all profits were ploughed back into the company. Then the company issued shares to the Canadian public and, by 1957, 16 percent of the stock was held in Canada, the balance being held by Hawker-Siddeley.

Early in 1946, in consultation with James Bain, Chief Engineer of Trans-Canada Airlines (now Air Canada), design work began on a commercial jet transport, a trans-continental passenger carrier designed to specifications drawn up by TCA. Bain had been impressed, when in England, with the potential of the jet engines being developed there, and wanted to see TCA become one of the first airlines to operate jet transports. TCA placed a provisional order for 30 planes. Edgar Atkin,

---

* Inter-departmental correspondence dated Dec. 15, 1945, from Howe's office to Crawford Gordon who was then one of his assistants suggested that the aircraft company at Malton should be established to design and manufacture jet engines as well as planes, to provide a nucleus for a new industry in Canada. It was suggested that the company at Malton should be set up as a private company if A.V. Roe could be interested.[1]

The Avro "Jetliner" Derwent jet engines being wheeled into position prior to installation.

Courtesy D. Rogers

James Floyd and Stan Harper were recruited from the parent company as Chief Designer, Designer and Adminstration Officer, a nucleus around which to build up a truly Canadian company.

Speaking at the tenth anniversary of the founding of Avro Canada and referring to his decision to establish in Canada, Dobson said he had been told that he was taking an awful gamble. He said, "Well, I don't agree ... You see, here was the way I looked at Canada ... I saw a great country full of natural resources, all kinds of metals, all kinds of minerals and oil, all kinds of capacity for growing wheat and other kinds of food, and yet it seemed to me ... lacking in the finer engineering developments and the finer developments in things like aircraft, aircraft engines and so on. And I couldn't imagine ... a nation with this sort of potential carrying on without demanding — not just asking, or thinking about it, but *demanding* — its own aircraft, its own aircraft industry, its own engine industry and indeed a lot of other industries too. But of course I was an aircraft man and so I said, 'All right. That's my field. I'm going to have a go ... And so, well, we had a go.'" He concluded by saying, "Whatever the future holds for us, let's just pursue it and stick together and go forward. The future will only belong to Canada *if* Canada, the people of Canada, have faith in the destiny of Canada and work like blazes to make that destiny come true ..."[2]

When work on the Avro Jetliner began, no American company had, at that time, a jet transport even on the drawing boards. The British Comet was in the design stage, but it would be developed for a different market. The Jetliner was designed to be powered by two Avon JL65 engines of 5,000 to 6,000 lbs thrust, then being developed in England. When it was learnt that these would not be available in time, due to domestic military demands, which take precedence in any country, the plane was modified to take four Derwent engines of about 3,000 lbs thrust each. This involved considerable redesign and some increase in fuel consumption. It is always a problem to find the right engine at the right time for any new plane. It was a particularly difficult problem for Canada with no engine industry of its own. The Jetliner, whose design was begun in 1946, made its first flight in August, 1949 — just thirteen days after the British Comet and just 25 months after the design of the four-engine version had been begun.

In the United States, when an airline requires a new type of plane, its own engineers work closely with the manufacturer's designers. For instance, American Airlines' Chief Engineer had worked closely with Douglas on the flight development of the DC—3 and shared credit for its final design. The Canadian airline, buying its planes abroad, was not accustomed to working closely with the designers in the continuing process of design and flight-testing. When the Derwent four-engine modified design was presented to TCA, they came up with new requirements as to the number of passengers, cruising speed and range. The plane had been designed to TCA's specifications, which called for a 36-seat aircraft with a cruising speed of 425 miles per hour, a still-air range of 1,200 miles, with 500 miles as the longest leg requirement. The new requirements called for a 40-passenger payload, cruising speed of 500 mph, a still-air range of 2,000 miles, with a 954-mile distance between stops. Also, since the ILS, or Instrument Landing Systems, had not been fully developed at Canadian airfields, they called for much higher fuel allowances.[3]

When production of the plane was already well-advanced, the Department of Transport also came up with a revised set of requirements for jet transports. The reserve fuel capacities they called for so far exceeded those of any other airline that they have never been met or even required of any commercial airline, including TCA, even on trans-Atlantic services.* Their estimated performance data for the Jetliner was considerably below that of the company; it also differed greatly from the much more detailed studies later carried out by Trans-World Airlines in the U.S. TWA flight-test data confirmed that the Jetliner would fulfil their requirements for most of their routes; using their accepted fuel requirements, it would have a 940-mile range with 40 passengers. The new fuel requirements presented by DOT would have imposed heavy and unacceptable weight penalties on any aircraft. TCA had obviously lost

---

* On its Toronto to New York flight, the Jetliner required only 9,400 lbs of fuel. The new reserve requirements would have called for 20,400 lbs extra for a total fuel load of 30,000 lbs for this short flight.[4]

The Avro "Jetliner" Design began 1946. First Flight August, 1949.

Pilot Don Rogers accepting world's first jet airmail for delivery from Toronto to New York. Postmaster-General and postal employee look on.

Courtesy D. Rogers

interest in the project, and its option on 30 Jetliners was dropped months before the first flight. Howe ordered work on the second plane discontinued shortly after.

However, a number of airlines in the U.S. and Europe had shown interest in the plane as had the U.S. Air Force. At least two American airlines had placed options for twenty to thirty Jetliners, and funds were allocated for the production of 20 planes. Howard Hughes had the Jetliner flown to California and kept it and its crew there for a month while he flew and tested it and had his airline engineers do an exhaustive evaluation. Some of their conclusions were:

"The direct operating cost per seat mile of the Jetliner compares very favorably with that of TWA's present equipment, yet reduces current trip times by as much as 30 percent between major centres of population.

Although this analysis was conducted on a conventional aircraft flight plan, which puts the jet transport at a decided economic disadvantage, the Jetliner compares exceptionally well with modern propeller-driven aircraft on a cost per seat-mile basis.

By making certain changes in the flight plan ... the overall economic picture can be improved still further — without any sacrifice in safety.

The Avro Jetliner, powered by [alternative] P&W J-57 engines can operate safely and efficiently over every TWA internal route except New York/Los Angeles, non-stop.

The Jetliner's high cruising speed enables it to cut present scheduled operating times by as much as 30 percent. This is undoubtedly the Jetliner's major contribution to air transportation.

The 'Jet Power' aspect of the aircraft ensures consistently higher load factors through its passenger appeal. The absence of fatiguing propeller vibration, the smooth, swift flight and the initial novelty of jet travel, collectively indicate an attractive and profitable operation.

Existing runways, even at minor airports, are in most cases more than adequate for scheduled Jetliner operation. The approach speed of the aircraft is entirely normal. The simplicity of flying and handling the aircraft reduces problems in pilot training to a minimum.

The numerous flights conducted to date demonstrated that the Jetliner does not present any severe traffic control problems which some anticipated for it. The fact that it can, if necessary, be operated in a conventional manner in the traffic and holding pattern and still show a profit is indicative of its versatility.[5]

On a flight from Toronto to New York on April 18, 1950, the Jetliner carried the world's first jet airmail. The crew were given a ticker-tape parade through downtown New York and a banquet hosted by the mayor, along with top media coverage. The Jetliner's record-breaking flights at half the elapsed time of conventional scheduled flights were a milestone in aviation history. However, when Avro asked permission to go ahead with the modifications requested by the potential customers to suit their particular requirements, C.D. Howe flatly refused to allow them the use of any floor space at all for the Jetliner, and told them to move it out.[6] He told them to get on with the CF-100 fighter; to stop work on the Jetliner, and *to concentrate on military planes*. Both planes, at very different stages, could easily have been dove-tailed into production. In addition to using the Korean war as an excuse, Howe, now Minister of Trade and Commerce, said publicly: "You can't build a plane without orders," although he was well aware of the orders and potential orders on the books. Perhaps, since TCA had decided not to buy it, they did not want foreign competitive airlines to have it. Or perhaps there were other reasons.

Jetliner on the world's first airmail flight; Toronto to New York, April 18, 1950. The U.S. press was congratulatory. In the race to get a jetliner into the air, Canada won, hands down.

Courtesy A.V. Roe

One of the Jetliners was never finished. The remaining Jetliner was flown for eight years as a company plane in Canada and the U.S., setting records and collecting flight data, without any design defects showing up. TCA officials are rumored to have admitted later that the Jetliner was one of the best aircraft they had ever had a chance to purchase and one of the easiest and cheapest to maintain. This fast turn-around capacity had been one of the design criteria. TCA had meanwhile bought the North Star, a modified DC4-M, produced by Canadair, for its Caribbean flights. Later, in 1955 it purchased the British Vickers Viscount turboprop, developed some time later. Eight years after the Jetliner first flew, the French 'Caravelle', using the same Avon engines which had been intended for the Jetliner, was being sold to world airlines, the market the Jetliner had been designed for.

The total cost of designing from scratch, tooling up and production of two radically new aircraft, by a new company, was *under $9 million*. The Jetliner was successfully flown just over three years from the time design work was begun. Each new plane has a long life of improvement and upgrading of the basic design, through successive Mark numbers. This is evident in the successive models of the Douglas DC series, right up to the latest DC-10 model. Shortly before the Jetliner was cancelled, Avro personnel, including Jim Floyd, designer of the Jetliner, took Dan Beard of American Airlines on a series of test flights on the Jetliner. According to Floyd, Beard commented, "You've got a bloody good aircraft there. I reckon it could be the DC-3 of the jet age."[7] With this eight-year lead, Avro could by now have been one of the world leaders in the manufacture of civilian jet aircraft. By the time the company could have begun again, it was too late. It was up against a now-alert U.S. industry, every firm heavily sup-ported by government orders, or assured of purchases from their own airlines, a good economic basis from which to obtain orders from other countries. The American industry had been taking a beating from the American aviation press for having been caught so flat-footed by Canadian enterprise which flew their Jetliner while the Americans didn't even have one on the drawing-boards. However, they had profited from the lessons learned "during its route flying over the continent which helped to pave the way for eventual entry of the American jet transports into airline service a decade later."[8] And at least they were saved the humiliation of seeing Canadian-designed and produced jet planes flying on American airlines. C.D. Howe later received a medal from the American aviation industry for his "services to aviation."

On a certain Saturday, early in 1957, after eight years of flying, the Jetliner had come in for a routine check and to have a new nose-wheel fitted. Several months of flying programme were scheduled. When the staff came to work on Monday morning, they found it had been cut in two on Sunday night, in such a hurry that not even the equipment had been removed or the plane properly dismantled. No one knew who had ordered it, or why. The "first Jetliner on the North American continent" was quickly reduced to scrap. The Smithsonian Institute had once asked for it, but it was not even kept for our own Aviation Museum. Why?

Well, it may be pure coincidence, but the *Saturday Evening Post* which appeared on the stands a few days later, carried a two-page colour centrefold that proudly advertised the new Boeing 'Jetliner', the 707. It was described as "America's first Jetliner, the only American jet airliner flying today."[9] Today? There never had been another in the U.S. but, when that ad went to press, the Canadian Jetliner had been flying for eight years, was still flying and had a full flying schedule ahead of it. When the ad appeared on the newsstands, the Canadian Jetliner no longer existed except as scrap. The advertisement went on to ask, "Why is Boeing so far ahead in the field of jet airliners? Because it has more experience designing and building long-range jet aircraft than any company in the world. And because Boeing, *back in 1952*, had faith in the future of jet transportation, and began actual construction *of America's first jet airliner*."* Was so far ahead because it had faith in the future? The Canadian Jetliner was *flying in 1949*, when Boeing did not even have one on the drawing-boards! Along

---

*More correctly, they had received a government contract to construct a tanker plane. Its design was modified slightly to become the 707 jet transport.

with the rest of the U.S. aviation industry it was still saying jets were not feasible, and was caught flat-footed. Would Boeing and the U.S. industry have been embarassed if the Canadian Jetliner had still been flying as it had been for eight years ahead of them? Would it have threatened the U.S. near-monopoly of world airlines? Would its presence, even in a museum have been disturbing to them? Or would C.D. Howe have found it embarassing for Canadians to know that we had been far ahead of the Americans, but that we had missed out because he had ordered Avro to discontinue production?

Just two years later, a new Government would be accusing Avro of not having developed a civilian plane to fall back on! But that is another chapter.

II The CF-100

Shortly after work had begun on the design of the Jetliner, the RCAF began discussions with Avro for the design of a fighter plane and drew up specifications for a long-range, all-weather jet fighter to be powered by two jet engines and to carry two men, a pilot and navigator, to meet Canada's needs for defence in the far north and for her overseas commitments.

The RCAF knew from wartime experience the difficulties in obtaining the type of plane to meet Canadian defence requirements, without expensive modifications or, indeed, of being able to obtain any first line plane from another country while still first line. At the time, no aircraft existed in the U.S. or the U.K. which met Canada's requirements of speed, range and all-weather reliability. No engine existed to power such a plane. In any case, foreign engines of advanced design are even more difficult to obtain in the quantities required, if at all, especially in wartime. The U.S. was concentrating on single-engine, single-seater planes. For high speed jets and long northern patrols in Canada the RCAF required twin engines and space for a navigator. Detail design was begun in May, 1947. Tooling and manufacturing of prototypes and 10 pre-production planes was begun in January, 1948. These were to be completed on leisurely-spaced production dates.

In 1946, the government had been about to close down a small company called Turbo-Research which had been set up

SIZE COMPARISON
DC-10 vs DC-3

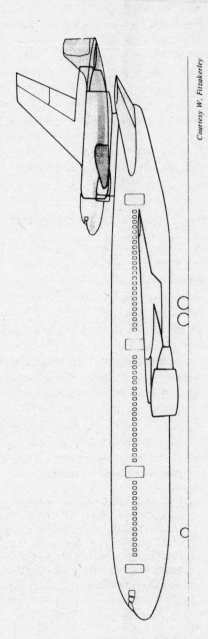

Courtesy W. Fitzakerley

in 1943 to do experimental design work on jet engines. It was suggested to Dobson that he get three others of the world's most famous aero-engine companies to go in with him to take over the company. When he approached the other companies they told him not to be a fool. According to Dobson they said that Canada had never built an engine, had never designed an engine, and never would. They said they could supply all the engines Canada would ever need. "Well", recalled Dobson several years later, "you can only imagine what I said to that. They didn't know the potential of Canada. But I think they know it now."[10] Avro bought the company and moved it and its engineering personnel to Malton. Work was continued on a small engine, the Chinook, and design studies were begun in April, 1947, for a much larger engine to power the CF-100. The first Chinook was successfully run on March 17, 1947. The first of the Orenda engines was test-run in February, 1949, and orders were placed by the RCAF for ten engines.

Government policy had been to establish a self-sufficient source of warplanes as well as of commercial planes. As James Hornick described it in October, 1951:[11]

"This meant developing radically new industrial techniques, setting up facilities to supply high-precision components, training not only a large working force within the Avro organisation, but counselling subcontractors whose only previous contact with aircraft was as passengers.

These were predictable prerequisites to the ambitious production program that was visualized. It was a back-breaking, time-consuming chore. To achieve self-sufficiency in aircraft production, Canada had to pay ... in time and money.

For the $50,000,000 invested to date, [Oct. 1951] Canada has acquired the foundations of a vital defense industry, invaluable experience in original aircraft and engine design, a hard core of skilled engineers and technicians, a plant full of scarce machine tools and two weapons of great promise, the Orenda and the CF-100.

Display model of Orenda Engine. *Courtesy Orenda Engines*

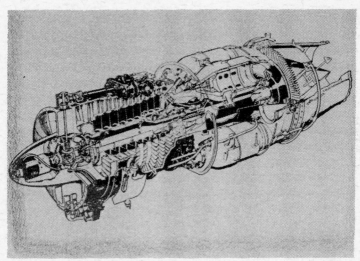

Cut-away view of Orenda Engine. *Courtesty A.V. Roe*

Experts from the United States and Britain have frequently expressed amazement at the technological strides of a company with only five years' background in the aircraft industry. They have been surprised, in comparing costs of similar undertakings elsewhere, and all that has been accomplished for $50,000,000.

Emphasis from the start was on design and development, not production. It was only in October of last year [1950] that Avro received the authorization to build production-line fighters for the RCAF. Originally, 10 pre-production models were to be completed on leisurely spaced delivery dates.

The Defense Department subsequently asked for 124 aircraft, to be delivered at the rate of five a month. Then it changed its mind. Deliveries were to be at the rate of 25 a month. Engines were to be built at the rate of 20 a month, then 50, finally 100.

Avro was totally unprepared for the assignment. It lacked forewarning, tooling and space. But the decision was made in Ottawa and on that decision was based a new concept of RCAF expansion....

RCAF planning proceeded on the assumption that Avro's production results would be as phenomenally successful as its miracles of design and development. The assumption was wrong.

Hornick forgot to mention that, in the years 1946-1949, Avro had also designed and produced from scratch the first jet airliner in North America and that it had flown in August, 1949.

It was only in October of 1950 that the government suddenly decided that the CF-100 should be put into full production at the rate of 25 per month. No such production rate had been previously suggested and no such production lines existed. To prepare for it required procurement of additional equipment, rapid tooling up, and hiring and training of additional workers. However, full production of the CF-100, first test-flown in January 1950, began late in 1952. After the outbreak of the Korean war it was decided to use the Orenda engine both on the CF-100 and on the older F-86 Sabre day-fighter, then being

Canadian Orenda turbojet engines were tested in the air in this converted Lancaster bomber. The Orendas are shown in the outboard engine positions.

Courtesy D. Rogers

produced under licence by Canadair of Montreal. The Mark 3 and Mark 4 versions of the Orenda engine were therefore redesigned to fit both the twin-engined CF-100 and the single-engine Sabre and to provide greater thrust and performance, and were moved into production. In 1949, as work on the first Jetliner neared completion, the first CF-100 and the Orenda engine were going into production. By the beginning of 1951, they were being produced at the rate of 25 airframes and 20 engines a month. Engine production was increased, first to 50 and then to 100 per month and, by June, 1954, the CF-100 was being produced at the rate of one per day.[12]

Production of the CF-100 and the Orenda engine in Canada was strongly criticized by the Conservative Opposition; but both the plane and the engine were very successful. They acquired a reputation for reliable performance in North America and Europe, where they were supplied at NATO's request. The CF-100 was the highest-rated, if not the only, truly all-weather long-range fighter in NATO. Because of its constant availability, Canada's NATO Division won the NATO gunnery competition against seven teams from five other countries, after also winning top trophies in the previous two years. The CF-100 had stolen all the headlines at the Farnborough Air Show in 1955. U.S. flier, Jacqueline Cockrane, set five world records in an Orenda-powered Sabre. While the cruising speed of the Sabre slightly exceeded that of the CF-100, the latter had a faster rate of climb: it could get up there faster and engage the enemy sooner.

Not only were the plane and the engine produced in less time than comparable U.S. or U.K. planes, they were also produced at less cost. The cost of each CF-100 delivered to the RCAF was approximately $100,000 less than the cost of a comparable U.S. interceptor. The delivery cost of the Orenda engine unit was approximately 10 percent lower than that of a comparable U.S. engine and 30 percent lower than that of a comparable British engine. The total cost of the CF-100 programme and production of 692 planes and spares was $450 million, or $650,290 each. The cost of the Orenda engine programme and production of 3,794 engines was $440 million, or $115,973 each. In addition, exports of both planes and Orenda engines

CF-100 production line at Avro plant, Malton, Ontario. Production reached 25 per month.

Courtesy A.V. Roe

to Belgium and other NATO countries earned $52 million in export sales for Canada.

When production of the Jetliner began, American suppliers and sub-contractors did not even bother to reply to requests from a Canadian company for bids on equipment. By the time the Jetliner and the CF-100 had flown, U.S. sales representatives came looking for business. Many opened branch plants and some even began to manufacture in Canada. When the first CF-100 flew, it had a high content of U.S.-made components and equipment; when the last Mark 5M was phased out in December, 1958, its Canadian content was over 90 percent. Similarly, in the first Orenda engine, U.S. content was over 95 percent; in the last ones, it was only 5 percent. The other 95 percent was Canadian content.

Avro followed a buy-Canadian policy and helped to build up a coast-to-coast network of Canadian suppliers and sub-contractors. Seldom, if ever, has a U.S.-controlled branch plant in Canada followed such a policy. Avro helped to build up new industries to design and manufacture in Canada everything from highly-specialized electronics equipment, to plastics, to machine tools, new metals and alloys, and equipment of every kind. Many of these firms had never before produced competitive, high-standard work of this type nor heard of working to ten-thousands of an inch. There had been little demand in Canada for high-precision work. Trained and assisted by Avro, many of them were, for the first time, able to bid on foreign contracts as well. Jobs were created in Canada, ranging from skilled shop workers to topnotch research, design and engineering teams. The Arrow programme later poured millions of dollars into the Canadian economy in the form of contract orders. For 1959 alone, these would have amounted to $25 million. Moreover, according to the *Financial Post*,[13] for every $100 million spent in Canada on domestic production, $ 65 million or more comes back to the government in taxes alone, instead of going out of the country. In addition to employees' wages spent in Canada on homes, furnishing, food and clothes, and the taxes accruing to the government, Avro also paid taxes on 16 percent of Toronto Township's assessment. These new developments created the

CF-100 with RCAF Squadron insignia.

Courtesy A.V. Roe

CF-100 in flight off coast of Britain.

Courtesy Don Rogers

basis of a growing network of high-technology secondary manufacturing in Canada, able to branch out and serve other Canadian industries and create new products for export. Canada was achieving world recognition. The slogan, "The twentieth century belongs to Canada" was beginning to achieve credibility.

III The Arrow

As the CF-100 was coming into production, the RCAF, knowing the lead time required to design, test and produce a new, more advanced plane, began to look ahead to a successor to the CF-100, to cope with the supersonic bombers the Soviet Union was said to be developing. They submitted specifications and design work began in the summer of 1950 on a more advanced plane, designated the CF-103. By the time detailed design had begun in 1951, the RCAF was aware that an even more advanced plane would be required and, in December, work was cancelled on the CF-103. The CF-100 was fitted with the more powerful Orenda Mark 4 engine to improve its performance while new specifications were prepared for a successor plane. In 1953, work was begun on the design of a radically new supersonic aircraft, to be known as the CF-105. Work was also begun on a new and more powerful engine to power the new plane as there was no such engine available elsewhere. Hawker-Siddeley of England put up the money for research and development of the new 'Iroquois' engine to have 20,000 lbs thrust and many new design features.

Two separate contracts were signed for the CF-105. The first covered the research, design, manufacture and flight-test programme for 5 research and test planes, to be fitted with the Pratt and Whitney J75 engines, for test purposes. The second was for 32 pre-production planes to be fitted with the much more powerful Iroquois engine; the engine would by then have completed its separate test programme. These were firm contracts. Further production orders were conditional on the results of the first two contracts. It was estimated that about 100 planes would be required to supply

Orenda jet engines are prepared for shipment to NATO bases in Europe.
Courtesy A.V. Roe

Jet engines after delivery in Germany.
Courtesy A.V. Roe

Canada's defence needs for the surveillance of our northern areas; and another 100 planes, to fulfill Canada's NATO commitments.

Normally, up to that time, when an aircraft company produced a new plane, it would first produce a prototype, a custom-made plane, before setting up an assembly line. The prototype would be exhaustively tested, faults discovered and all necessary design changes carried out; only then, when certain that it would meet its specifications, would the production assembly line be set up, complete with tools, jigs and fixtures. Avro decided to eliminate this expensive and time-consuming process through intensive preliminary research, design and model testing. Research and testing costs could be higher but this would be compensated for by later savings in months of time and labour which would reduce production costs on all succeeding planes. The first plane would come directly off a complete production line with further production models coming along behind. This had been attempted only once before. Convair tried it with the F102, designed to fly at Mach 1.5 or about 1000 mph. But when it came off the assembly line, its best speed was about 632 mph or Mach 0.95, less than the speed of sound.* The F102 had to be completely redesigned and the very expensive production line, tools, jigs, everything, dismantled and rebuilt. Even the CF-100, designed to be sub-sonic only, had so far exceeded its specifications that it had reached supersonic speed in a dive.

Avro gambled on the skills of its designers and engineers. An intensive research, design and testing programme began. New and stronger alloys and new methods of machining them were tested and developed. A special autoclave was installed to accommodate new methods of bonding large metal components. Avro was performing 70 percent of all research being

---

*Mach 1 is the speed of sound in still air on a "normal" day, that is, when the temperature is 519 degrees Rankin (59 degrees F.). Mach 1 is about 767 m.p.h. at sea-level. The formula for deriving the speed of sound in miles per hour is $33.7 \times$ square-root of t, where t is the temperature in degrees Rankin. Since the temperature decreases with altitude, the speed of sound also decreases with altitude. At 36,000 feet or above, Mach 1 is about 665 m.p.h. Since the best cruising speed for most jetliners is 40,000 feet, the Mach number is usually expressed in terms of miles per hour at 40,000 feet. At that altitude, a speed of Mach 2 is 1330 m.p.h.; of Mach 3 is 1995, or just under 2000 m.p.h.

Air Marshall W.A. Curtiss, Test Pilot Bill Waterton, Minister of National Defence Ralph Compney, A.V. Roe President Walter N. Deisher, with first CF-100 at Malton.

Courtesy Aviation and Space Division, National Musuem of Canada

done in Canada. One shop foreman alone had over forty Canadian patents to his credit. The results were being made available all across the country to suppliers and sub-contractors, as well as to U.S. aircraft companies. Most research done in Canada by branch plants, even when supported by Canadian grants, is patented in the name of the parent U.S. company and is then unavailable to other Canadian firms. It becomes an 'import cost' even to the Canadian branch plant. This was not so for Avro.

The pre-testing programme was extensive and thorough. A mock-up of the cockpit was built and tested by the test pilots to check visibility and instrument location under simulated flight conditions. To test the various aircraft systems, each complete system, electrical, hydraulics, air conditioning, etc., was mounted on its own test panel for complete testing of individual systems. Scale models of the complete plane were constructed for wind-tunnel tests. Free-flight models were constructed to 1/10 scale to simulate in every way the behaviour of the actual plane. Nike missiles were used to launch them from the north shore of Lake Ontario at Point Petrie. So realistic was their flight pattern that, on one occasion, they are said to have touched off a 'scramble' of U.S. fighter planes based in New York State. This part of the programme was later moved to the facilities at Wallops Island, Virginia, to take advantage of their more advanced telemetry equipment.

The Iroquois was the first engine to be designed with a fixed air intake able to operate from Mach 0 to Mach 2. The engine was tested at NASA (National Aeronautical Space Administration), at the NACA (National Advisory Committee on Aviation) Lewis Flight Propulsion Laboratory in Cleveland and at the high altitude engine test facilities at Tullahomo, Tennessee. It established records for the highest dry thrust ever recorded by a turbojet in North America, for highest inlet temperatures ever encountered in the tunnel without adverse mechanical effects on the engine, and for normal relights following induced flame-outs up to the 60,000 foot capacity of the tunnel. Demand for wind-tunnel time is so great, that time must be reserved in advance. Failure in the programme means going to the bottom of the waiting list. The CF-105 pro-

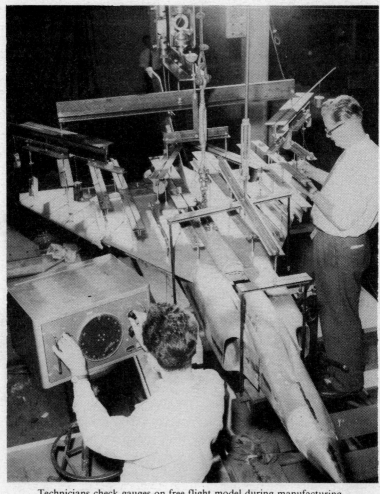

Technicians check gauges on free flight model during manufacturing.

Courtesy W. Fitzakerley

grammes were so well-planned that A.V. Roe never had a programme failure, something of a record.

Every phase of the test programme was monitored and a film record maintained of the production processes and test programmes.   Leading U.S. aircraft producers submitted many requests for the loan of these films. Avro designers and engineers were the first foreigners ever to be invited to visit certain aircraft firms in the United States. Teams from other countries toured the Avro plant to study the new processes and technologies. James Floyd, designer of the Jetliner, was the first non-American designer ever to win the U.S. Wright trophy for excellence in aircraft design.

On display at the Air Show in Dallas, Texas, in 1958, the Iroquois engine attracted great interest from the U.S. aviation industry and from the USAF. By the time the first Arrow was rolled out for flight tests, the results of the pre-production test programme and wind tunnel tests were well known to the U.S. aircraft industry and to the U.S. Air Force. By the time the first Arrow flew, they were well aware of the potential of both the plane and the engine. U.S. aviation magazines were giving it wide coverage, all of it favourable.

The first CF-105, the Arrow Mark I, was rolled out of the assembly bay on the afternoon of October 4, 1957. News programmes that morning had carried an account of the launching of the first Russian sputnik. Military men and the media, both U.S. and Canadian, had been saying for years that Soviet technology was far inferior to that of the U.S., that their repressive political system did not allow for excellence. On that bright, sunny day, those 'experts' were somewhat in a state of shock. The Hon. George Pearkes, the new Minister of National Defence, spoke at the ceremonies to the dignitaries on the platform and to the large crowd gathered on the tarmac. He suggested ominously that "the missile age" had arrived.

During the next several months, the first Arrow underwent extensive and thorough ground-tests. On the morning of March 25, 1958, the rumour went around that the Arrow was going to fly. The roof of one of the low buildings was a good vantage point and it was soon crowded with personnel. In the distance, along the runway, the Arrow came into view — a great, sleek, white bird, rapidly growing in size. As she approached, she lifted smoothly from the runway and was in the air for the first time. Cheers went up as she gained altitude. A few moments later the Arrow, piloted by Jan Zurakowski and accompanied by the chase planes, had disappeared into the sky. The first flight had begun at 9.51 a.m. of March 25, 1958. On successive flights Arrow exceeded all expectations. On its seventh flight, even with the smaller Pratt & Whitney J75 engines, it achieved a speed of just under 1,400 mph, or about Mach 2, while climbing and without trying for any record.

The first five Mark I's, with the P. & W. engines, came off the assembly line in succession for flight tests. The remaining 32 Mark II's, to be fitted with the powerful new Iroquois engines, were following along in successive stages, nearing completion, all the parts on hand, all sub-assemblies ready to roll up to the production line as each plane moved along. The Iroquois engine had simultaneously been undergoing separate flight tests in a flying test-bed, a converted B-47. There was no fighter in existence, except the Arrow, with a sufficiently advanced airframe to test it.

The first Iroquois engines had been installed in the sixth and seventh Arrows, the first Mark II's. They were almost ready to roll off the assembly line on February 20, 1959. They were expected to set a new world speed record.

IV The Government

On December 14, 1956, the Progressive Conservative Party, after a long term out of office, had selected as their new leader a criminal lawyer from Saskatchewan who had acquired a following in western Canada, by means of his talent for evangelistic oratory. In Canada as elsewhere, the longer the government remains in office, the more people become critical and ready for change. The Liberal Party had been in power continuously since 1935. A further factor was C.D. Howe's arrogant mishandling of the TransCanada Pipeline issue and his imposition of closure to get a Bill passed in time for construction to begin. The Bill proposed that the government provide a guarantee of funding costs up to $8 million.

C.D. Howe, born and educated in the U.S., was one of the few businessmen ever to sit in a Canadian Cabinet. He was a man who liked to get decisions made and then get on with the job; during the war and after, he had become the most powerful Minister in the Cabinet. Far from being a popular orator, he had little patience with oratory and obstruction. Canadians, in and out of Parliament, were so unaccustomed to this kind of Minister or politician that he became widely distrusted.

The special skills of Canadian politicians usually lie in pleasing the crowds and winning elections. Diefenbaker, campaigning on his 'vision' for Canada, barnstormed across the country and, in the ensuing election of June 10, 1957, the Liberals lost by a whisker and the Conservatives romped in to victory. The margin was too narrow for comfort, but a second election called the following March, brought in the Conservatives with one of the largest majorities in Canadian history.

Canadian elections rarely throw up enough good talent to form a highly competent Cabinet, even if chosen on merit alone without political considerations. This government was no exception. Also, most Ministers were chosen not so much for their competence as for their personal loyalty to the Prime Minister. The leader himself distrusted the Opposition, the civil service, the press, and even some members of his own Party. This somewhat paranoid outlook was most evident with respect to the Liberals or anyone who had ever worked for them when they formed the government. The Chairman of the Board of A.V. Roe at the time was Crawford Gordon who had formerly worked under C.D. Howe when Howe was Minister of Defence Production. This relationship became an important factor in later events.[14]

In the new government, an elderly, retired army officer, Major-General George Pearkes, became Minister of Defence. His Deputy Minister, later Minister of Defence Production, was a Raymond O'Hurley, who described himself as a 'former forestry expert'. He had been a timber-grader and, reputedly, a bagman for the Duplessis provincial government in Quebec.

Technicians work on free flight model prior to launching.

Courtesy A.V. Roe

The expertise and qualifications of these two new appointees as to defence matters was very soon apparent. Time after time, it was obvious that they did not know what they were talking about. Some, but not all of this, was due to the Prime Minister's tendency to vacillate and to make decisions without consulting his Ministers. Prime Minister Diefenbaker himself, in repeated statements, both in and out of the House, frequently contradicted himself.

When spell-bound by great oratory, how many really question what is said? Who notices that what is actually happening in the country is quite different from what the leader is glowingly describing as his 'Vision' for Canada? Diefenbaker publicly deplored Canada's heavy dependence on one country, the United States, and announced a policy of "strengthening Commonwealth ties."   The Royal family was solemnly referred to on every possible occasion. However when, in response, Britain offered Canada a free trade agreement, it was very quickly rebuffed and nothing more was heard on that matter. More important, but realized only belatedly, was the acceleration in the rate and extent of takeover and control of Canadian resources, enterprises and industries, by the United States.

The Liberal government, in the previous decade, had paid off a considerable portion of the war debts and had accumulated a considerable surplus. The Conservatives had quickly depleted this huge surplus and were going heavily into debt. Part of this was attributed to the huge and unnecessary $6.4 billion government bond conversion loan engineered shortly after the 1958 election, reputedly to benefit the financial houses that had supported the Conservatives. To provide funds for the purchase of the new government bonds by the banks, the money supply had been increased by twelve percent, followed by the inevitable inflation. The economy was suffering and the government, in the face of public criticism and declining popularity, had to find some very visible evidence of their presumed efforts to cut costs and save the taxpayers' money. In such efforts, 'visibility' is always, then as now, the main criterion in selecting the target.

Thus, as 1958 passed the half-way mark, the economy was in trouble, the public was uncertain, and the Prime Minister's

Electrical Systems test panel.

Courtesy Canadian Aviation Historical Society

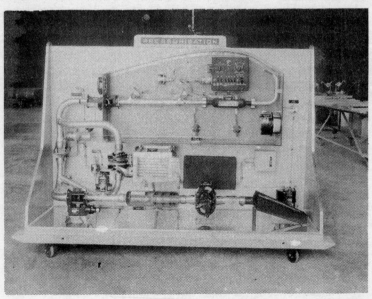

Pressurization system test panel.

Courtesy A.V. Roe

popularity, according to the polls, was declining even more rapidly than that of his party. Oratory is no substitute for solid management skills in the leadership of a large country. Diefenbaker had to make some magnificent gesture at saving money for the taxpayers. He could not touch the welfare programmes he had promised during the election; subsidies to provinces, grain growers, dairy farmers and to transportation, were also sensitive and would not have been sufficiently spectacular. The hundreds of millions being spent on Navy destroyer escorts and on Argus planes for coastal patrol were seldom mentioned, although, due to many modifications and changes in equipment, the cost of the ships and planes had gone far above the original estimates.

But there was the CF-105, the one part of our defence costs which we were spending in Canada, that had received the most publicity and acclaim from abroad, and which every one could see. One could roll out nice, round figures of hundreds of millions 'saved'. You didn't have to mention that this had been and would be spread over several years; you didn't have to mention how much of this money came back in taxes, nor how many jobs it created; nor how much it had purchased in research, development, stimulation of the economy, and the actual production of 37 planes as well as new, modern engines; you didn't have to mention how much industry, earning power, manufacturing development of every kind and of a growing export capability would be lost; nor what it would do to the flow of skilled immigrants Canada had been told she needed so badly, nor to the skilled Canadians who had been kept here because there was challenging work to do. You didn't have to mention what it would cost to suddenly terminate the contract, or the cost of buying alternative equipment outside of the country, if we could; you didn't have to mention that *it wouldn't really save us anything at all*. It would simply throw away all we had already spent plus the growth and development across the country which had resulted, and would leave us more dependent than ever on the U.S. for both military policy and procurement, as well as for our advanced technology. But except for a small number of

Canadians, few appreciated the consequences.

The Arrow was the perfect sacrifice. It was a large and visible programme; many Canadians resented any ambitious programme for Canada; it was easy to frighten them with exaggerated figures as to cost. Scrapping it would achieve more than one objective at one stroke. But first, public emotions had to be aroused to support such an action, and the action had to be skilfully planned for maximum effect.

In October, 1958, led by *Maclean's* magazine,[15] the mass media swung into action. The Canadian people, believing the myths with which they had for so long been indoctrinated, had much to do with the events which followed; they unquestioningly believed everything the Prime Minister and the media told them. Canadians were willing to sell their future, believing they would thereby save a few bucks. The irony of it is that, when the costs were added up, it was found that Canadians had saved nothing at all, even in the short term; in the long term, they had lost more than most of them would ever know.

---

1 Howe, C.D., Correspondence Files, National Archives of Canada, Ottawa
2 Dobson, Sir Roy, Speech at 10th Anniversary Dinner, A.V. Roe Canada Ltd
3 Floyd, Jim, "The Avro Story," *Canadian Aviation*, 50th Anniversary Issue, 1978
4 *idem*
5 Trans World Airlines, *Operational and Route Analysis: Avro Jetliner*, May 5, 1952
6 Howe, *loc. cit.*
7 Floyd, *loc. cit.*
8 *idem*
9 *Saturday Evening Post*, Feb. 16, 1957, pp. 64-5

10 Dobson, *loc. cit.*

11 Hornick, James, *Globe & Mail*, Toronto, Oct., 1951, *passim*

12 *ibid.*, Oct. 10, 1951

13 *Financial Post*, Toronto, Sept. 20, 1958

14 Brown, J.J., *Ideas in Exile*, McClelland & Stewart, Toronto, 1967. Brown claims that Diefenbaker's hatred of Crawford Gordon became "a key factor in the cancellation of the whole Arrow programme."

15 *Maclean's*, Oct. 25, 1958

The four men who controlled all phases of engineering necessary to create the Arrow. From left: R.N. Lindley, Chief Engineer; J.C. Floyd, Vice-President Engineering; Guest Hake, Arrow Project Designer; Jim Chamberlin, Chief of Technical Design.

Courtesy A.V. Roe

Chapter 3
Count-down

On September 23, 1958, Prime Minister Diefenbaker announced that "in view of rapid development of missiles for both defence and attack" and on the "detailed advice from military experts" on the nature of the attacks on North America that might be expected in the event of a major war, his government had reviewed the Canadian Air Defence programme. According to the "preponderance of expert opinion", manned aircraft would be less effective in meeting this threat by the 1960's than had been expected.

He stated that Canada was therefore acquiring from the United States, the missiles and equipment for 2 Bomarc missile bases, and would install the Semi-Automatic Ground Environment (SAGE) electronic system being developed for the guidance of these missiles. He also stated that, because of mounting costs, the contract for development of the Astro-Sparrow fire-control and missile programme would be discontinued. This would result in a saving of $330 million on a production run of 100 aircraft, thus reducing the cost of the CF-105 "from $12-1/2 million to $9 million each". The Arrow would be modified to accomodate an existing American fire-control system. In view of these developments, the CF-105 would not be put into production *at this time*. The development programme would be continued until the following March when the programme would be reviewed again. After this announcement, he left for a leisurely trip around the world.

As designer James Floyd has remarked, in an effort to meet Canada's obligations as the "first line of defence of North America" in the event of a nuclear war, the Air Force requirements as presented to A.V. Roe were so advanced that they could scarcely be met with then current technology. In fact, such requirements have been met by few, if any, service aircraft up to this day. However, the multiple problems had been solved and the design approved. The company then ran into the same problems of obtaining a suitable foreign engine that had been encountered in the development of the Jetliner. A new engine, more powerful than the Orenda was therefore developed and put into production, to power the CF-105. These two projects were enough for the company, and they preferred to utilize a fire-control system already tested and in production. But the Air Staff required that the aircraft be guided by "the most sophisticated automatic flight and fire control system yet envisaged". This became the Astra-Sparrow programme. RCA-Victor of Montreal was given the contract to develop the Astra system under the direction of A.V.Roe.* It was a very costly programme; Avro was afraid that these costs would later be charged to the costs of the Arrow, and this in fact turned out to be the case.[1]

It was well known that the contracts Avro was already working on and which were nearing completion, were firm contracts. The costs of research, development, design, tooling, manufacture or purchase of parts and components for all 37 pre-production aircraft had already been incurred. Five of the aircraft were already flying; two more, the first Mark II's, were almost complete and ready to fly and the remaining 30 were right behind on the assembly lines. In addition, on fixed contracts, cancellation charges, both to Avro and to the many suppliers would be heavy. Thus, no one considered that these contracts were involved. The contract for production aircraft, however, had always been conditional, dependent on results of the first two contracts and on political decision. Therefore, it was logical to assume that Mr. Diefenbaker was referring to the production contract, as stated in the Prime

---

* Development of the Sparrow missile was let to Canadair of Montreal.

Minister's announcement.

Most of the media appeared to have reached the same conclusion. Then *Maclean's* magazine of October 25, 1958 appeared. It contained an article by Blair Fraser, *Maclean's* Ottawa editor, entitled "What Led Canada to Junk the Arrow?" It began :

> "Never, not even in June, 1957 [date of the first Conservative victory] has Prime Minister Diefenbaker met the press *with such well-earned glee* as when he announced the discontinuance of our all-Canadian supersonic fighter aircraft, the Avro Arrow. Both times the prophets and soothsayers had been wrong, but there was a difference. In the case of the Arrow, the ill-starred reporters and their ill-informed sources were misled not just by lack of fore-knowledge, but even more by *lack of faith*. The plain truth is, nobody thought the government would have the courage to make such a painful decision. (Italics added.)

Fraser went on to say that, when the Arrow was designed, neither the U.S. nor the U.K. was developing a similar plane. However, now the U.S. had changed its mind and decided to modify the F104 to produce the F106, *which would be equivalent to the Arrow*; there would be no chance therefore, to sell the Arrow to the United States. The F106 would not, of course, be operational for two years, but, in the meantime, *its predecessor, the F104*, would be available. Since the U.S. would therefore not buy the Arrow, it would be too expensive for Canada to produce. The cost would be *ten million dollars apiece* for an order of two hundred.*

This same issue[2] contained an editorial that claimed, among other things that the Arrow was "a very obsolete fighter aircraft" and that the decision was "a logical military decision ... on military affairs, arrived at for military reasons." *Maclean's* piously added: "And that, we trust, is the only basis on which this country will ever make a military decision" not on the basis of other factors such as economic benefit, unemployment, or industrial development.   The editorial con-

---

* This statement contained many clear errors. The F106 was not remotely comparable to the Arrow; it was not developed from the Lockheed F104 but from the Convair F102 of which it was a modified version; the cost per plane was wildly inaccurate and did not even conform to Diefenbaker's inflated estimates.

cluded: "But what, we'd like to know, is so difficult about making up our minds to stop manufacturing a military aircraft *that has outlived its usefulness*." (Italics added). Such errors of both fact and conclusion will be considered later.

These articles were followed in November and December 1958 by a series of three articles by Fraser on Canadian defence and NATO requirements.[3] In these articles, Fraser himself refuted the statement that the Arrow was "obsolete" by disproving the implied claim that manned interceptors had been replaced by missiles such as the Bomarc. Yet he claimed that the F104 would serve until a modified version, the F106, would be ready two years later. The F106 would be an end of the line plane, a modification of the F102, not the F104, and was a stop-gap plane with a short service life. It would not compare to the Arrow in range, speed or performance, if it flew at all. Further modifications were, in fact, cancelled. It carried only the pilot. Fraser admitted that one man was no longer sufficient to perform the tasks required of an interceptor at supersonic speed; therefore, he said, the U.S. had now begun development of a system of Semi-Automatic Ground Environment computer (SAGE) to control the flight of both Bomarc missiles and interceptors. The costs quoted by Fraser were wildly inaccurate, especially when calculated on the same basis as the comparative costs being quoted for U.S. planes. The cost quoted by the company to the government for 100 planes would as of then, be $3.6 million each; the cost for 200 would drop to $2.5 million each. This is quite a far cry from the $10 million each for 200 as given in the article. Fraser's figure was four times the actual price!

With respect to possible purchase by other governments, the CF-100 had won sales to other countries *after* going into production and proving itself in performance. So have other planes produced by de Havilland and Canadair. Government representations to the United States as to sharing of defence production contracts had had an effect on sales of both the CF-100 and the Canadian built Sabre F-86 to NATO countries. Therefore, no one could possibly say that other countries would not buy the Arrow until it was in production and had proved its superior performance in service. No other plane would be available for several years which could remotely approach the Arrow's performance. It would fill a large gap even in a 'tough market.'

The prestigious U.S. magazine, *Aviation Week* reported that:

> Arrow is bettering its predictions ... Estimates are that the Orenda-Iroquois engine ... will give the Arrow a top speed of better than 2,000 miles per hour, or in excess of Mach 3 at 30,000 feet and above. The price will be $3.6 million per aircraft for 100 Arrows, as of now. *[They got it right.]* Speculation is that it will be difficult for foreign governments as well as that of Canada to turn down a Mach 3 aircraft that is flying in early 1959. This would be several years before other Mach 3 aircraft now in development, and would give Canadian industry an achievement that could not be ignored. [4]

A "Very obsolete aircraft?" Not exactly! An aircraft that Canada would find very difficult to turn down? Oh no! As *Maclean's* said: "What is so difficult about making up our minds to stop manufacturing a military aircraft ...?" Not difficult at all as *Maclean's* knew. It has never been difficult for Canadian governments to stop the manufacture of anything designed or produced in Canada, unless manufactured by a U.S. subsidiary such as Canadair,* or unless taken over by an American company in return for financing not available in Canada, or unless it was too small to offer competition to any American industry and its sales. Canadian governments have been doing it for almost a century.

The *Maclean's* articles unleashed a torrent of stories, columns and editorials in the popular press. It was as if the whole Canadian media had been waiting, with editorials already written, for someone to give the signal that now was the moment to release them. These repeated and enlarged on the errors, the distortions and omissions of fact. In fact, as fast as one mis-statement was proven false, they produced new ones, equally false. This powerful and vocal lobby also effectively controlled the opportunity for any public reply. Only

---

* Until recently, Canadair was a subsidiary of U.S.-based General Dynamics Co. which also owns Convair and other American subsidiaries. Canadair manufactured, under license, a number of planes designed by Convair and other aircraft firms in the U.S.

one Toronto newspaper would publish even a short letter, correcting facts. A short statement given by Crawford Gordon, A.V. Roe President, at the express invitation of *Maclean's* magazine, was attacked by Pierre Berton as a "lobbying effort, master-minded by the firm of Cockfield-Brown" (the former government's advertising firm.)

The Toronto *Telegram* cancelled the daily column of a long-time regular columnist who dared to discuss the Arrow and the national and international consequences of its cancellation.[5] The column was not reinstated until all reference to the Arrow was dropped.   Editorials by John Bassett, editor of the Toronto *Telegram*, which he claimed to be the result of "much careful research" from authoritative sources, contained the most ridiculous errors of easily-checked facts.[6] Letters sent to the *Telegram* to correct the most obvious errors, were neither published nor acknowledged. Of course, few of these editors or reporters knew anything at all about aircraft, defence, advanced technology and the effort it takes to acquire it, let alone the enormous developmental and industrial spin-offs which result from technological advance, as well as from domestic production versus foreign purchase. But editors and reporters should at least know how to check facts.

Ranking officers in the armed forces were muzzled.[7] One was transferred from Ottawa, reputedly because he stated facts the government didn't want to hear. Air Marshall Slemon, second-in-command at NORAD headquarters in Colorado, was allowed to talk to reporters only once. In reply to direct questions he stated that, yes, manned interceptors would be required for defence for the foreseeable future, but no, no interceptor to equal the Avro Arrow would be available anywhere for several years. He made it quite clear that these were simply statements of fact and did not involve advice to government; that policy decisions were the sole responsibility of the government. Most newspapers published only the first part of his reply. He was severely reprimanded in the press and in Parliament for making these two factual replies. There were even angry demands for his recall and demotion. The Ottawa *Citizen* and the Montreal *Gazette* accurately reported his remarks and attacked the Government's efforts to muzzle its military experts.[8]

The Hon. Mr Pearkes, who apparently didn't know the difference between a bomber and a transport* was, meanwhile, again working hard to convince the public that the Arrow was completely useless. Having told *Maclean's* and the public that we couldn't sell the Arrow to the U.S. because they still had the F104**, he now claimed that *we couldn't use it for NATO either.* He said the Arrow could not operate without SAGE and there was no SAGE in Europe. There was, of course, no SAGE anywhere when the Arrow was designed. SAGE was developed as a guidance system for 'unmanned' missiles such as the Bomarc. Even in 1958, there was as yet only one station set up, in the New York area. It was not available in the rest of the United States, let alone Europe, or in the far North, although he implied that this was the only place where the Arrow could be used. The Arrow was, of course, designed for use both in NATO and in the far North and without SAGE. Pearkes must have been confusing the SAGE system with the TACAN system, an airborne ground-navigation-aid system then operating in the U.S. and southern Canada.

The Astra-Sparrow programme then being developed in Canada had been undertaken in conjunction with the USAF and at the request of the RCAF to provide greater range in guidance and fire-control systems than was available with existing U.S. equipment. This would be especially useful in the Canadian Arctic. However, when Canada took over its development, the USAF withdrew its support. On September 23, 1958, Diefenbaker cancelled the programme and then or-

---

* Shortly after his Cabinet appointment, Defence Minister Pearkes visited A.V. Roe. On being shown the B-47, the well-known bomber being used as a test-bed for the Iroquois engine, he seriously asked: "Where do they put the passengers?"

** When Defence Minister Pearkes went with his delegation to Washington, ostensibly to sell them the idea that the Arrow would be a logical contribution for Canada to make as her share of the Defence Production Sharing Agreement, they turned the tables and sold him the Bomarc instead. The Bomarc was being criticized as ineffective and vulnerable, and was about to be phased out. Our purchase helped to prevent its cancellation and to reduce Boeing's production losses. It reminds one of a Canadian delegation which went to Washington a few years previously to confer with Sinclair Weekes of the U.S. government. As Weekes with his group left the conference room, he was overheard by Canadian reporters to remark: "Well, I guess we fixed them." They later sold us the F104 also.

dered Avro to contract for the purchase of the MG-3 system, produced by Hughes Corporation in the U.S.* and to make the necessary modifications to the CF-105. Its range would be sufficient for use in Europe and, to a certain extent, in the North. Pearkes seems to have been confused by a lot of things, but he must certainly have known this, since it was the responsibility of his Department. However, his blatant misstatement concerning SAGE was picked up by George Bain of *The Globe & Mail*. It apparently did not occur to him to suggest that our Honourable Minister of Defence didn't know what he was talking about. In his article "What wings for the RCAF Abroad?" in *Globe Magazine*, Bain accepted Pearkes' statement that, because it couldn't operate without SAGE, the Arrow "was probably never intended for use in Europe."[9] By cunningly implying that the Arrow could neither be sold to any other country such as the U.S., nor be used in NATO, Pearkes was, of course, deliberately making nonsense of the whole development and making fools of the Air Staff who had laid down the specifications. This must have been Pearkes' deliberate intention. Either that, or he was too badly misinformed to be the Minister of Defence, entrusted with such far-reaching decisions.** George Bain accepted this misinformation at face value and proceeded to analyze the alternatives available as replacements for the RCAF in Europe, excluding the Arrow from any consideration or comparison.

The public attacks and controversy surrounding the programme began to affect the company personnel. For several years, U.S. aircraft corporations had been trying to woo employees away from Avro. One company, after searching all over the United States for a specific kind of electronics expert, found the man they wanted at Avro and offered

---

* Pearkes persisted in referring to the Hughes system as the MA-1 system, which was a production version designed for use with the single-seater F106. It was not designed for and never intended for use with the two-man CF-105.

** J.J. Brown, in *Ideas in Exile*, makes these comments: "In general, on the government side, the people involved were far too small for the size of the project. Diefenbaker, a small-time Prairie lawyer, was far out of his depth when it came to making decisions about the world military aircraft industry ... To cope with such sophisticated enterprise, Canada had a criminal lawyer from the Prairies and Gen. Pearkes from Victoria, the epitome of nineteenth century protocol and intelligence."

him about double the pay he was making, plus a fully-paid course at the university of his choice. Every so often, U.S. companies would rent hotel space in Buffalo, N.Y. for the week-end, and beam radio advertisements from Buffalo stations inviting Canadian aircraft personnel to come over for interviews. They had had little success, in spite of offers of pay and benefits far above what Canadians were making at Avro. As long as there was meaningful work for them in their own country, they would stay. Now, however, buffeted between attacks from the media, tongue-in-cheek reassurances from the government and the mounting uncertainty concerning the future of the programme, there was danger that key men would be lost and essential teams would be broken up. In her column in the Toronto *Telegram*, titled "Rabbits for the Eagle", Judith Robinson summed it up very well:

> In Ottawa, front bench politicians are still repeating the old form of words. Questioned in the House, questioned in their offices, they say it over again: A final decision regarding production of the CF-105, the Avro Arrow, will not be announced until March 31.

> But in Toronto the — shall we say eagles? — are gathering this week. In Toronto newspapers, American aircraft producers and their subsidiary aviation engineering firms are advertising for engineers and technicians. Already from such U.S. firms as Curtiss-Wright, groups of executives have moved into Toronto hotels and passed out the word that they are there to interview top-flight aviation experts who may wish to consider leaving Canada for more certain and rewarding employment in the United States.

> One such group started interviewing Monday and has found the material offered so good and so plentiful that it has prolonged its stay until Wednesday night instead of leaving today.

> By the time it and a couple more delegations like it have come and gone it may not matter very much what the politicians decide in Ottawa. The team that designed and built the Arrow in Canada for the defense of Canada will be broken up. The men who invested seven years of their professional lives and their engineering genius, enthusiasm and skill to the production of the best and fastest interceptor aircraft now

flying in North America will write off the investment as lost and leave for the United States.

Canadians will then be able to put the millions their betters have saved for them on the Arrow into the unemployment relief fund."[10]

In this atmosphere, Charles Grinyer, head of the Engineering Division at Orenda Engines, finally tendered his resignation to the company. Within fifteen minutes, the Minister of Defence Production was on the phone from Ottawa. O'Hurley begged Grinyer to withdraw his resignation, *to go on and finish the job.* Grinyer said he could not work for the government any longer under these conditions, that he could not ask his men to stay and use their very competent brains on work which was going to be wasted. The assurances given him by the government were so convincing that Charles Grinyer withdrew his resignation. The next morning, he called together his supervisors, repeated the assurances given him by responsible Ministers of the Crown, and asked them to stay and to persuade their men to stay.

In November, 1958, officials of the Company went to Ottawa to inquire about the possibility of going ahead with alternative projects. They sought permission to release personnel from the Arrow contract to proceed with other development work. They were assured that the Arrow programme had *not* been killed; that the "development contract" for 37 aircraft, and the "research and test programme" *were not in question.* They were also assured that they would probably get a production order for at least fifty aircraft. It was well-known in the industry that this was the minimum that the Air Force had asked for, so it sounded logical. This assurance was given to the Company by at least four Cabinet Ministers, including the Acting Prime Minister. Mr. Diefenbaker was still travelling around the world.

At the same time, *in November,* after the government had cancelled the Astra-Sparrow development programme with RCA-Victor in Montreal,* Avro was given the further contract to obtain and install the alternative Hughes MG-3 missile and fire control system now available in the United States and *to make the necessary modifications in design* to accomodate the

* Canadair, Montreal, had the contract for the Sparrow missile.

new system.* Avro had previously been told to design the Arrow around the Astra-Sparrow equipment. This represented only one of the many delays and costly changes in requirements originating with the government or the RCAF about which Avro could do nothing, but which added to both the time and cost of the Arrow. On receipt of this contract from the Canadian government, the Hughes Aircraft Company in California undertook a major redesign of its production line, at considerable cost, in order to accomodate both the new Canadian contract and the existing contracts it had with American firms. With this new directive *in November*, it would have been difficult for the company to assume that the contract had been cancelled the previous September, as asserted by *Maclean's*, by the Toronto *Star* and the *Telegram*.

Still later, in December, 1958, officials of the Company wrote to Ottawa and made appointments to try to arrange for alternative projects and an orderly slowdown, if there were any chance of the Arrow being cancelled. Five times in one week, they were given written appointments; five times they went up to Ottawa and back. Two appointments were broken before the time set; three others were cancelled after they had waited for hours in O'Hurley's office. They went to Ottawa again on Saturday. This time they saw, not the Minister, but a lower-level department official, who had no authority and could tell them nothing. Probably O'Hurley had no authority either. Prime Minister Diefenbaker was still travelling around the world. When asked later in Parliament whether or not the company had been consulted before February, 1959, Pearkes said merely: "Members of the company have been in Ottawa on a number of occasions." Diefenbaker went further: "No one from the company contacted the government or tried to see them," he said.

What the company had been told in September — by the government, not from press reports — was to get the price

---

* J.J. Brown, who was working for RCA-Victor at the time, refers to the cancellation of the Astra-Sparrow programme as though it represented the actual cancellation of the whole Arrow project. He apparently was not aware that Avro was, at the same time, given a new contract to substitute the Hughes system and was told to go ahead with the necessary design modifications. Also, contrary to Brown, there was no shut down of the company at that time.

down by installing the MG-3 Hughes fire control system and to speed up the delivery date, to facilitate the giving of a 'production contract'. This had been confirmed in November and in December by Cabinet Ministers. Therefore, in spite of the press campaign, Avro was working at top speed to fulfil its contract with the government, on final assembly of the first of the Mark II aircraft, on modifications to accomodate the MG-3 system, and on the installation of telemetry equipment on the sixth, seventh and eighth aircraft, the Mark II's, for the research and test programme.

The author of this book was responsible for the installation layout drawings for the telemetring equipment in the second Mark II. It included equipment which filled the large weapons bay plus hundreds of tiny copper tubes and electrical wiring which were threaded through the aircraft structure, from each area to be monitored, to the equipment fitted into the weapons bay. On February 18, 1959, the shop foreman in charge of the installation called the author to come down to the assembly line. He proudly showed off the installation and explained how beautifully it had fitted in. They shook hands on a good and expert installation. There were many Avro workers like him, the best there were and proud of the work they were involved in.

Everyone at A.V. Roe was aware that the promised review on March 31 might tell them there would be no production order; but completion of the development contract, completion of the research and test programme and compilation of the tremendous amount of extremely valuable data available from this programme would ease any slowdown on the Arrow and the commencement of work on alternative programmes. The first Mark II Arrow had already been fitted with the new, powerful Iroquois engines and was ready to roll out to Flight Test to begin its test programme. The second and third Mark II's were right behind. They had each been fitted with masses of delicate test equipment for checking every phase of engine performance and flight characteristics at various altitudes and speeds. Everyone expected that the Mark II would easily break the world's speed record. Even the Mark I had almost done so without trying.

1 Floyd, James, "The Avro Story," *Canadian Aviation*, 50thAnniversary Issue, 1978
2 *Maclean's*, Oct. 25, 1958
3 *ibid.*, Nov. 8, 22, Dec. 6, 1958
4 "New Hope for CF-105," *Aviation Week*, Nov. 10, 1958, p. 31
5 Judith Robinson, *Telegram*, Toronto
6 Editorial, *Telegram*, Toronto, Jan. 20, 1959
7 "Defence Chiefs Warned by PM on Airing Views," *Globe & Mail*, Ottawa bureau dispatch, Jan. 16, 1959
8 *Gazette*, Montreal, Dec. 2, 1958; *cf.* Connolley, Greg, *Citizen*, Ottawa, Dec. 1, 1958. Connolley was among the news reporters visiting NORAD headquarters in Colorado.
9 Bain, George, "What Wings for the RCAF Abroad?", *The Globe Magazine*, Feb. 14, 1959
10 Robinson, Judith, "Rabbits for the Eagle," *The Telegram*, Toronto, Feb. 10, 1959

Chapter 4
Black Friday

The morning of Friday, February 20, 1959, begins as a normal day. There is the usual hum of work in the design office, consultations over drawings at several tables, the occasional trip to the Records Section for blueprints or to the library for some technical report. Occasionally, one of the engineers from the Stress Section or from Technical Design walks in to confer with a group over some detail design problem. There is an underlying atmosphere of both apprehension and expectation throughout the company. Statements from politicians and media have been conflicting and disturbing. But the first Mark II Arrow with its powerful Iroquois engines will roll out within a day or two to begin its test flights and it is expected to set new records which NATO and NORAD will not be able to ignore.

Sometime about mid-morning, one of the men is called to the phone. A few minutes later, he walks slowly back into the design office. Someone speaks to him, but he doesn't answer. Then he says, "The Arrow has been cancelled. My wife heard it on a news broadcast." No one quite believes him. Such an important and crucial decision could not be just casually announced over the radio, with no prior notice to the company! The Defence Production representative at Avro can't believe it either. He contacts Ottawa by phone to find out if it is true. He is stunned!

Nearly two hours later, the Company receives its first

notification from the government. The voice of the President, J.L. Plant, comes over the public address system, announcing that he has *just now* received from the government a telegram which reads as follows:

> TAKE NOTICE THAT YOUR CONTRACTS BEARING THE REFERENCE NUMBERS SET OUT BELOW INCLUDING ALL AMENDMENTS THERETO ARE HEREBY TERMINATED AS REGARDS ALL SUPPLIES AND SERVICES WHICH HAVE NOT BEEN COMPLETED AND SHIPPED OR PERFORMED THEREUNDER PRIOR TO THE RECEIPT BY YOU OF THIS NOTICE STOP <u>YOU SHALL CEASE ALL WORK IMMEDIATELY STOP TERMINATE SUB-CONTRACTS AND ORDERS STOP PLACE NO FURTHER SUB-CONTRACTS OR ORDERS AND INSTRUCT ALL YOUR SUB-CONTRACTORS AND SUPPLIERS TO TAKE SIMILAR ACTION STOP</u> YOU ARE REQUESTED TO SUBMIT TO THE DEPARTMENT OF DEFENCE PRODUCTION OTTAWA ONTARIO FOR CONSIDERATION ANY CLAIM WHICH YOU MAY HAVE AS A RESULT OF THIS TERMINATION STOP* (Emphasis added)

There follow instructions as to submission of claims and then a list of contract numbers which are now terminated. A similar telegram has been received by the Vice President of Orenda Engines, Earl K. Brownridge.

The contract numbers listed refer, not to a further "production order", but to the existing "development contract" for the 37 pre-production aircraft and the Iroquois engines and the "research and test program". Absolutely nothing is left. Even a request from NATO for modifications to the CF-100 has been ignored! And this is February 20, not March 31. There has been no prior information or consultation with the company, no prior permission given to the company, as had been requested, to release men for other projects, nor any consideration of such projects. After eighteen months in office, the government has no defence plans in existence, no alternative contracts, no integrated 'defence-sharing' orders from the U.S., promised so often and so glowingly by the government. If the government knew the Arrow contract would be cancelled, alternative plans should have been arranged by now, to go into effect at once.

If this were, as *Maclean's* had assured us, a "purely military decision" taken by a responsible government, aware of the dislocations it would cause, some program would surely be in hand to ease the transition, to retain the highly-skilled work

* See Appendix I

force and the know-how it has taken Canada so long to acquire. It takes years to put together a top-notch research and development team, or a design and production team such as the ones Avro has built up. Once scattered, they are lost for ever.

The only work left that the company can legally continue is a small contract for CF-100 repairs and one with the United States for the experimental Avrocar. No one knows how much work will still be done on these, nor who will be kept on for these small jobs which cannot absorb more than those who are currently working on them, certainly none of those who have been working on the Arrow, or on the Iroquois engine. The reshuffling of personnel, if any, will have to be worked out, in the light of this sudden termination. For very good and sufficient reasons, the company is forced to announce that all employment is terminated as of now, and the plant closed, at least temporarily. Even if the Company were to ignore the terse order of the telegram, "YOU SHALL CEASE ALL WORK IMMEDIATELY," it cannot charge to any contract one hour of work after receipt of the telegram. Even then, Avro is still obligated to pay the three weeks' termination pay to every worker.

In a few hours, by telephone, on the following Monday, one man cancels all the sub-contracts which have been placed across Canada and in the United States in the past five years. Two Avro engineers are down at the Hughes Aircraft plant in California, where the whole assembly line has just been redesigned to accomodate the November order from the Canadian government, for the MG-3 fire control system. They are there when the phone call comes through to Hughes. The official who answers slams down the phone and furiously swears that never again will his company accept a contract from a Canadian government.[1]

On Monday morning, a large area of the shop has been cleared. Employees are lining up to register for severance pay and to fill out employment applications. Accounting, auditing, payroll and personnel departments are working around the clock to deal with the massive effects of the sudden cancellation and to ease the most immediate problems of 14,000 employees. In the design offices, a few have come in to pick up their books, tools and equipment. Except for these activities, there are very few around. Department supervisors and their key men are at their desks. One man is on the phone all day, answering calls from U.S. firms wanting to hire individuals, whole teams or groups. By now, they know them by name and by reputation. For almost a decade, these same firms have been putting on the pressure to get Avro designers and engineers, offering special inducements to lure them from Canada. Now they are a free gift from a Canada that no longer wants them and considers them no loss. American firms can now pick and choose as they wish.

When the company closes down on receipt of the termination order, Diefenbaker suddenly becomes alarmed. The scenario isn't working as planned; this may become a political 'boomerang.' So the Prime Minister turns on the company and publicly accuses it of closing down "in order to embarass the government." How quaint, coming from Diefenbaker! As Paul Hellyer, the Opposition defence critic points out in Parliament, "The Prime Minister did not anticipate the extent of the consequences of the short circuit which he caused by pulling the switch on that Friday morning. He seemed to be hurt, as well as surprised." Diefenbaker apparently believed that Avro would absorb the shock of his malicious and irresponsible bungling and carry 14,000 people on its payroll for free, to save the government the embarrassment caused by its own action—a government that has just pulled off the final act in the Prime Minister's monstrous, playful 'game' with the company, in his programme to destroy it.

As a matter of fact, if the company were to continue, it could prove infinitely more embarassing for the Government. But, regardless of the terms of the notice of termination, what can 14,000 people do whose work has just been cancelled without notice — just stand there and look at it for two weeks, knowing that it has all been utterly wasted? Or should they go down and watch the cutting torches which Diefenbaker and O'Hurley will shortly send in to destroy in a matter of days all evidence of the outstanding and record-breaking products of seven years of effort and achievements?

Even a small-time courtroom lawyer should know something about contracts. Government contracts are standard forms. So are terminations. So are the penalties for cancellation. Prime Minister Diefenbaker casts his eyes to the skies and, with righteous self-gratification, tells the country that he has cancelled the contracts to save the taxpayers the millions of dollars which have been wasted on this extravagant project! He does not tell them that, in addition to destroying everything this money, already spent, has paid for, it will actually cost more from now on, just to cancel the contracts as he has cancelled them, than it would have cost to complete the contracts and finish the rest of the 37 aircraft and the research and test programme. He does not tell them that A.V. Roe has signed a contract with Curtiss-Wright in the United States for production of the Iroquois engine under license, the first such contract ever signed by the U.S. with a Canadian company. He does not tell them that France has made enquiries to the government concerning the purchase of 300 Iroquois engines and that both the U.S. and the U.K. have been trying to negotiate to purchase some of the Arrows which are already flying, since they have nothing comparable and these would be immensely valuable to them. If this were "a purely military decision" made with due deliberation by a responsible government, concerned with Canada's economic well-being, every effort would be made to recover these extra millions in foreign sales for Canada, to help pay for the expenditures. But Diefenbaker is not really concerned with saving anything. He is certain that he can fool the poor taxpayers and keep them in blissful ignorance of what is really going on.

A small-town lawyer may not know anything about economics, defence or global military matters, or the importance of technological know-how to a country hoping to play a developing role in the twentieth century. But he should certainly be mature enough not to bring disrespect and contempt upon his country by his eccentric and paranoid behaviour. If he dares to assume the highest position as leader of the government, consideration for his country's welfare and good reputation abroad would be paramount, not the pursuit of personal animosities or political advantage.

But a small-time criminal lawyer will probably derive a gleeful delight from playing what he has come to regard as his 'adversary' as a cat would play with a mouse. Only on this assumption do the inexplicable events of the previous few months fall into place: the Prime Minister's ambiguous statement of September 23, made with the "well-earned glee" noted by *Maclean's* Blair Fraser; his immediate departure for an extensive, leisurely and needless trip around the world; the confusion, conflicting statements and evasion which characterized supposedly responsible government Ministers and officials left, during his absence, to look like fools without any authority, knowledge of intentions, or direction, attempting to evade and temporise while the press did its hatchet job.

Diefenbaker, on his way around the world, must have savoured every moment of it with malicious delight, like a small and sadistic boy watching a fly trapped in a cobweb. Then, on his return, he must have held his finger to the wind, found that the news media had done its con job on the unsophisticated public and, with true courtroom drama, moved in for the sudden kill.

But this was not a virtuoso small-town courtroom display. It was the supposedly responsible government of a nation operating on a world stage. Not only was Canada's role as a member of the international community in jeopardy; the future of the country's technological development, international reputation, and its very political, economic and military independence were in question.

The sudden cancellation of the Arrow and Iroquois programmes has been followed by the exodus of thousands of highly-skilled personnel and their families to the U.S., the U.K. and Europe, and the closing down of many smaller supply industries. In the wake of the shock-waves induced by these events, the government and the press have begun to issue a series of conflicting statements. The media has hastily tried to retrieve its credibility, while the Prime Minister has attempted to shift all responsibility for the havoc from the government to the company.

The press, perhaps taken aback by the rush of events which its campaign has helped to precipitate, has published exaggerated reports of the numbers called back after the cancellation, in an effort to down-play the effects. According to a Toronto *Star* headline of February 24, Prime Minister Diefenbaker claims "Avro Firings Needless; the company

Roll-out ceremony, Malton, October 4, 1957. *Courtesy A.V. Roe*

knew that fifty million dollars was available.''[2] But in the House of Commons Liberal leader Lester Pearson states that he has searched the estimates over the whole period and can find nothing that would allot such money to A.V. Roe for any purpose whatever. Three days later, the *Star* declares, "The jobs of 1,000 Avro technicians were pulled out of the fire today by the Diefenbaker government, but another 11,000 received their severance pay." According to the *Star*, the government would "share with the company the payroll cost of an 'essential nucleus' of technical personnel for the next six months".[3] But these are merely those who have been finishing up the odds and ends of the CF-100 programme and those working on the Avrocar funded by the USAF, along with personnel staff and maintenance. Donald Fleming, Minister of Finance, makes it clear that the Government has offered "no proposals to the company officials during the four days of talks held [in Ottawa] this week". Pearson suggests that these talks are six months too late.

The Toronto *Telegram* on the same day reports, "Government to Share Brains Pool cost: 3,000 Avro Jobs for Six Months: Recall 1,000 Engineers". It advises that "Cost of the wage-sharing programme to the Government has been estimated at $1,500,000 to $2,000,000".[4] There never were more than three to four hundred engineers at A.V. Roe. By the time a small percentage of them are recalled, most of them have already gone to the United States or abroad. Even for those who remain in Canada, six months' make-work on nebulous projects does not look very interesting compared to the work they could do on advanced projects in other countries.

With a record of outstanding achievements to their credit, not only in research and development, but in the production of the most advanced interceptor in the western world and the most powerful aircraft engine, these designers, engineers, technicians and other employees have now had their work taken away from them and given to the United States to be done in American factories. The headlines now read, "Arrow Killed: Canada to Buy U.S. Planes". The real lobby has accomplished its purpose.

Or has it? Destruction of the Arrow programme and dispersal of its design and production teams may have met the objectives of most of the press-supported lobby. But even this, as it turns out, is not sufficient retribution to prevent such an audacious development from ever happening here again. There is something prescient of the Nixon paranoia in the final scenes of this unseemly chapter in Canadian history.

During the next few weeks those who are left in the design office observe men whom they assume to be maintenance staff, moving about the now almost-deserted design and engineering offices with large, wheeled garbage containers. Into these goes everything that can be found in the offices, in the desks and shelves, in the Records Department and the Blueprint Section. Drawings, blueprints, thick volumes of specifications, performance standards and records, operating manuals, test programme data, all are thrown into the containers. Word has gone around that no one is to touch anything. A few who guess at what is happening salvage the ocassional drawing or manual, but little is rescued.

Slowly, the grapevine picks up the rumour that all these records, drawings, blueprints and data are not being collected as valuable irreplaceable property to be kept in a safe place along with other valuable research and development records. They are being collected *to be destroyed*, down to the last scrap, along with the photographs, technical films and scientific and research data obtained by the expenditure of so much cost and painstaking effort over the past few years. The taxpayers paid for it. It is valuable. Other companies, especially in the United States, have been constantly requesting access to it and are willing to pay for it. This is incredible! But even this is not enough!

Sometime within the next few weeks, those in the design offices begin to notice acrid odors coming from the direction of the shops and assembly bays. It smells like a charnel house. Once again, the rumours begin. One after another, men drift down to the shops to see if they are true. Down in the shops and bays, new crews have taken over. Like men from Mars, they are dressed in masks; wielding blow-torches, they are reducing to scrap all the parts and finished components which had been ready to move onto the final assembly line. Then they begin on the assembly line, with its complete and almost

CF-105 leaving for hanger after roll-out ceremony.

Courtesy A.V. Roe

complete Mark II aircraft. They move up through increasingly complete aircraft, right up to the two wholly complete, brand-new first Mark II Arrows, which had been almost ready on February 20 to be rolled out and flown.

Legend has it that, when the vandals reached Rome, they had never seen a modern civilisation or a city like Rome before. They did not understand what the houses, the buildings, the underground heating systems, the baths, the technology, the art work, the books and treasures were for. They meant nothing to these savages from the northern forests. So they smashed the city and burned it, then sat down and ate their raw food out of the broken pieces of marble. The citizens of Rome, if any were left in the city, must have felt much the same as do the men who now stand and cry as grown men seldom cry, as they watch the torches slowly melt down and cut to pieces the magnificent airplanes which they have spent seven years of their lives designing, creating and building. Very few venture down to the shops again as, later, not only the planes, but the whole specially designed assembly line, ready for production aircraft to roll off one after the other without further set-up costs, along with the tools, jigs and fixtures, everything, is reduced to scrap metal and hauled out to the scrap metal trucks to be sold to dealers for a few cents a pound. This is all that remains of what the Canadian taxpayers' money had bought!

The five completed, tested and flying aircraft, the Mark I's, are still on the tarmac by the Flight Test hangars. Both the U.K. and the U.S. have approached the government with requests to purchase at least some of the planes. They are far in advance of any other planes now flying. Even as research and test planes, they are worth millions. The Royal Aeronautical Establishment in England has been trying to obtain two or three of the existing flying Mark I Arrows for test and research, since there is as yet no other comparable plane available for this purpose in the Western world. Use of these planes, as well as of the test data, would speed research and development work on similar planes still in design stage in Britain and the U.S. It would give the Western world at least some small return for the $300-odd million investment Canada has made in this most advanced interceptor. If Canada cannot

Ready for ground handling test, November, 1957.

Courtesy Canadian Aviation Historical Society

or will not use it, surely she can allow Britain the use of three of them, with the other two to provide spares, so that it would not be a complete and total loss. The several million dollars Britain has offered to pay for them would also help to defray the cost to Canada.

According to very reliable information, the R.A.E. wants them so badly that only the *political* implications involved have prevented the British Government from making a formal, public request for them on behalf of the R.A.E.[5]. However, the Diefenbaker Government has flatly refused to consider this request. It has already begun to dismantle these five flying and proven Mark I Arrows with somewhat frantic haste. There is an odd sense of urgency in the speed with which the almost completed Mark II Arrows have been put to the torch and the multi-million dollar production line reduced to rubble. Now it would seem that even the existing planes are to be dismantled as quickly as possible to forestall any possibility of any of them ever being used again. Is it all just to save face? If so, it is a rather high price to pay to cover up one man's blunder.

Members of the Opposition, reporters and others have been asking questions in Parliament and outside, trying to find out what is going on. This is turning into an unprecedented riot of senseless destruction seldom seen before in a 'civilized' country. Members of the press ask to be allowed to visit the plant to photograph the planes they have heard are being cut up. O'Hurley replies to their request by saying flatly, "*No Arrows are being cut up*. We cannot allow photographs for 'security reasons.' These planes are fitted with the secret MA-1 fire control systems." As O'Hurley surely must know, workmen have been busily cutting up these planes with torches for a week. He gave the order. As O'Hurley also must know, none of the Hughes MA-1 (or, correctly, MG-3) fire control systems has ever been fitted to the Arrows, *nor have they ever been in Canada*. Some empty boxes were tried for size then removed, pending structural modifications to accomodate them. O'Hurley's own Department of Defence Production is responsible for the MG-3 system, which was to replace the Astra-Sparrow system, that the government has also cancelled, as well as for the destruction of the planes and everything else. It would be too kind to label such answers as double-talk.

Still later, Frank Lowe of *Weekend* Magazine, questions the

Minister of Defence concerning the fate of the five flying aircraft. He is told that there is no question of these flying aircraft being destroyed, that the government "is trying to find some use for them". Paul Hellyer, the Opposition defence critic, quietly advises Lowe that, if he can gain access to the company fence that parallels the Derry West Road, he can see these aircraft being destroyed at that very moment. *Weekend* Magazine proceeds to rent a helicopter and to fly a photographer over the site. They are quickly chased off by the airport tower but not before obtaining pictures that show the last five Arrow aircraft being cut up into scrap which is then piled into bins and trucked away. These pictures are to be published in *Weekend* Magazine but not until August 14, 1959, when the public has lost interest.[6] A similar picture also appears in *Aircraft* Magazine of November, 1959. It is apparently too dangerous to publish them at the time.

First the Jetliner, and now the Arrow! But this time, there are 37 aircraft, seven of them complete, the other 30 nearing completion as they progress down the assembly line. When the Jetliner was scrapped, the company had other contracts for the CF-100. This time, there is nothing left.

Scrapping the Jetliner had evidently not been enough to eliminate the threat of Canadian competition. The company had come back with the Arrow. This time the destruction would have to be complete. Was it good Canadians who made that decision? We perhaps shall never know. But, Canadians carried it out.

---

1 From conversation with the author, and the author's personal experience
2 *Star*, Toronto, Feb. 24, 1959
3 *ibid.*, Feb. 27, 1959
4 *Telegram*, Toronto, Feb. 27, 1959
5 Internal memorandum, A.V. Roe Co. Ltd, Malton
6 From conversation between the author and former editorial staff, *Weekend*

First flight of Avro Arrow, March 25, 1958. Note rotation of main under carriage as it retracts into storage space in thin wing.

Courtesy A.V. Roe

Chapter 5
The Real Target

The election of 1958 brought Mr. Diefenbaker such an over-whelming majority that he had a practically free hand politically. Within a short time, he began to carefully prepare public opinion for his attack on A. V. Roe and the Arrow. Purchase of the Bomarc missile planted the idea in the public mind that we were up-dating our forces to meet the challenge of the 'missile age', — few appreciated the fact that it was useless against ballistic missiles. Because we now had the Bomarc, interceptors were obsolete, therefore the Arrow was already obsolete, although the Bomarc was merely a back-up weapon for interceptors. When overwhelming evidence disputed any such argument, he proceeded to the argument that the Arrow was useless in any case, since it could not operate without SAGE, therefore it could not be used in NATO. We could not sell it to the United States either since they already had supersonic planes, and were commencing the design of the F108 which would be equivalent to the CF-105 Arrow. Except for the experts, few understood that none of the existing planes approached the performance of the Arrow, or that the F108 would not be operational for almost a decade. It was, in fact, later abandoned; this raises questions as to why it was begun at this particular point in time and given so much publicity.

Having established the belief that the Arrow could find only limited use, the matter of cost could now be introduced. Here was an issue of course, which could arouse Canadians more than any other, and the Prime Minister played it to the hilt, using the most wildly exaggerated figures in order to arouse the public against any further expenditures. In his estimates, he included costs of all the research, development, new material and process research, test programmes, Astra-Sparrow development, costs of weapons and armament and even, in one estimate, the cost of airport improvements. On the contrary, in the case of the Bomarc, he gave the public a cost of only $20 million, although the cost of each base only, without the missiles, was $120 million apiece and the one-third to be paid by Canada was $80 million plus the cost of the missiles themselves. Similar costs were given for 'alternative' American plane purchases.

Having proceeded from the military argument to the economic argument, he then began to attack the company directly, and the deep underlying animosity became apparent. Added to his other accusations, Diefenbaker accused Avro of being a "lobby", protesting piteously on television that "no one will ever know the pressure which has been brought to bear on us". This was a strange charge as the media had closed off almost all channels for the company to make any statement to the public, even to correct simple errors of facts presented in the press; and Diefenbaker had publicly told the armed forces to keep quiet.[1] Air Vice Marshall Curtis and Air Marshall Slemon alone had expressed their views as to the need for interceptors and the non-existence of any plane comparable to the Arrow.

One particular event from the summer of 1958 illustrates the kind of paranoia behind this charge. At that time, the CBC was preparing a programme to celebrate fifty years of flight in Canada. In order to provide contemporary material and to illustrate Canada's latest achievements in aeronautics, A.V. Roe offered to the CBC a choice of the films it had made of the test and production programmes and the in-flight performance of the CF-100 and the Arrow. It paid Pierre Berton the compliment of asking him to give the accompanying commentary. In return, Berton issued a vicious public blast against the company, labelling this offer of film a "lobbying tactic" masterminded by the advertising firm of Cockfield-Brown. The CBC programme, as eventually shown, was merely a commemoration of the 50-year-old flight of the Silver Dart which just happened to be made in Canada, plus the exploits of Canadian fliers in World Wars I and II and in the Northern bushlands, flying largely foreign-designed aircraft. For some strange reason, it would not have been fitting to tell Canadians that they had come a long way since the Silver Dart and were, a half-century later, leading the world in the design and production of advanced aircraft. Very strange, in a country claiming to be modern and 'developed'! Strange that Canada alone, of all the countries in the world, must hide from its own people, like a guilty secret, any real industrial or technological achievements. The myths must not be disturbed. A good question would be who profits from such strange behaviour; it is certainly not Canada.

After this episode, in order to avoid any appearance of pressuring the government, Avro even suppressed publication of a detailed and comprehensive study it had made concerning the use of interceptors in the Arctic, and of how to meet and solve the problems of living and operating conditions to be encountered there. Such a study has now been undertaken by NORAD for the use of the USAF in the Canadian Arctic, where it is suggested that the USAF should take over the defence of Canada's northern areas. Truly, the government is satisfied to be a satellite country, guarded by the troops and planes of a foreign country.*

In the world of legal sleight-of-hand, it is an old trick to accuse the other side of using certain tactics. Then, while the jury carefully watches the other side for any sign of such tactics, you yourself can proceed to use them with impunity. Diefenbaker is a master of sleight-of-hand, and the charge of lobbying was just such a tool. It served to divert public attention from the real lobby that swung into noisy, unremittant ac-

---

* In 1959, there were already some 8,000 U.S. military personnel in Canada. It has been estimated that at least 4,000 additional U.S. military personnel would be required here if they were to be assigned the role of defending the Canadian north as suggested.

tion following *Maclean's* issue of October 25, 1958.*

In an effort to put on the company the blame for the sudden closure, the government charged that the company should have anticipated the cancellation from press reports. Since when have companies been able to cancel contracts on the basis of press reports? Would they ever get another contract if they did? Anyone trying to determine his contractual obligations on the basis of the hysterical articles in the press during the previous five months would have suffered a mental collapse. The government now says that the company should have known of the cancellation six months or even a year before it happened. But, to justify the government's confusion, Pearkes himself told the House on March 2 that the decision depended on answers from Britain and the United States, and that he himself "did not have the final answer until a few weeks ago". Did only Mr. Diefenbaker know? Or was even he still plotting the best moment for the kill?

Now that the media had convinced the public that the vague September announcement constituted a cancellation, Diefenbaker felt free to say that "he told the company in September." What he *did* tell the company in September was to get the cost down by installing the new Hughes MG-3 fire control system, to speed up the completion date, and that a production order would then be possible. This — the production order — would be reviewed on March 31. A.V. Roe proceeded on this directive. Would any sane company drop seven years of unremitting and outstanding work, so near to completion, on the basis of that directive, or of conflicting press reports and rumours? Would any sane company expect a responsible government to throw away, so near to completion,

---

* When later, Canada found out that we did need advanced interceptors after all, and began shopping around for suitable replacements in the U.S., shortly after the cancellation of the Arrow, no one noticed the intense lobbying being carried on in Canada bv. rival U.S. aircraft manufacturers, which ranged from public flying displays of their planes in Ottawa, to full-page newspaper and magazine ads, touting the rival virtues of their planes' performance and cost in order to influence the Canadian public. There wasn't a word from Diefenbaker, deploring the 'pressures' of this lobby, or from Pierre Berton or *Maclean's* magazine objecting to this high-pressure lobbying *by a foreign country and its corporations*, being carried out in Canada. Perhaps they paid more for their ads than A.V. Roe did. Certainly, there were far more of them.

all the results of the work already done under the first two contracts?

The government also charged that A.V. Roe should have had alternative programmes on hand, *especially commercial projects*. This is a particularly bitter charge. The government didn't mention that, when the company produced the first commercial Jetliner in North America, eight years ahead of the United States, the previous government ordered them to abandon it and "concentrate on military aircraft", and that they were not allowed the use of even the small amount of floor space required to make the flight-test modifications necessary to obtain foreign orders, nor were they allowed to accept any of the orders and potential orders they had received. Perhaps the memory of C.D. Howe's famous and misleading remark that "you can't build a plane without orders", by which he had justified the scrapping of the Jetliner, kept the Opposition relatively quiet while the Arrow was being scrapped. By the time Avro could have begun again on commercial design, they had of course, lost that eight-year lead. Even the one flying Jetliner had been completely destroyed, so that Canadians would never even remember it.

The government also failed to mention that they refused to discuss any of several current alternatives Avro had under study, or to agree to the release of personnel from the Arrow programme for other work. Avro was 'under contract' to finish the Arrow and Iroquois programmes within the time specified, until the day it was notified *officially* that they were cancelled. The government also ignored the fact that the September statement said only that the Arrow would not be *put into production at present*, and that the programme was to be reviewed on March 31. The statement did not even suggest that the "development programme" and the "research and test programme" would not be finished according to the existing, almost-completed contracts.

Statements of both Diefenbaker and Pearkes were masterpieces of obfuscation. When asked in Parliament whether he or officials of his Department had conferred with any officials of A.V. Roe before the announcement to advise them that *all contracts* would be terminated weeks before the announced date of review, Pearkes made a most illuminating and typical statement: "The officials of the company have been in Ottawa within the last two weeks"; they have seen "the *report in the press*" which had been put out, and "the statement by the officials of my Department which were *reported in the press* when the estimates were tabled, clearly showing that there was enough money *either* to continue the development or to cancel it. There was no hesitation. There was no attempt to confuse anybody. It was clearly stated that *both were possibilities*". Well, it may be inexcusable, but this layman must be pardoned for being confused. If enough money is provided in the estimates to *continue* a development, one does not conclude that it will be cancelled, unless so advised! The confusion engendered by statements made by Diefenbaker and Pearkes, both before and after the cancellation, was shared by many commentators both in Canada and elsewhere.* Perhaps it is just as well for Mr. Pearkes that he chose the Army for his career so long ago. He would have been in a pretty mess if he had cancelled his contracts in industry on the basis of press reports or of such statements as the above.

Government statements that the United States would not

---

* This confusion has been noted by other writers who have tried to follow government statements during this period. Some of their comments, while couched in as diplomatic terms as possible, have been devastating. For instance, in commenting on Diefenbaker's hasty decision to sign the NORAD agreement shortly after his election, without any proper consultation with either his Defence Committee or with the Cabinet itself, McLin remarks that the Prime Minister's only statement was an attempt to implicate the Liberals in the decision. He notes that, "This was an early example of a Diefenbaker trait which was to show itself on later occasions; he found it easier and/or more congenial to attack the former government or the Opposition than to explain what his own government was doing." He also remarks that, in the course of debate "the government tended ... to undermine its own arguments," and that "fear of political embarrassment, not military logic" dictated the course they followed.

He contends that some of the confusion engendered "lay in the tendency of the Diefenbaker government to set forth its policies not in the clearest terms possible but in what (it thought) were the most politically palatable terms." He noted, with respect to Defence Minister Pearkes, that he would make statements which, on more than one occasion, later had to be modified. He suggests that "The reader who finds [Pearkes'] comments less than clarifying has a good deal of company in current editorial comment." In general, he concludes that the Conservatives had a "tendency to act furtively and conceal information," a course which was politically inspired but, in the long run, politically unprofitable.[2]

In his Memoirs, there is a similar attempt by Diefenbaker to tailor the facts so as to flatter himself and his government and to make the whole confused and deplorable event sound like a masterpiece of clear thinking, planning, far-sighted logic, magnanimity and "patience."[3]

buy the Arrow, made before it had been put into production, and Pearkes' statement that it couldn't be used in NATO and had "probably never been intended for use in Europe," along with Diefenbaker's equally wild and contradictory figures as to costs, had one purpose only: to convince Canadians that the Arrow they had produced was a useless and expensive plane, with no future except perhaps a small role in Canada's far northern defence. Even here, since there was no SAGE in the North either, the USAF would presumably have to take care of us, especially in western Canada, which was "too far away for Canada to defend" according to Pearkes.[4]

A purely military decision would have required only the cancellation of the Arrow production programme on the grounds that interceptor aircraft were no longer needed. A purely economic decision would have required only that no further funds be expended on the programme except those required to recoup as much as possible of the costs through sales contracts with France and the contract with Curtiss-Wright of the U.S. for manufacture and sale under licence of the Iroquois engine; it would also have included the sale of the flight-tested and flying aircraft to the Royal Aeronautical Establishment in Britain, as requested. The Prime Minister's personal vendetta against the company may have required the obscene destruction of millions of dollars worth of finished and almost-finished planes, of tools, jigs, fixtures and masses of expensive production and test equipment. It could have accounted for the total lack of concern as to any further contracts to the company under defence sharing arrangements, all of which were directed to Canadair; and for the lack of any action taken to retain the technological and engineering personnel. But the effects were even more wide-spread and devastating than this.

In the fall of 1958, the *Financial Post* pointed out how widespread would be the effects of a cancellation of the Arrow programme. It carried a list of major suppliers across Canada whose contracts would be cancelled. About 650 major subcontractors were working on purchase orders for the Arrow. These orders would total, during 1959, expenditures in Canada of about $25 million. According to the *Post*, the livelihoods of nearly 100,000 Canadians would be affected, as well as the fate of dozens of new industries, particularly in electronics.[5] Due to the scarcity of any other large Canadian industries which make a practice of purchasing supplies and components from *Canadian* sub-contractors, many of these companies still relied mainly on orders A.V. Roe had placed with them. Many had not yet had time to expand their markets in Canada and abroad.

The treatment meted out to these new and growing industries by the Canadian government was disastrous. Apparently there was no limit to the swathe Diefenbaker would cut in order to complete the destruction. There was no limit to his single-minded determination to "save face" even to the extent of sending Canadian companies into bankruptcy. Over three months after the cancellation of the Arrow programme, an internal memo was circulated stating that:

> No effort has been made to date to settle termination contracts with any of the hundreds of companies involved. One company has spent three months preparing and filling out the required termination forms, only to have a new set of forms sent out saying that the existing ones are now replaced. They are now forced to spend three month's additional work on the new forms. No interest is being paid by the Government on the money they owe to these firms. Many of them are owed from hundreds of thousands to millions of dollars for investments already made in plant equipment and tooling and for complete parts and equipment already supplied complete for the first 37 aircraft. Many of these firms are facing bankruptcy as a result. However, if these contract termination charges were to appear in the Government's budget in the current year, it would become obvious at once to even the most thoughtless Canadian that we had not only lost a $300 million investment, but that it had also cost us as much to scrap it as it would have cost to complete it ...[6] *

But bankrupt companies are evidently a small price to pay to avoid giving the lie to Mr. Diefenbaker in his claim to have saved the taxpayer millions of dollars. To prevent the public from knowing how high a cost it would have to pay for his sudden cancellation of the existing contracts just 40 days

---

* This was confirmed by officials of a number of the companies involved.

before they would have been reviewed in any case, the Government delayed the settling of its termination contracts with any of the hundreds of companies involved so that the costs would not appear in the estimates for the current year. Perhaps he hoped that, by the time another year had passed, apathetic Canadians would have lost interest.

Not only were Canadian companies affected. The press attacks against A.V. Roe and the Arrow extended to everyone who worked there. Old wartime attitudes towards the thousands of workers who had been recruited to work at the same plant during the war, when it was called Victory Aircraft, were revived and applied to the new company and its employees. Malton is not far from what was then the sleepy town of Brampton. Aside from the local Dale Florists who grew roses and shipped them all over the country, there had been little industry there up to that time. The surrounding area was fine farmland and the local population were largely shopkeepers and prosperous farmers. Many of them resented the growth of the town as new arrivals, many of whom worked at A.V. Roe, bought or built houses in the area. They also had the traditional suspicion, then shared by so much of Canada's population, of 'office' workers, trained in professions such as engineering or technology. They tended to regard them, not as 'real' workers but as overpaid loafers. A whispering campaign against the new residents spread around the area. *

The whispering campaign was picked up by the press. As a result, after the cancellation, those who did not go to the United States or to Europe, were not only being refused work in the Toronto area, but were being insulted into the bargain. They were maligned, their work belittled as 'wasteful', 'useless' and 'obsolete'. All the catch-words used by the press concerning the Arrow were directed against those who had worked on it. The press referred to them as 'overpaid' although few of them had been making as much as the average Toronto-area school teacher and they had none of the security. Engineers at A.V. Roe earned less than some newly-

---

* This would not be possible in the Brampton of today which has been submerged in the spreading new industrial municipalities of Bramalea and Mississauga, most of whose residents now work in Toronto or in large local industries. Whether it is better or worse is a moot point, but it is very different.

arrived real-estate salesmen, who require only a three-month part-time course in order to qualify. Such was the atmosphere that even unskilled or unemployed workers in the Toronto area showed a vicious satisfaction in the closing of A.V. Roe. They believed the government's statements as to the enormous amount of money that had been 'wasted' and was now being 'saved'. They did not, of course, realize that this was just what other large companies wanted — the elimination of a developing industrial enviroment that could result in increasing numbers of jobs at higher skill levels and better pay, bringing increasing prosperity for everyone. Instead, high unemployment forces wages down (or did at that time) and increases profits. Even the workers were divided against each other. It is easy to con Canadians into believing the myths that we are too small and too poor to do anything for ourselves in Canada — even to our own eventual cost.

The wide-spread rumours about the so-called high pay at Avro and Orenda should have been well-exploded by the much higher offers from the United States that Avro personnel had been turning down for years, because they preferred to work in Canada as long as there was challenging work to be done. If further proof were needed, the following incident, typical of many, should give those rumours the lie. After the Arrow cancellation, a former engineer from Orenda applied to Atomic Energy of Canada for a job. AECL is one of the few other Canadian corporations that require people with training and experience in high technology. AECL has had trouble getting and retaining qualified personnel since its pay scales are comparatively low. Towards the end of the interview, the question of pay came up. The engineer was told, "Of course we can't offer you the fabulous pay you received at Orenda; we can't afford to throw money around the way they did." They then made their lower and more 'sensible' offer — which was $600 a year *more* than he had been making at Orenda.[7] (In 1959, that was a large difference). The same thing happened to those who applied for work at U.S.-owned Canadair in Montreal. Because of the whispering campaign against Avro, Canadair had gained an unearned reputation for paying lower wages and, therefore, of being more 'efficient' than Avro. Perhaps their wages were lower for their office help and shop workers. But the pay they offered their engineers was better than that paid at Avro[8] . Perhaps some circles in Canada rated Canadair more highly than Avro because, according to the rumours, it was doing more to keep down the standard of living in Canada.

Maclean's was not quite disinterested either. Apparently they also believed the whispering campaigns. They went even further. They phoned one man from Avro three times following February 20, telling him they had just the job for him, requiring a man "with experience and education". When he finally went down for an interview, they offered him this wonderful job, at $19.50 a week. "But", they said, "when you really work into it, you can make a lot more than that — even as high as $28 a week. And we only work a 30-hour week here. You would appreciate that."[9] It was certainly fewer hours than he had worked at Avro, and it is nice to know that people at *Maclean's* had it so easy. We trust that, even in 1959, most *Maclean's* employees made more than that. But what impelled *Maclean's* to invite an unemployed man, whose industry they had done their best to destroy, down to their expensive new building just to insult him? Just how deep is the hatred in Canada of any Canadian success story, and what is the source of this vicious and self-defeating attitude?

To work for the government on development and production contracts is always a gamble, subject to every kind of insecurity, from every change in the economic and political atmosphere, to changing requirements imposed by officials who haven't done their homework, to dealing with politicians who are inexperienced or worse. In Canada especially such projects have to contend with an atmosphere that is inimical to Canadian investment in long-term research and development projects — an inherent suspicion of and unawareness of the benefits to be derived from high technology investment and a tendency to drop any such investment before it pays off, if it hasn't shown immediate returns. All of this is in addition to the usual hazards of any scientific and industrial development, especially in Canada, where the pressures of U.S. competition are so great. A.V. Roe had surmounted the technological and development hurdles and had twice beaten the American competition by several years. The company had gambled on advanced designs for three aircraft and two engines and had come up with winners in every case. In the short space of ten years, these few hundred graduate engineers, designers and technicians had built up the best team in aircraft research and design on the North American continent, if not in the world. They had done it in spite of the drain of good personnel to the United States. Anyone who knows anything about research and development and the production of new, advanced designs knows of the terrific pressure on any project. Time is of the utmost importance in the race to produce the best, ahead of the rest of the world, in order to be competitive (unless one has a 'protected' market, as American companies appear to have). In most countries, if they succeed, it pays off; but not in Canada, or for Canada.

There was, of course, little other work here for these designers, engineers, and technicians. Most of the research done in Canada was now gone. Other plants could not absorb them. They did not even answer applications. One man had a job almost secured until he said he had formerly worked at Avro. He was immediately told he needn't bother to apply. That same firm later turned down a contract which involved high-quality, close-tolerance work which they were unable to handle. Is this what scares them — the need to meet modern demands and methods, to be competitive in Canada? Another man sent out applications to 47 firms across Canada. Only 20 took the trouble to answer. They had nothing. He regretfully and bitterly left Canada to work in the United States for Minneapolis-Honeywell, from whom Canada imports a great many products because they are not produced here. One engineer went to 37 'Canadian' firms in the Toronto area in a week. All require a great deal of engineering and design work. They all told him the same thing: "We do not hire engineers in Canada. All our design and engineering *is done by the parent company in the U.S.*" He went to work for North American Aviation in Columbus, Ohio. His products and his taxes now produce revenue for the United States.[10]

Avro and Orenda between them employed between three and four hundred engineers. There are few other large employers and, of the jobs available for engineers in Canada, the general opinion is that over half of them are so routine, uninteresting and undemanding that they could be handled by a reasonably intelligent graduate of Toronto's Ryerson Institute of Technology. To handle the type of work which was considered routine at Avro and Orenda, most of these firms would demand someone with a Ph.D.

The top-notch engineers and technicians from A.V. Roe were, of course, picked off by U.S. firms immediately after cancellation. Even those who didn't want to leave Canada soon found they had to join the others as there was no work for them in Canada. Avro had one of the top designers on the continent and one of the best mathematical experts. It had one of the only three authorities on high-pressure systems in North America. Thirty men, with their families, went to work for the National Aeronautical and Space Administration (NASA) on space vehicles for the U.S. government. They were specifically asked for. Over one hundred were taken on by North American Aviation. Others went to Lockheed plants in Georgia and California, to Boeing, Rhor, Vertol and Grumman, among others. One is now in charge of off-shore drilling rigs for Boeing. Another became project engineer on the landing gear for North American Aviation's Apollo project. One became Development Project Manager, Launching Systems, for the Boeing Aerospace Program. Another is Chief Designer and Vice-President of Fokker Aircraft in the Netherlands.

Canada's only expert in hydrofoil design did not want to leave Canada but, due to lack of either funds or government support for Canada's successful hydrofoil project, which was left dangling, as usual, until other countries could catch up, he now works for the U.S. government's Department of Ships.

One Avro engineer became Vice-President and Director of Westinghouse (Canada), another became Vice-President and Director of McDonnell-Douglas (Canada). His job now is to sell us planes produced by his company in the United States. There were many more of the same outstanding ability. One U.S. visa office in Ontario alone, issued 2,600 visas in the first three months of 1959. Their holders were, in most cases, lost to Canada forever.

But, according to John Deutsch, of Queen's University and

one of Canada's 'leading' economic advisers and spokesmen, Canada is "a large, empty land, empty of people, capital and skills." Does he ask why?

The noisy campaign waged by the government and the press against Avro and the Arrow spread far beyond Canada. The reputation given to this Canadian company and its aircraft, by the Canadian government and press, spread abroad even to people and officials who knew nothing about aircraft. A nice black eye for Canada and her technical ability! The abuse heaped on the Arrow here and the speed with which it was destroyed created the impression abroad among those who were not familiar with it that it must have been a total failure. As a result, the following episode, can and did happen. It is doubtless typical of reactions throughout the world; no other country could imagine a government behaving in such a manner for any other reason.

An American engineer who had visited Avro regularly for years in connection with his company's equipment and who knew the Arrow and its performance well, was talking to an official in Washington shortly after the cancellation. He mentioned the Arrow. The official said, "That was a real mess. They had to cut it up real fast so people wouldn't know how bad it was". The American engineer blew up; he protested, "It was a better plane, with fewer bugs in it than I have ever seen come out of an American factory. It was better-built, took less testing, cost less, took less time to develop, and required the most minor changes in design. Look at all the basic redesign most American planes have to go through before they are up to scratch. The first Arrow off the line, without a prototype, flew seven times in the first 25 days, went supersonic on its third flight, and even recorded two flights in one day; it was expected to break the world's speed record in a short time." Then he recalled the U.S. official's response: "That couldn't be true. No government would be crazy enough to scrap a plane like that and then buy them somewhere else. It must have been a flop. Look what they did to it." The American told us this story and was still hopping mad. But as he admitted, "What could I say? His last remark just can't be answered."[11]

Arrow landing after first flight. Note speed brakes deployed.

Courtesy Canadian Aviation Historical Society

This familiar story would be believed only in Canada. The reaction of a Japanese mission which visited England and the U.S. shortly after the cancellation was later reported in a Japanese magazine. The Canadian decision to cancel an advanced Canadian plane and replace it with a U.S. plane, which was then being phased out and replaced by its own country appeared quite incomprehensible to them.

When questioned in Parliament later about the fate of the large quantities of almost completed test data that had been collected, the government indicated that "it will not release the test data because, although no Western power is interested in either the engine or the airframe, it feels that the information possibly could aid a potential enemy".[12] This statement like many others exceeded the bounds of legitimate error. Other countries had, of course, shown considerable interest both in obtaining the existing planes and in purchasing or manufacturing under licence the Iroquois engine, as the government well knew. As to the release of the test data, it was not its acquisition by potential enemies which concerned the government. One should remember that the Arrow was destroyed, not so that no one could find out how *bad* it was but, contrary to the Washington official's logical conclusion, so that Canadians would never find out how *good* it was. All the test data was destroyed.

In the course of development, production and testing, Avro made film records of research, methods, processes, flight testing and so on. Many high-technology firms do this. They are invaluable records and Avro's were more detailed and complete than most. Many companies loan such films all over the country to firms and to groups that ask for them. Even films on Soviet rocketry are available to groups in Canada. One would think that the production of the CF-100, the Jetliner and the Arrow, as well as of two very advanced aircraft engines, along with the development of new metal alloys and new fabricating processes, were part of the 'History of Flight' in Canada. Yet when Avro offered one such film to the CBC, it was called a 'lobby'! So perhaps the next episode could have been predicted.

Some of the films produced by Avro were rated as among the best and most informative industrial films ever made. One film on *Flutter and How to Combat It* won the highest award given in the U.S. for an industrial film. Neither the film nor its award received any publicity in Canada. But a firm in the U.S. which had heard of it wrote, shortly after the cancellation, asking to borrow it. These films are extremely useful to other firms and save them from duplicating work done elsewhere. We pay dearly in Canada for access to this kind of information from the United States, if and when we can get it. The U.S. firm was told, "The film is not available." When Avro engineers protested, they were told by a government official, "You fellows seem to think the Arrow was important. Forget it! *It never existed*. Get that into your heads."

It never existed! Forget that Canadians ever designed and built the Jetliner, the Arrow, the Orenda and Iroquois engines, or the *Bras d'Or* or any of the other firsts that Canadian individuals and companies have to their credit. Above all, make sure that all evidence is destroyed; it might disturb the myths — that Canada is a "large, empty country, empty of people, capital or skills." Otherwise, we might get the idea that we were just smart enough to take our own raw resources and produce much of our own domestic requirements as well as producing enough distinctive products for export that we could compete with other countries, even, perhaps, with the U.S.

Not one of the three A.V. Roe planes can be found in Canada's National Aviation Museum; it is full of planes from other countries or of other countries' designs manufactured here under licence.* The exhibits range back to and including the Silver Dart. On a recent visit to the Museum, the author found an original Iroquois engine up against the wall of the Museum and went over to read the label. There was nothing, not even a name, to identify it, although every other exhibit had a large sign beside it, giving its name and its history. On being queried, the attendant replied, "We have asked for a sign a number of times but the answer has always been 'NO'." Asked why, he seemed at a loss for a moment, then said: "I expect that it is still politically explosive."

Even twenty years later? But then, Diefenbaker is still alive.

---

* There is, of course, the U.S. F-104, which replaced the CF-100 and the Arrow.

The author sincerely hopes that, in such an atmosphere, the attendant does not lose his job and that the magnificent engine does not somehow also disappear from sight, along with the Jetliner and the Arrow. The result of "a purely military decision."

---

1 "Defence Chiefs Warned by PM on Airing Views," *Globe & Mail,* Ottawa bureau dispatch, Jan. 16, 1959
2 McLin, Jon, *Canada's Changing Defence Policy, 1957-1963*, Johns Hopkins, Baltimore, 1967
3 Diefenbaker, Rt. Hon. John G., *One Canada*: *The Tumultuous Years*, Macmillan, Toronto, 1977
4 Lowe, Frank, "Is the RCAF Obsolete?", *Weekend*, Vol. 9, No. 33, Aug. 14, 1959
5 *Financial Post*, Toronto, Sept. 20, 1958
6 International Association of Machinists, internal information memorandum
7 From conversation between the author and a former Avro engineer
8 *idem*
9 Signed affidavit from former Avro technologist; and the author's personal interview.
10 From conversations with former Avro engineers
11 From conversation with a U.S. company representative
12 *Aviation Week*, Mar. 2, 1959
13 Reply by government official to A.V. Roe personnel, Malton

Chapter 6

A Purely Military Decision: Canadian Style

According to *Maclean's*, the decision to stop production of the "very obsolete fighter aircraft, the Arrow," was a logical military decision, "a decision on military affairs, arrived at for military reasons. And that, we trust, is the only basis on which this country will ever make a military decision," not on economic factors, such as loss of the whole existing investment, unemployment of several thousand workers, or the loss of further millions of dollars worth of industrial production. The making of war equipment, according to *Maclean's*, has only one legitimate object. "That object is military defense — not pump-priming on behalf of business, not the preservation of full employment; the object is military defense and nothing else. If we ever lose sight of this simple fact or even waver from it by the slightest degree, capitalism will deserve all the libels heaped on it by its most envenomed critics. And the society we seek to defend will be no longer worth defending."[1]

This makes magnificent reading. It sounds almost like a tract in response to Marx. It would be nice if it were true. But even if it were, it would be quite irrelevant to the decision to cancel the Arrow.

Prior to the the procurement of any military hardware, three kinds of decisions must be made. First, there is the political decision, determined by a country's foreign policy and by the alliances it has contracted. This determines whether or not a country requires defending or, perhaps as *Maclean's* would put it, is worth defending. Once the political decision has been made, two other decisions remain. The second, or military decision, concerns the kind of armed forces required, the role they are to play and the military equipment they require. These decisions are, in most countries, taken on the basis of the perceived defence needs of the country itself and on the basis of mutual decisions reached within its alliances as to the role it should play. These decisions determine the kinds of equipment required. The third decision then becomes a purely economic decision as to where to obtain such equipment, so as to obtain the best and most suitable equipment possible, and to receive the maximum over-all value for the millions expended.

If we reneged on all of our military agreements in NORAD and NATO, cut off all spending on defence equipment and let a foreign country take over our defence, few economic decisions would have to be made, although it would still cost us a considerable amount, as some European countries have discovered. The question of the resulting satellite status is one that Canada could probably learn to live with; we have had considerable practice. But we have not yet completely reneged on our commitment to NATO, although we have come close to it in the past decade or so. Although we are almost at the bottom of the list of NATO countries in terms of percentage contributions, we do spend relatively large amounts on military equipment.

Once we have decided on what equipment is required, which is a military decision, usually made on the basis of thorough consultation with military advisers at home and alliance partners abroad, the only remaining decision is an ecomomic one. Put briefly, it is whether we buy abroad, adding enormously to our already huge deficit in imports, and getting nothing in return in the way of technological development, employment, huge tax returns and, eventually, in the possibility of further profits from foreign sales, or whether we spend the money on production at home and at least derive some of these additional benefits.

From an economic standpoint, the history of Canadian government pump-priming to produce even a few jobs, to the tune of millions of dollars donated to U.S. corporations to establish branch plants in Canada, or merely to move to a different area to relieve unemployment; the construction of enormously expensive facilities and infrastructure for the sole benefit of foreign companies, plus the handouts to regional areas to promote inefficient and uneconomic developments, must be read to be believed. Few of these have repaid the cost either in technological leadership, in the development of distinctive products or exports, in the encouragement and support of Canadian domestic suppliers or even in very many sustainable jobs, even at a low skill level. There is really no economic reason why production of Canadian technologically advanced aircraft, either civil or military, is less deserving of such subsidies, if one can call domestic purchase a subsidy, than many of the foreign enterprises we have in the past, or are now, subsidizing.

But *Maclean's* considers the loss of millions of dollars worth of industrial production and growth and the immediate unemployment of many thousands of workers irrelevant, so let us concern ourselves with the purely military aspects of the decision and the way in which it was made. If this was a purely military decision, certainly no such military decision was ever carried out in a stranger manner. A purely military decision would have been carried out in a responsible way, after thorough consultation with experts in all related fields and after well-informed public and private discussion. A responsible government would have had a well-defined alternative military policy in hand before sending this programme and all it had cost down the drain. It would already have taken steps to implement a mix of programmes, especially under the Defence Sharing Agreement with the United States (for what that was worth), and including modifications to existing planes as requested by the RCAF. Such moves would have prevented as far as possible the complete dislocation of the industry and the loss of at least some of the design teams concerned, which Diefenbaker "claimed" he was trying to prevent. If only considerations of military needs had been involved, we would certainly have attempted to salvage from the project as many of the economic savings as possible. We could have accepted France's inquiry as to purchase of 300 Orenda-Iroquois engines, and the agreement with Curtiss-Wright to manufacture and sell these engines under licence in the United States. This is the way in which other countries pay off their development costs. We would have sold to the U.S. or the U.K., both of whom had asked for them, some or all of the already fully complete and flying Arrows, and have put at least one in our own Aviation Museum, so that future Canadians could have some pride in our capacity to produce leading products. With that kind of decision, if it were justified, few people would have too much quarrel. None of these things occured. The consensus of military opinion both here and in the U.S., military advice from Canadian experts, requests from NATO for an interceptor like the Arrow, the preservation of independent sources of supply for Canadian military equipment, the future of the industry and of the design teams which had finally been built up with so much effort, from around the world — these were the last things considered by the government. In fact, the purpose was quite different.

Contrary to *Maclean's*, cancellation of the Arrow did not represent political courage. Diefenbaker perceived it as a political and, even more, as a personal triumph. That, as a purely military decision, his action was a disaster, and ran counter to military intelligence in both Canada and the U.S. did not concern him in the least. Neither did its effects on Canada's future economic development or our reputation as an independent modern country. It is doubtful that Diefenbaker knew anything about any such matters, military or economic. Political oratory was his business. His oratory on his "Vision" of Canada's future was heady stuff. He also got quite a bit of mileage out of his 'mission' to free Canada from the overpowering dominance of one country, the United States, and to strengthen ties with Britain and the Commonwealth. The only results of all this oratory were that he angered and offended the Americans beyond measure through his ignorance, posturing, rudeness and indecision while, at the same time, he made Canada an object of contempt to be easily manipulated. He rebuffed the British offer of a free trade agreement, made in response to his oratorical flights about closer trade ties with the Commonwealth. The results of his deeds were, in the long run, the exact opposite of his words, and we were, five years later, more tightly bound to the U.S. empire, both militarily and economically, than ever before.

The making of a purely military decision with respect to the procurement of military equipment involves consideration of many complex factors. Since few government leaders have the necessary expertise to make such decisions on military grounds rather than on the grounds of political expediency, it would seem essential to call in the necessary experts and conduct a thorough investigation into all the statements made and evidence given. It would seem of prime importance that those who are given the responsibility to decide on the procurement of expensive equipment are themselves as well informed as is humanly possible.

If such decisions are to be supported by the public — and this decision relied tremendously on arousing popular emotion — then the public must also be given at least a clear statement of factual information, rather than emotional press releases and blatant and deliberate mis-information on the part of the government. The government's advisers on military, economic and policy matters must be heard, in public and in private, rather than being muzzled and told to keep quiet while the government gets its advice from Washington, where the priorities and responsibilities are quite different.

Whether purchased abroad or produced at home, military equipment is expensive. It is essential to know what role it is expected to perform and whether or not it can do so effectively. In the case of equipment purchased abroad, this is even more important, since few other domestic benefits will be gained from it. No country can afford to select such equipment on the basis of ignorance, personal prejudice or short-term political expediency. Yet, since 1958, Canada's record in this respect has been a sorry picture of waste and mismanagement. It has resulted in the purchase of ineffective equipment, has saved us little money, if any, and has provided few benefits of any kind, economic or otherwise. For most of the period, our role in NATO has therefore been little more than a token gesture. As for NORAD, well, of course, the U.S. will look after us. But should we really spend so much money just to look so silly? If we do spend it, we should at least have something more to show for it?

A purely military decision would first consider the role a piece of equipment is required to perform. Military planes, Bomarcs and so on, are designed to perform in a specific manner, to carry out specific roles within a specific 'game plan' or scenario; that is, in the kind of situation which the experts believe to be possible or probable, and in the kind of action we will be required to take according to our military and foreign policy commitments.

Different roles require, with few exceptions, quite different types of equipment produced to different design specifications. To choose the right equipment able to deliver the necessary performance, without agreeing on the role it is expected to perform, will result at best in inefficiency, and at worst in a complete waste of military funds and a gap in our defences. This is particularly true of aircraft. *Wings Magazine* recently carried an excellent analysis of the considerations which should enter into such a choice and the extent to which Canada has ignored any such fundamental military considerations, both in 1958-9 and since.[2]

Current roles for military aircraft range from interception (usually high-level), to strike/interdiction, through open-air combat, (the dog - fights of the last wars), to attack and close air support, usually carried out at low level. The design parameters for each role are different, in some cases quite radically so. There may be two or three overlapping characteristics common to adjacent roles, such as interception and strike-interdiction, but these points are few. To increase them imposes a performance penalty against one role or the other, or both. "The most difficult trade-off comes in the attack and close air support mission," for which the aerodynamic requirements are quite different from those for other roles, as are the electronic and fire-control requirements.

The proliferation of ground-to-air electronic defences has affected the type of war plan envisaged. The Americans still consider open-sky, air-to-air combat ability a prime requirement and are able to force this concept (and their planes) on some of their allies. As Wayne Ralph notes, the Americans have "invincible faith in their own technology" in the face of the bristling ground defences of Europe. Other

European countries, by contrast, claim that this type of combat ability might be applicable if future wars were to be fought over the Arizona desert, but would be unthinkable over densely populated Europe, and would be suicidal for planes and pilots. Their planes are therefore designed for low, treetop-level attack, to knock out tanks, trains and supply routes, and to provide close air support for ground action. They contend that nothing above tree-top level would survive for very long. In this latter role, it would be supremely wasteful to use expensive, highly sophisticated planes since "the cost of one plane lost would be higher than that of hundreds of tanks or trains destroyed." On the other hand, for high-level interception roles, the most sophisticated airframe, engines and electronic equipment, preferably carried in the plane, are required. The ease with which ground control systems like SAGE can be jammed makes the latter important.

Due to these conflicting design requirements, no designer really claims to be able to produce a plane with more than a dual role capacity, in spite of their companies' glowing press releases. There are some similarities between interception and interdiction requirements, such as high wing loadings, and some strike capacity may be added through use of a variable geometry wing, but the cost is high. There is also some trade-off between interception and air combat roles, with the addition to the latter of radar and radar controlled missiles. But to design an air combat or interceptor plane which is also efficient as a low-level attack and close air support plane presents a conflict in design requirements. According to *Wings'* analysts, an attack fighter that can defend itself is "historically a rare combination."[3] The manufacturers of some of the planes being offered to Canada in 1978 make this claim.

Disagreement over future scenarios in Europe and the best type of plane to meet the apprehended threat is compounded by confusion as to the planes that will be available to NATO. Ray Braybrook comments: "Please don't ask where Canada stands on this, as the country's defence scenario (if it exists) is the great impenetrable mystery of the aviation business." In some countries, unfortunately, equipment is frequently chosen, not on the basis of its required performance, but "on the basis of price and political expediency."[4] As a result, either the roles must be altered to suit the planes, or the planes must be modified to fit the roles which they are actually required to perform. Either process is costly and inefficient. It does not produce a well-planned and coordinated defence. In Canada's case, it has resulted, since 1958, in a long series of costly expenditures on weapons systems which did not meet Canadian or NATO requirements, or which were expected to perform roles for which they were not designed. Most of them were selected on the basis of lowest 'first cost', or according to which firm offered the most apparently attractive package of 'off-set' goodies, few of which brought much benefit, if any, to Canada. These are economic and political criteria. They are not the criteria of a "military decision."

As a result of changing conditions in Europe, Canadian requirements for its NORAD role may now require planes with different characteristics than those required for NATO, unless the two roles have been well-defined and co-ordinated in advance. In such a case, purchase of smaller orders of two different planes, one primary and one secondary, for the different roles, might be considerably cheaper in the long run. We might then have to forego some of the supposed benefits of the off-set programmes, but their benefits so far have been largely political.[5]

In 1958, however, this was not a problem. NATO had asked Canada to provide another high-level, fast interceptor to replace the CF-100 and Sabre interceptors. The Arrow was designed for just this role, with its high thrust-to-weight ratio, thin, delta-shaped wing, its speed and high rate of climb. This also made it admirably suited to interception and surveillance patrols over the Arctic, with its two engines for added safety over Arctic wilderness and with both pilot and navigator to assist in navigation and fire control in its high-level interception role. The government cancelled it, but not for military reasons as they claimed.

Neither in 1958-59 nor now does the Canadian government appear to have had any clear policy concerning either Canadian domestic defence needs or its role in NORAD or NATO. As Wayne Ralph points out, there is little military input into the government's White Papers on defence; there appear to be no 'scenario writers' in Ottawa, and we have become "just carbon copiers of other nations."[6]   When the new and inexperienced Diefenbaker government rushed to sign the NORAD agreement so soon after its election, it did so without any consultation with its Cabinet Defence Committee, the Cabinet, or of course, Parliament.   Presumably, there was little time for consultation with its armed forces.   The bargaining positions we might have maintained as our price for joining what would be, in effect, a very unequal bilateral alliance, were thrown away.   We therefore effectively lost any control over our own defence priorities, which are, in many respects, quite different from those of the United States, and over our choice of military equipment and production.   There is, therefore, as in so many areas, little room left for any independent Canadian policy; our direction as to policy, weapons and procurement is laid down in Washington to a very large extent.   Our NATO policies must be fitted into these NORAD parameters, or the cost would be prohibitive.   The result of this lack of any independent or coherent policy in Canada has since 1958, been a ludicrous series of conflicting policy statements and a series of inept purchases of equipment which, as *Wings* points out, seldom met Canadian requirements and, in some cases could perform no successful role in any conceivable scenario.[7]

Let us consider the Canadian experience as compared with the American method of arriving at a "military decision".   Of course, contrary to *Maclean's*, no decision as to military procurement, in any country in the world, including Canada, is ever based on purely military factors alone.   Economics, costs, employment opportunities or jobs lost, export business to be derived, foreign policy, and the need to support technological development in the home country, all enter into such decisions, certainly in the United States and Britain.   The latter factor is considered especially important to any country hoping to achieve or retain a place with other advanced nations, since, as noted before, it provides one of the most effective stimuli to all kinds of technological developments. This is not to provide an argument for defence production *per se*; but it is an argument for procuring this equipment at home if we are going to buy it in any case.

In the United States, whatever other aspects are involved,

the purely military aspects are thoroughly explored in public as well as in private, and final decisions are at least based on the best military evidence available. When the U.S. government must make decisions on military procurement, a bi-partisan Congressional sub-committee is activated whose business it is to hold hearings, call witnesses and cross-examine them to find out all the facts and assess them. Every available expert is called and questioned exhaustively on matters within his expertise. This was being done in the United States in 1958.[8] General Partridge, the U.S. Chief of NORAD, the North American defence alliance of which Canada was now a member, had concluded several days of testimony before the U.S. Senate sub-committee. All except strictly 'classified' evidence was being released to the American public, so that they would be well-informed on the issues at stake. It was, of course, also available to the Canadian Prime Minister and Minister of Defence.

Let us review the arguments brought forth by the government to defend its cancellation of the Arrow/Iroquois programmes. The government had just acquired two Bomarc bases and contracted to pay one-third of their cost. To justify both this purchase and the Arrow cancellation, Diefenbaker claimed that we had entered the missile age; any potential enemy would, from now on, be concentrating on missiles. We were therefore acquiring the Bomarc missile, presumably to meet this new threat, although this was not explicitly stated. Therefore all interceptors would shortly be obsolete; therefore the Arrow was obsolete, even though it was the most advanced interceptor in the world at the time. But even if interceptors were still required, there were others, just as good, which would be available. Later, of course, economic arguments as to our alleged inability to sell the plane to our allies, or to use it in NATO, and the resulting high cost to Canada for a plane of such limited utility, were brought into the debate. Let us therefore compare the statements made by our government (without any supporting evidence being provided by their experts or advisers) with the evidence given by the U.S. Chiefs of Staff before the U.S. Senate sub-committee.

Diefenbaker: "The bomber threat against which the CF-105 (Arrow) could be effective has not proved to be as serious as was forecast. Potential aggressors now seem more likely to put their efforts into missile development than into increasing their bomber force.''

General Pearkes: ''We believe that the CF-100 is capable of dealing with the bomber that the Russians can send over to this country. It will be touch-and-go as far as ... the Bear and the Bison are concerned, but they have that aircraft(sic) in very limited numbers.'' ''The indication has been that the Russians are not continuing the production of any type of bomber more advanced than ... the Bear and the Bison ... that the number is extremely limited and ... these are the only two types which could reach this continent and return again.'' (Touch-and-go should hardly be good enough for our Minister of Defence, if the bombers are loaded with nuclear airborne missiles.)

General Pearkes: There is no longer a bomber threat — but General Pearkes has asked the U.S. to take over the defence of Western Canada for us, with manned interceptors *against manned bombers*. General Pearkes said — he really did — that our Western provinces were ''too far away for Canada to defend.'' Too far away from Canada? So we are now going to improve our western airfields to accomodate U.S. interceptors which are ''obsolete,'' so that the U.S. can defend Western Canada for us, since it is too far away from Canada to defend, because we scrapped the Arrow which could have defended it, because there was no bomber threat we would have to ask the U.S. to defend us against. Are you confused? You should read General Pearkes' explanations in Hansard of February 23, 1959.

Diefenbaker: ''We believe any potential aggressor will concentrate on missiles.'' He went on to say that $20 million paid for Bomarcs would give ''equal coverage to the same area'' as $780 million for Arrows. At the Company's firm price to the government, as of then, $780 million would purchase over 300 aircraft, or over 25 squadrons, enough for NATO and for NORAD and we would still have enough left to defend Western Canada and to sell to other countries.[9]

Meanwhile, testimony being given to those who had the last word in NORAD policy was quite different, as was the considerable evidence from military sources and other observers: General Twining, USAF: ''The Russians are now building a new bomber far beyond the capabilities of the Bear and Bison long-range bombers. We do not know what it is yet, but it is an advanced heavy bomber." (It was nicknamed Bounder and everyone in the air forces and industry had been aware of it for quite some time, except General Pearkes, who did not talk to his military advisers.)

General White: "The advantage of the bomber over the IC-BM is (that) it can carry multiple nuclear weapons—a much bigger yield and variety and can be deployed. It has greater potential for use in limited war."

General Partridge, Chief of NORAD: "At the present time the Soviets can attack us only with bombers ... Our intelligence estimates are that they will improve the quality of their bombers and, in a few years, will have a supersonic bomber force. This means that we must not only maintain the defences against bombers which we have, but we must also improve them, so we can counteract a supersonic attacking force." He noted that the U.S. was equipping its forces with supersonic interceptors, but that the RCAF interceptor, the CF-100, was now "of older design." He also said:

— the aim of the North American Defence Command (NORAD) is to hit an attacker as far away as possible, *i.e.*, over the Arctic.

— Bomarcs are useless for this function and are intended only as "defence in depth" to give the SAC (Strategic Air Command) time to get off the ground and away, and to provide "limited point defence."

— like the Bomarc, Early Warning Radar Lines, such as the Canadian DEW Line and Pine Tree Line, cannot identify radar signals as intruders, or tell the type of attack, if any. For this, there has to be a man in the interceptor.

He added that, for these and other reasons, they needed "the fastest, highest-flying, longest-range interceptor available" for as long as they could foresee. Unfortunately, he said, until the F108 is in service several years from now, there is in the United States "nothing now available except the F101."[10] (The F101 had a speed of about Mach 1.3, less than 1000 mph, and a range of 600 miles at most. It was not comparable to the Arrow in any way, nor to the proposed F108).

As for the F106, so widely promoted by the uninformed

Canadian media, it was never even considered in the United States for such a role. As Hellyer remarked in Parliament, to compare the Arrow to the F106 was like comparing a car to a horse and buggy. It was a last modification of the early F102, was never designed for NORAD, and any further developments were cancelled.

Canadian Aircraft Industries magazine reported "Both Britain and the U.S. are developing new advanced interceptors against the manned bomber. They know that Russia is developing very high altitude supersonic bombers and that the first line of defence against the bomber is and will continue to be the manned interceptor. The U.S. are bringing along the F108 to cope with even faster, heavier bomber threats anticipated years hence."[11] The Arrow could have done it in 1960, several years before the F108 would be ready, and could have kept ahead of any future developments.

General Macklin of the Canadian Armed Forces was quoted as saying:

> Even now, Canadian armed forces cannot complement each other in the simplest operation of war. Not one of them can carry out a strategic decision of its own Government without help from some other country ... We have an Air Force armed with obsolete jets, strategically hog-tied to the USAF. It has no air transport, strategic or tactical, that can lift the army with its equipment. It has no tactical aircraft that can intervene in a land-battle. The RCAF is preparing to give up air warfare and get right down to earth to fire untested, obsolete U.S. anti-aircraft missiles. It will soon wield no more power than a flock of common barnyard hens.[12]

All of these opinions and information were available to Diefenbaker and Pearkes. They were doubtless quite aware of it. Most writers tend to give Diefenbaker the benefit of the doubt and to suppose that he might honestly have believed the statements of himself and of General Pearkes. Then the charge would merely be incompetence! However, the manner in which he destroyed the Arrow and his subsequent behavior towards the company prove rather conclusively that incompetence was only one factor. That alone could not account for his destruction of every trace of a great plane.

The informed opinions of the U.S. Chiefs of Staff and other experts were the exact opposite of statements made by the government of Canada. They confirmed the statements of Air Marshall Slemon in 1958 for which he was so severely reprimanded. The Canadian armed forces were warned to keep quiet, or else. They were denied any proper input into this "purely military decision."

Compare this treatment of Canada's top military advisers with the manner in which U.S. military experts are consulted and questioned. Pearkes, instead of getting his information concerning Canadian defence requirements from his proper military advisers and informed authorities, went to Neil McElroy, Secretary of Defence in Washington. McElroy was quite rightly concerned with the defence of the United States, not of Canada. He would fit Canada into the pattern best-suited to *their* defence, *their* production needs, *their* full-employment picture, choosing for Canada weapons which would keep American factories busy and bring to the U.S. government the income received by them in offset payments for military sales abroad. This brings down the cost of *their* defence budget, through domestic manufacture and large foreign sales, but raises *our* costs. After all, McElroy was responsible to the American people; he selected the war strategy and weapons that in his judgement best protected the United States — but not necessarily Canada; the planes and equipment which would provide the most jobs for Americans, not Canadians. The latter is supposed to be the job of our Minister of Defence and our government. From the standpoint of U.S. military planning, Canada is expendable.

Leroy Pope in a United Press International dispatch from New York wrote:

> Canada's hesitancy over the Arrow fighter plane looks to some cynical Americans as evidence that Canadian nationalism is hardly skin deep.
>
> Official Washington and the U.S. Air Force and Aircraft Industry leaders say it is an excellent bet that the Diefenbaker Government will abandon the Arrow come March 31. Thereafter, it is figured, Canada will have to buy not only the Bomarc missile with its SAGE ground equipment, but also will either have to buy a new U.S. fighter plane for use by the RCAF during

the next ten years, or turn over the primary defence of Canada to the U.S. Air Force.

From the narrowly professional point of view, simply adding the whole of Canada to the vast defence perimeter of the U.S. Air Force makes good sense to the U.S. generals. They won't say so for publication because the striped pants gentlemen in the State Department would be too annoyed, but privately the military men say—"even if Canada does build her own planes for her Air Force, they wouldn't count for much. The responsibility would soon fall on us in case of real trouble. So why encourage the Canadians to go to all the trouble and expense?"

Naturally, the U.S. aircraft companies would far rather see their planes man the Arctic defence line than see Canada's Arrow not only manning the Canadian skies, but taking over a segment of the NATO business the Yanks have long regarded as their own preserve.

If Canada is really determined to have an air force equipped with her own planes, some observers say, she will build the Arrow regardless of whether the U.S. agrees to buy it for NATO and NORAD.

But Americans note that so far, the protests in Canada against the proposal to abandon the Arrow do not sound very tremendous. Indeed, those Canadians who say 'We can't afford the Arrow unless the Yanks will buy it' seem to have the dominant, if not the loudest, voices.[13]

Now, let us consider just what the "narrowly professional point of view" of U.S. generals might be. In the balance of her article entitled "Rabbits for the Eagle", Judith Robinson ties it all together very well:*

But before we agree that unemployment relief is the better bargain for our money, let us get a few other alternatives straight, for they concern us.

U.S. defence planners, quite rightly, from their point of view are no more interested in the safety or survival of Canada, as Canada, than the U.S. Attorney-General is interested in Canadian sovereignty. Their task is the defence of the United States and its

---

* First part of the article was quoted in the previous chapter. After this article, the Toronto *Telegram* cancelled Robinson's column. It was not reinstated until she dropped all reference to the Arrow or defence.

people.   Canada can provide *for the defence of the United States* three things: a narrow margin of time, distant early warning signals, and rocket bases.   Just those three things.

Manned supersonic fighters based in Canada have no place in U.S. defence plans.   U.S. supersonic fighters to combat a second-wave attack with manned bombers on U.S. power and communication centres will, according to plan, be based in the United States.   The margin of time provided by Canada makes that possible and preferable.

True, manned supersonic interceptors based in Canada might be useful in defending *Canadian* centres from attack; *but what U.S. defence purpose is served by defending Canada*?   If a rocket attack on the United States were to be launched across the Pole and were to succeed in the first round, that would be that.   If the U.S. were to survive and launch a counter-attack, the attacker, according to plan, would be driven back from the north half of North America and the initial gain won back.

For Canada?   Don't be silly.   For the 'American Way of Life'.   *Canada as an area of desolation*; dead, blasted and contaminated; a no-man's land half a continent deep would be an asset from the point of view of U.S. defence planners.   It would provide manoeuvering space; the necessary thousands of empty square miles above and across which two world powers would battle for domination of each other and the sun and moon and stars.

It is Canada's role in any all-out war that can be foreseen by realistic defence planners looking at things from the Pentagon in Washington.

Canadian defence planners, no less realistic, see another less dismal role as possible for Canada in the defence of North America.   As they see it, the ability to play that role effectively and the possibility of thereby saving Canada from utter destruction in any war of giants would depend on the sort and number of manned fighters with which Canada's northern defences were supplied.   The possession of *and the ability to produce in adequate numbers* a jet interceptor of the required range, speed, manoeuverability and firepower might make the difference between utter destruction and partial salvation to Canada in such a war. So what are we doing?

We are leaving it to politicians in Ottawa to decide, *with the help of U.S. Secretary of Defence McElroy,* whether we can or cannot afford to produce the CF-105 for the use of the Royal Canadian Air Force.

... 'The bald eagle, chosen emblem of the United States of America, lives for the most part on carrion,' according to the books, 'but will not infrequently take living prey such as rabbits.' *Such as rabbits!*[14]

If you think this sounds fantastic, you have only to read U.S. military and service publications, releases from the missile and space planners, or the following excerpt from a speech by Lyndon Johnson when he was Senate Majority leader:

The United States should strengthen our strategic air force auxiliary, and expand our research and development programmes, speed up the development of the intermediate or intercontinental missiles, strengthen our educational system, provide a top level information service, military planning, establish a new defence weapons development agency, streamline the decision making process, accelerate the nuclear submarine programme, eliminate overtime limitations, increase co - operation with our allies, build shelters and store food and machinery as a precaution against a Russian attack, build as quickly as possible the early warning system capable of detecting missiles.''

Johnson goes on to say that control of outer space means total control of the earth:

From space *the masters of infinity* would have the power to control the earth's weather, to cause drought and flood, to change the time, raise the level of the sea, divert the gulf stream and change temperate climates to frigid. Therefore, our national goal, and the goal of all free men must be to win and hold *the ultimate position from which total control of the earth may be exercised.* (Italics added)[15]

It would appear that it might at some time in the near future, as in the Cuban crisis, be urgently important for Canada to have the freedom to formulate her own independent foreign policy and the equipment with which to carry it out, rather than being totally dependent on the United States for both. But from the '' narrowly professional point of view'' of the planners in Washington, that must not be allowed to happen. It would not be hard for the brilliant Public Relations boys in Washington to confuse and frighten the elderly General Pearkes with their huge array of missiles, planes, space projects and talk of push-button warfare, and to convince him that he, as Minister of Defence for Canada, was way out of his depth and we had best leave it all to them. It is doubtful that he understood what they were talking about. It was not quite fair of Diefenbaker; he should have saved his old friend such embarrassment.

---

1 *Maclean's*, Oct. 25, 1958, p. 4

2 Ralph, Wayne, "The NATO Scenario," *Wings*, NFA Issue, Summer, 1978, pp. 18-22; *cf.* "The Myth of the Multi-Role Fighter," *ibid.*, pp. 23-7

3 *ibid.*, p. 26

4 Braybrook, Roy, *Air International*, Dec., 1975

5 "The Myth of the Multi-Role Fighter," *loc. cit.*

6 *ibid.*, p. 21

7 *ibid.*, pp. 18-22

8 U.S. Senate Sub-Committee Report, 1958

9 *Hansard*, 1958; *cf. Globe & Mail* and *Star*, Toronto, 1958, 1959. *passim*

10 *Globe & Mail* and *Star*, Toronto, 1958, *passim*

11 *Canadian Aircraft Industries,* Oct., 1958

12 Macklin, Gen., public statement, Nov. 11, 1958

13 Pope, Leroy, United Press International dispatch, New York

14 Robinson, Judith, "Rabbits for the Eagle," *Telegram*, Toronto, Feb. 10, 1958

15 *Missiles and Rockets*, April 27, 1959. Lyndon Johnson was then U.S. Senate Majority Leader.

Chapter 7
Alternatives

When Defence Minister Pearkes went to Washington in 1958, ostensibly to sell them the Arrow as the Canadian contribution to the vast array of equipment being produced in the United States for the defence alliance, U.S. Secretary of Defence Neil McElroy talked him into paying for the installation of two of the U.S. Bomarc bases instead.* They were of no use whatever to defend Canada. They were designed solely to protect and provide warning time to the U.S. Strategic Air Command (SAC). To do even this, they required nuclear warheads, but no agreement to make these available to Canada had been secured by the Diefenbaker Government. However, the suggestion was eagerly seized upon by Pearkes and Diefenbaker. By claiming that the 'missile age' had arrived and that, by buying the Bomarc, they were 'modernizing' the armed forces, they could justify the cancellation of the Arrow which they claimed was now 'obsolete'.**

---

* It has been stated[2] that Pearkes asked the U.S. for the two Bomarc sites to be located in Canada. This seems unlikely, as the U.S. had already been surveying sites in Canada for SAGE installations, and promptly suggested the sites in Canada where they would like to station the Bomarc bases.

** American defence analyst Jon McLin remarks that, in the face of "an overwhelming body of testimony to the contrary," the argument that the need for manned interceptors would disappear "exceeded the bounds of legitimate disagreement."[3] The Diefenbaker government showed a strong tendency to ignore the facts in their statements as long as they served the political purpose. For instance, Diefenbaker stated on September 23, 1958, that the Bomarc which Canada was acquiring could accomodate *either* a conventional or a nuclear warhead, which was contrary to fact.

Clean aerodynamic lines of CF-105 Arrow are evident in this flight photo. Even when fully armed, all armament is carried internally in weapons bay, which lowers momentarily for firing rockets. Most U.S. fighters are festooned with externally mounted armaments which affect aero dynamic performance.

Courtesy A.V. Roe

There were several bits of information which McElroy evidently failed to pass on to Pearkes and Diefenbaker, or which they chose to ignore. One was that the Bomarc was even more useless against ballistic missiles than was a manned interceptor. The Bomarc was designed solely for use against manned bombers. Moreover, it would bring down these bombers over mid-southern Canada rather than over the far North, as interceptors could do. Since, to be effective, Bomarcs needed to be fitted with nuclear warheads, the scenario becomes interesting, especially for the residents of North Bay, Ontario and of LaMacaza, Quebec, where the Bomarc bases were installed.

When the public and presumably the government belatedly found out about the need for nuclear warheads, which would be held under the control of U.S. military personnel, the resulting protests posed a political threat to Diefenbaker and he hastily denied any intention on the part of the government to introduce nuclear warheads into Canada. Why then did he bring in the Bomarc which required them? As Paul Hellyer pointed out: "...if there is one thing that is more useless than an armed Bomarc it is an unarmed Bomarc."[1] The second such bit of information concerning the Bomarc was the fact that the Pentagon had decided to discontinue any further production or purchase of the Bomarc on the grounds that it was too costly, too vulnerable to attack, and had very limited capability, compared to manned interceptors. However, the agreement with Canada gave Boeing a reprieve, and made cancellation more difficult. In a hearing before the U.S. Committee on Appropriations later, one Congressman pointed out: "If we scratch Bomarc, we have stuck the Canadians for a whole mess of them and we have another problem on our border." He also pointed out that the Bomarc had cost between $3 and $4 billion to develop, and the operating costs amounted to at least $20 million per year.

In defending the Bomarc, Secretary MacNamara stated that they would draw enemy missiles which might be used on other targets; "as they are deployed, they draw more (enemy) fire than those Jupiter missiles will."[3] The latter were located in Italy and Turkey. Apparently, Canada was also expendable. The Bomarc was a rather expensive decoy, but Canada needed something to justify the Arrow cancellation, and immediate purchase of a substitute U.S.-built interceptor would have been politically touchy. The cost of the Bomarc-SAGE package to Canada, including additional radar stations to fill existing gaps, was $125 million, one-third of the installation costs only.

Diefenbaker stated on television that $20 million paid for Bomarc would "equal the protection of the same area" as would be provided by $480 million worth of Arrows. To say that this was not quite accurate is an understatement. Ten squadrons, or 120 Arrows, would cost, even at the higher price, less than $450 milion, since the given price for 100 was $3.6 million each. The spares and missiles were less expensive than those used by the Bomarc. If the missiles were taken aloft and not used, they and the Arrow would return to be used again. One squadron of Arrows could fly sixty missions in just five flights each and be as good as new for further missions. They could range farther and intercept intruders far to the north of populated areas.

One base, or squadron, of Bomarcs would cost an estimated $120 million at least. Two bases would cost $240 million. *If used to defend Canada* as implied by Diefenbaker, the minimum requirement to equal the coverage of ten Arrow squadrons would be at least ten bases, at a cost of $1,200 million. Each base would be equipped with 60 to 100 one-shot missiles, good for one mission only. The cost of missiles was $400,000 each for a total of $24 to $40 million per base. Once fired, even in error, they do not return. Sixty missions flown from one Bomarc base would leave it with no missiles and a replacement cost of at least $24 million. The SAGE system, developed for Bomarc guidance, would cost an estimated $100 million. The Bomarc and the interceptor were not interchangeable; they were complementary.

Diefenbaker announced that we were paying one-third of the cost of two bases and, in fact, gave the figure of $80 million in Parliament. But to the public he quoted the ridiculous figure of $20 million. It sounded better. According to estimates mentioned in Parliament, $20 million would about cover the cost of building the roads and clearing the sites for the two bases. If this was our total contribution to our

Canadian defence, it was so paltry as to be meaningless. Of course, Bomarcs were to protect the Strategic Air Command only; any protection for Canada was purely illusory. Missile bases are costly installations, which cannot be moved, and missile range is limited, that of Bomarc 'B' being about four hundred miles; it cannot distinguish friend from foe, must wait for identification from an interceptor or from the ground, which might be too late, and its guidance system is vulnerable to jamming. It is effective only against manned bombers. It is useful only as second-line 'area defence' against the same targets against which the Arrow would have been the first-line defence.* Today, the government's arguments appear rather stupid; but these were the arguments the government used in 1958 to con the public into supporting the cancellation of the Arrow, and they worked.

Eventually, some of the considerable and damning evidence as to the limited usefulness of the Bomarc and the continuing development of more sophisticated bomber fleets must finally have gotten through to Pearkes. The earlier arguments, to the effect that manned interceptors like the Arrow were now obsolete, were replaced by new charges as to its usefulness and its cost. First, Pearkes declared that we couldn't sell it to the U.S. because they were belatedly beginning design work on the F-108, disregarding the fact that there would be a time gap of several years before the F-108 could be operational even if it were successful. He then followed this by claiming that the Arrow was "probably never intended for use in Europe," because it could not operate without SAGE and there was no SAGE in Europe. Someone should have told him that there was at that time only one pilot installation in the U.S. and certainly none in the Canadian far north. It was being developed as a guidance system for the Bomarc missile. It is not certain whether Pearkes just grabbed this argument out of a hat, or whether he was confusing it with the TACAN system which is an airborne navigation aid, while SAGE is a tactical vector control system operating through a central ground station. Pearkes was confused by a great many modern military facts and was far beyond his depth most of the time. However, the

* See Appendix 11

public was even less informed than Pearkes. By getting them to believe that the Arrow could be sold neither to the U.S. nor for use by European members of NATO, he had achieved his purpose. If the Arrow could play only a very limited role in Canadian defence needs, it would be far too costly for Canada to produce.

It is interesting that no writer, with the exception of George Bain of *The Globe and Mail*, picked up Pearkes' contention as to the need for SAGE. However, even the adverse evidence concerning Bomarc versus interceptors, and the obvious lack of any other plane capable of replacing the Arrow didn't cause Pearkes to hesitate more than momentarily.

Although the U.S. estimated that the Soviets had from 1,000 to 2,000 bombers then current which were capable of attacking the United States, and although information about the new, supersonic Russian bomber had been available for some time, Pearkes told us, "There is no bomber threat," and cancelled the Arrow. Then he said that there may be a bomber threat, but they have only the Bear and the Bison, and only a few of those, and the CF-100 won't really be obsolete for two or three years. It would be capable of dealing with those bombers, although "it will be touch-and-go as far as combat between the CF-100 and the Bear and the Bison are concerned but, as I pointed out, they have that [sic] aircraft in very limited numbers." Since these were the ones that could reach Canada, it would seem that they were the ones Pearkes should have been concerned about. As pointed out earlier, Pearkes seemed to get his information from very different sources than did U.S. and Canadian experts.* Even assuming that he had been correct, it should leave one a bit uneasy to have a Defence Minister who is satisfied with an older plane whose chances in combat with nuclear-armed bombers is merely "touch-and-go".

Furthermore, the CF-100 production had been discontinued. What would we do for replacements? On February 20, 1959, Pearkes assured us, "Perhaps the most efficient [bombers] which the Russians will have in the very near future, could not be engaged by the CF-100 in its present form; but if

* This was pointed out at length in an article entitled "Intelligence Schism" in the U.S. magazine, *Aviation Week*, March, 1959, p. 26.[4]

we add certain other equipment to the CF-100 ... then I believe the CF-100 will be able to engage effectively the majority of Russian bombers.'' The Arrow programme had been cancelled that morning. As Opposition Leader Lester Pearson pointed out, ''In February 1959, they are giving further study to what will take the place of the CF-100 and it will not be the CF-105 [Arrow]. If they have been engaged in these studies, why were they not concluded before such an important decision was taken ... to end the Arrow and disrupt an important section of the industry?''

To explain away its failure to have as yet any defence plans whatsoever, the government claimed that it was waiting for the visit of General Loris Norstad, Chief of NATO, the following May, to let the government know of NATO's requirements. It was expected that on such an important matter the government might at least allow him to speak to a closed session of Parliament, in order that all members might have some information, and such a request was made by the Opposition. Although General Norstad was in Canada for several days, according to Diefenbaker ''he had to leave for the Continent immediately'' after his two-hour session with the Cabinet. This was in direct and disgraceful contrast to the way in which other governments hear information, and in the United States, not only give it to every member of Congress and Senate, but also release all but classified information to the public. It was strongly rumoured that the reason for this secrecy was to prevent any knowledge from reaching the Canadian people of what NATO or NORAD had requested Canada to provide as part of her obligations to Western defence. It was also suggested that the government was so deeply in debt that they could not afford to announce publicly any plans for defence spending whatsoever. So we would either renege on our commitments, or the government would commit itself to further vast sums of money for defence without informing the Canadian people of what was being done.

Compared to the publicity and public controversy accorded to cancellation of the Arrow programme, this was a strange course of action, indeed. But of course, we were supposed to be 'saving' money by cancelling the Arrow. Announcements of NATO commitments, on the contrary, would be a case of the government 'spending' money. According to Jon McLin of the University of Alabama, these commitments also related partly to whether or not Canada had, when purchasing the Bomarc missile and the Lacrosse (later known as the Honest John) missile, made a decision on the use of nuclear warheads. The Washington press revealed the existence of an agreement in principle, but the government at once denied that any draft agreement was in sight. As McLin points out, this "was in the fashion of things to come" and he comments on the succession of ambiguous statements made by Diefenbaker, which amounted to "artful policy pronouncements, committing him to nothing".[5] Diefenbaker himself, in his memoirs, gleefully reveals that he would, when speaking, frequently change the direction of a statement in midstream, thus creating the *impression* of saying something which, later, in the written account, no one could "catch him out" on. These evasions, ambiguities and indecisions in policy and statements were, largely, a response to real or imagined political hazards of any decisions, not the result of military arguments. They eventually resulted in a loss of confidence, both at home and abroad, in the capability of the government to adhere either to a policy or to international commitments.

When Pearkes spoke of adding "certain other equipment to the CF-100," it would be interesting to know what he meant. Two years before , the Air Force had placed a requirement for a new and up-dated version of the CF-100 to be known as the Mark 6 with, among other things, accomodation for air-to-air missiles. The design work had been completed and the first trial installation flown when the Conservatives came into office. One of the first things they did was to cancel the program for political reasons. It was a case of all the money, time and effort being thrown away, merely to allow the government to tell the public that they were 'saving money.' This should have been seen as a premonition of the future. Of course they didn't save any money at all. All the work already done was scrapped but, later, the most necessary changes were incorporated in what was known as the Mark 5M. The public, of course, was told about the 'saving', but there was no mention of the later expenditure. This is surely a most inefficient and wasteful way of 'saving money.' Would the changes Pearkes referred to merely reinstate the abandoned Mark 6? It would have been useful when it was cancelled; it was now two years too late.

Since there was no longer a bomber threat, the Arrow was now obsolete, having been "overtaken by events" as the government claimed. But now that it was gone, Pearkes stated with a straight face that even the CF-100 was *not* obsolete; it would be useful for several years, as long as there was a "manned bomber threat" in fact. Of course, it could not fly faster than 600 miles per hour, and the Russian bombers already flew faster than that, while the first Arrow had already flown at almost 1,400 m.p.h., or Mach 2, and was expected to reach Mach 3 with its new engines; but the Arrow was "obsolete". Apparently only the Arrow was "overtaken by events". Were these "events" quite different from the military events to which Pearkes attributed this odd situation?

According to the dictionary, to be "obsolete", all need for such an object must have disappeared or something else, definitely superior, must be available to take its place. It had been amply proven by now, even to the government, that the first condition was not true. Let us then consider the second condition.

The CF-100 was a previous-generation plane, certainly not superior to the Arrow which had been designed to replace it. Although Pearkes now said that it would not be obsolete for several years, the government immediately began to look all over the world for some other interceptor to replace it. They really did not have a very good choice. There was nothing available that was remotely comparable to the Arrow and there wouldn't be for several years. Moreover, the government was learning to its surprise that it would cost almost as much to buy even an inferior plane, or to manufacture it under license, as it would have cost to continue with production of the Arrow. The rock-bottom price per plane which it would have cost to put the Arrow into production on the existing production line was turning out to have been a real bargain, compared to tooling up from scratch just to produce an American plane under license and to incorporate the modifications which would be required to make it suit Canadian requirements.

Having accepted Pearkes' statement that the Arrow couldn't be used in Europe, George Bain[6] suggested that there were three possibilities open to Canada: that our NATO Air Force be withdrawn entirely; that Canada replace manned aircraft with ground-to-air missiles; or that an aircraft of U.S. design be bought or built under license in Canada to re-equip the Air Division. Since NATO had requested *more high-level manned interceptors*, it was likely that the Air Division in Europe would get another round of aircraft, regardless of any decision taken by the government as to the home defence squadrons. He noted that the English Electra was not sufficiently advanced and the F-108 would be too late. Only the F-106 would be available to Canada at the right time. Certainly, the plane would be American, either the Convair F-106 or possibly the North American F-108, "although the three to four years in which the Air Division ought to be re-equipped might need to be stretched if the latter were chosen." The F-106 was a late modification of the F-102, with little scope for further up-grading and with a limited service life - a stop-gap aircraft. Just to modify it from the F-102 had cost $150 million.* Production of later models was discontinued shortly thereafter.

Canadian Aviation magazine published a comparison of the F-106 and the CF-105 Arrow:

> The CF-105 has been widely recognised as the most advanced interceptor in the free world at its present stage of development. The belief that the U.S. has an aircraft with the performance capabilities of the CF-105 presently in production, *is erroneous*. The F106, the latest of the American Century series now in production, has been singled out in a number of reports and commentaries following the Prime Minister's speech, as comparable to the CF-105. *This is not the case.*
>
> The F-106 is a single-seater, single-engine plane, therefore lacking the twin-engined CF-105's margin of

---

* This was almost half the cost of designing from scratch a radically new and advanced plane, researching suitable new metal alloys, new methods of forming and machining them, new bonding methods, new development and test programs, the flight testing of five complete aircraft and the almost complete production of a total of 37 aircraft in the case of the Arrow.

safety for long patrols over isolated areas which are the everyday duty of Air Defence Command squadrons.

The CF-105 with the same amount of armament as the F106, is far above the range of the F106. Operating at the same range, it can carry much greater fire-power. It has a much greater intercept and kill capacity. With two more powerful engines than the F106's one, *it is much superior*. The F106 was not designed for and cannot fill Norad's requirements for a long range interceptor.

That Norad's chiefs and defence planners are still seeking a plane similar to the CF-105 is proved by the development work now begun in the U.S. on the F108, a twin-engine, two-man interceptor. It is still in design and engineering stage, therefore three or four years away from production and *several more years away from operational service*. The CF-105 would be available for squadron service in 1960.[7]

At the time, the United States was plugging the Republic F105 for sale to NATO countries on a 'shared production' basis, and several countries had accepted it. Republic hoped to be able to bring the price *down* to about $2 million apiece, if the NATO countries *purchased the plane in quantity*. Although it was as heavy as the Arrow, it had only one engine, and therefore had less speed and rate of climb. To manufacture it in Canada would have cost as much as the Arrow, since a Canadian company would have to tool up from scratch and start the whole production process again from the beginnning. Of course, no design work would be done in Canada. All of that, plus the tooling up of the whole production line had already been done on the Arrow; plane after plane could have rolled off the assembly line from the moment the go-ahead was given. This would not be true of any U.S. plane manufactured under licence in Canada. Further, if equipped with a sufficiently powerful engine to serve RCAF and NORAD requirements for Arctic patrol and interception, and the modifications necessary to accomodate a new engine, the F105 would have been more costly than the Arrow CF-105. It would still have had only one engine and no space for a navigator. Canada, of course, did not buy it, although it was probably the best plane then available. We were looking for a really cheap plane.

When it became obvious that the Diefenbaker government had done a flip-flop and was now looking for an interceptor after all, every U.S. manufacturer with surplus planes on his hands got into the act.   Their opinion of the Canadian government's ability to make intelligent decisions as to air procurement was so low that they believed they could sell them almost anything, as long as it was cheap. They were not far wrong.   Several companies lobbied intensively in Canada, placing large ads in Canadian newspapers and magazines and making extravagant claims for their planes and for the advantages to Canada of their 'off-set' programmes.   The major contenders were the F-101, the F-104 and the F-156N.*   The F106 was no longer a contender; the U.S. had none to spare and had discontinued production. Then, as now, Northrop took the most aggressive action in its onslaught on Canadian public opinion. In its open lobbying, it also took liberties with the facts. It advertised the F-156N as a plane designed, according to the President of Northrop, "expressly for our allies in NATO," a statement which was somewhat less than accurate. Northrop also put on well-advertised flying demonstrations in Ottawa for the benefit of the government and the Air Force. Pierre Berton didn't say a word about "lobbying".

The F-101, by McDonnell Aircraft, was a somewhat dated, surplus U.S. plane.   The version which was eventually acquired by Canada had been sitting unused on the Arizona desert. It carried a two-man crew. It could be fitted with either nuclear or conventional missiles and the Canadian version eventually carried nuclear-tipped MB-1 Genie missiles as well as non-nuclear, conventional Falcon missiles.

The F-104, by Lockheed Aircraft, was a small plane with very short wings, which had been developed during the Korean war for a very specific 'area defence' role. It was said that Lockheed had practically been given Fort Knox to quickly develop a plane which could climb very fast and chase off the MiG's which were attacking American lines almost at will. It killed a good many pilots before its downward ejection seat was modified. It also had, from 1969 to 1973, the highest accident rate of all single-engined planes in the USAF. For two-engined planes, the F-101 held the record.[7] (We bought both.) The F-104 carried little in the way of electronic

* See Appendix III

equipment for any kind of attack except air combat. Since no suitable role had been found for it with the USAF, it was offered by Lockheed for sale to U.S. allies in NATO as a nuclear strike plane. In this role, it was a reasonably effective and sophisticated piece of equipment.

The F156N, out of Northrop, probably had the oddest history of all. It was too bad that Mr. Pearkes didn't know what everyone else knew about the F156N, that 'new' plane being advertised in Canada as a plane "designed for the first time, expressly for our allies in smaller countries," according to the President of Northrop. Did Pearkes know that the cute little thing was actually a converted trainer that had been developed five years earlier — *not* "for our allies", but for the U.S. Navy — but not quite acceptable and so never ordered into production, until later revived and modified to sell to Third World countries as part of a U.S. Military Assistance Programme? The F156N was re-designated the F5A and F5B. As to its qualifications for Canada's defence needs, Wayne Ralph had this to say: for its new role "... it had to be strategically useless, while fulfilling a tactical need for countries *with a modest level of technical expertise*. The aircraft fits this role admirably."[8] Northrop had probably heard of the Folland "Gnat", developed some time earlier in Britain for a similar role. Canada had just developed both the Arrow and the Iroquois engine, but the Canadian government must have concurred in Deutsch's description of Canada as "a large, empty land, empty of people, capital and skills."

The first plane purchased by Canada to replace the CF-100 and Sabre F-86 for its NATO divisions was the F-104. It was bought in 1960 and renamed the CF-104, or Starfighter. It was manufactured under license by Canadair in Montreal, after political pressure was brought to bear on Lockheed to allow its manufacture in Canada. About 340 were produced between 1960 and 1964, about 200 of them for the RCAF. The initial base cost was supposed to be about $1.5 million each but this was an off-the-shelf price only and the actual cost was closer to $2 million. Once again, as in the case of Bomarc, the politicians appeared not to have understood what they were buying. Since it was purchased to perform a nuclear strike role in NATO, it required some modification to carry conventional bombs and was far from efficient in this role. However, because of the outcry over nuclear warheads, it was given a conventional role. Our forces in NATO were now equipped with two weapons systems which were designed for a nuclear role but which were forced to perform with conventional warheads. The Honest John missiles carried, instead of nuclear warheads, a load of sand in their noses.

Some commentators have claimed that, when later used as a low-level nuclear strike aircraft, the CF-104 made the Canadian division in Europe one of the most powerful strike forces available. Equipped with conventional bombs without the requisite fire control systems, it was assigned to a role for which it was not designed. Production of the plane provided years of work for Canadair, plus additional years of work on overhaul and modification of both airframe and electronics systems, which added to the original cost. There was, of course, no original research and design work involved for Canada. It was merely 'manufactured under license'. McLin argues that the largest defence orders placed in Canada since 1959, such as the production of F-104 fighters for Canada and for NATO countries under the Mutual Defence Assistance Programme, were uneconomic and were based on the political need to provide larger orders to Canadian industry than were justified by economic competition. He claims that any economic production sharing would require the effective integration of Canadian defence industries with the U.S. defence industry,[10] probably a desirable goal from the U.S. point of view.

The next Canadian acquisition was the F-101, which was purchased in 1961 for use with NORAD for North American defence and renamed the CF-101, or Voodoo. Its cost was nominally estimated to be $1.5 million each, but it was part of a complicated exchange arrangement and it is difficult therefore to determine the actual cost to Canada. Diefenbaker described the purchase as a three-part deal, in which Canada would purchase the Voodoos and, in return, would take over from the United States the full cost of operating Pine Tree Line radar sites for the future. In addition, the U.S. would purchase $200 million worth of F-104s manufactured by Canadair for NATO under the U.S. Mutual Defence Assistance Programme; Canada would pay 25 per cent of the shared cost of this programme. In 1960, Canadair had negotiated an offer from the Military Air Transport Service (MATS) of the USAF for the purchase of its C-44D4 freighter. However, the sale was conditional on Canada's purchase of either the U.S. F-106 or the earlier model F-101, armed with the Genie MB-1 nuclear missile. The Canadian government hesitated for so long that MATS bought 30 jet transports from Boeing. Six months later, the government decided to buy the modified F-101, which could use either nuclear or conventional weapons, and purchased 66 of them. Canadair of course, had lost the order for the freighter, worth approximately $400 million, and the potential follow-up orders that could have resulted.[11]

The F-101 was equipped to carry both the AIM-4D Falcon, a guided missile with a conventional warhead and the MB-1 Genie nuclear-tipped but unguided missile. It was bought by Canada and equipped with conventional missiles for the same reason as in the case of the previous weapons. Having first flown in 1948, it was technically out-dated, but a reasonably servicable plane. It is difficult to understand just why it was selected except that the U.S. was happy to sell them to Canada since maintaining them on the Arizona desert was unproductive. Later, under a Liberal government, the Voodoos along with the Bomarcs were equipped with nuclear warheads. It is claimed that the weapon they carry requires the pilots "to perform escape manoeuvres to avoid the effects of nuclear blast from this dated weapon, which is in long term impact as hazardous to the crews carrying it as those who are fired at."[11] Its main asset appears to be that it carries a 2-man crew, a definite advantage in the Canadian north.

In 1963 an interesting comment appeared in a Japanese aeronautical magazine. It spoke of a Japanese mission which had earlier visited England and the U.S. At the time of their visits, commented the writer, the U.S. was dropping the old F-101 in favour of the newer F-4, while Canada was scrapping its advanced fighter, the CF-105, and replacing it with the F-101, then being discarded by the U.S. It commented that the requirements for the Arrow that were laid down in 1953 had been exceeded, and that the Arrow was an excellent, advanced design. The Canadian decision appeared quite incomprehensible to them.

The last fighter purchased by Canada, the CF-5, was an updated version of the Northrop F-156N. "It represented a programme which no Canadian scenario could possibly employ - but that did not stop us from buying it. Whereas other acquisitions reflected poorly thought out scenarios, or disproven ones, the CF-5 mirrored no politcial stance or objective that could survive scrutiny."[13] Designed for border defence for small Third World countries and for point defence such as 'clear air' dogfights, Canada used it in an air-to-ground bomb attack role. From 1966 to 1971 Canadair produced 115 for Canada, and 105, called the NF-5, for the Netherlands. For the Canadian role the plane was totally misapplied, but it "had one redeeming feature to politicians - it was cheap."[14] Cheap? For this small, dated plane, Canada paid what amounted to about $2 million apiece, twice the cost of the plane in the U.S. and almost as much as the quantity price of the large, twin-engined, advanced Arrow. One-third of them were mothballed; there was not enough money left to set up the necessary RCAF squadrons. Some of them were later sold by Canada to a third country. Northrop sued the Canadian government over this third-party sale and the Canadian government was forced to pay $9.2 million in settlement of its claim.[15]

All of the military planes manufactured in Canada since 1958 have been produced by Canadair. The company, originally Canadian Vickers, produced Catalina/Cansos during the war in a plant built by the government in a suburb of Montreal. In 1944 it became Canadair Ltd., and in 1947 was bought by The Electric Boat Co. of Groton, Connecticut. The new conglomerate, which also owned Convair in California, was renamed General Dynamics Corporation. It now has twelve divisions which manufacture ships, submarines, missiles and rockets as well as aircraft, and are involved in radar, test equipment, satellite ground stations, navigation equipment, limestone and coal mining and asbestos (in Canada). During the 1950s, Canadair built, under license, 1,815 Sabre F-86 fighters. Since then, they have produced 37 Bristol-Britannias(CP-107 Argus); 38 CL-44 D4s and CL-44-6s; 10 CC-109 Canadair/Convair Cosmopolitans (Convair, who designed it, sent up the jigs from California); about 400 F-104 Starfighters; 190 CL-41s (CT-114 Tutors); 115 Northrop F-5Gs (CF-5A-15); 18 Lockheed CP-140 (Aurora) patrol planes; plus a $100 million order for parts and maintenance, and a $68.3 million order for CL reconnaissance drones. They also received the contract for production of Bomarc wings and ailerons after the Arrow was cancelled. Total value of that contract was about $17 million, of which $2 million was for components and tooling alone.

Canadair has produced, not counting the Sabre order, about eight hundred planes for the Canadian government since 1959. Many were built for export, including the F-104 order for NATO. It has also received multi-million-dollar orders for parts and maintenance. It has had no trouble obtaining government financing. Subsidies received in 1958-59 from the government for production under license of the CL-44 for two American private non-scheduled airline companies amounted to $4.00 apiece from every Canadian, according to the *Financial Post*. The government is also subsidizing Canadair on the Aurora contract by over $11 million, merely to work out the final plans. Final cost of the Aurora is estimated at $57 million each. None of these planes were designed in Canada. All were foreign-designed planes manufactured under license by a subsidiary of a U.S. conglomerate. They brought little to Canada in the way of technological development, but production of the Sabre alone is said to have provided over half of the total profits of General Dynamics Corporation in the U.S. during that period. Canadair was purchased by the Canadian government in 1976. It will undoubtedly win whatever sub-contracts are let in Canada for the new fighter programme.

It is evident that Canada can obtain foreign sales for a plane produced in Canada once it is in production and flying, even for the "uneconomically produced" F-104. This lengthens the production line and keeps cost down. Of course, all of the planes sold, except for the CF-100, were *designed* in the U.S. or U.K. and were produced in Canada by Canadair, at the time a wholly-owned U.S. subsidiary. They created no Canadian capacity for research and design that could lead to further development, and few spin-offs to build up supporting industries. These may be vital considerations.

The lack of any effective Canadian military or defence policy since the 1950s has been commented on by both military and non-military observers. Canadian indecision and changes in policy have caused difficulties in both NATO and NORAD. Without a policy, it is impossible to make rational decisions. As noted, Canada acquired four weapons systems in the 1960s which depended on nuclear warheads to be effective. These were the Bomarc, the Honest John missile, the F-104 Starfighter and the F-101 Voodoo. McLin claims that the Arrow also was intended to be equipped eventually with nuclear missiles, and that the Sparrow and Falcon missiles were merely provisional weapons.[16] If so, the $100 million spent by the government on the Astra-Sparrow program, later cancelled, would seem to have been particularly foolish. These costs were, of course, charged by the government to the Arrow program. In every case, the government, for political reasons, then rejected the nuclear weapons needed to make these systems effective. None of them were equipped for the roles they were called upon to perform.

Canadian purchases of foreign planes since 1958 have seldom justified either their choice or their cost. Although each of them would have been reasonably effective in the roles for which they were designed, these were not the roles for which Canada required them. Canada bought the wrong planes for the wrong role and then used them for purposes for which they were essentially ineffective. Canada had little choice, of course; she now had to take what was offered. Neither have the much-vaunted offset programs offered as 'bait' by each U.S. manufacturer in its effort to sell its planes to Canada lived up to their glowing promises. Once the contract has been won, interest in such programmes on the part of the U.S. companies concerned has rapidly declined, and the benefits, in employment or in the use of Canadian technical resources, have been very small. There have been no effective penalties for non-fulfillment.[17]

Once again in 1978, the U.S. aviation industry is putting together tempting packages of off-set programmes in an effort to sell their respective planes to Canada. They have even given the competition a sporty new designation, "The New Fighter Aircraft Programme for Canada". Planes being offered and widely advertised in the Canadian media, include General Dynamic's F-16, Grumman Aircraft's F-14 Tomcat, the Mc-Donnell-Douglas F-15 Eagle and its F-18A, and the Northrop F-18L, advertised with astounding audacity in Canada as the CF-18L, a Canadian-only designation. The only non-American plane proposed is the Panavia Tornado, produced by a European consortium. Little information is publicly available as to their proven or predicted performance, or as to their cost, probably a subject for negotiation, as part of a package deal. Price is rumoured to range from about $6 million each for the Northrop F-18L to over $16 million each for the Grumman F-14, without taking extra costs for modifications into account.* If past experience is any guide, the final choice will depend less on the capabilities and role of the plane, than on which one appears to offer the most economical over-all deal to Canada, whether useful or not.

The 1970 government White Paper, "Defence in the '70s," outlined a policy that emphasized the so-called "Third World Option". The policy stressed defence of Canadian sovereignty, of the North, the coastal areas and fishing zones. Foreign policy appeared to favour "getting out of NATO, standing up to Uncle Sam, halting the multi-national takeover and saving our Arctic and coastal ecology."[18] But Canada's approaches to the European Economic Community concerning economic ties were met with questions concerning her contributions to NATO. (This neatly avoided the touchy question of increased trade relations with Canada, in which the EEC has shown little interest). Since 1975, there has been an almost complete reversal by the government of the 1970 White Paper policies. Defence Minister Danson and the Chief of the Defence Staff, Admiral Robert Falls, now advise us that fulfillment of NATO commitments is "almost inseparable" from North American defence and the protection of Canadian sovereignty. As a result, Canada has embarked on a programme costing over $4

---

*Recent information indicates that these price estimates are much below probable current price tags.

billion to re-equip Canada's armed forces. The programme includes the purchase of 18 Aurora anti-submarine surveillance planes at a cost of $1.2 *billion*, of 130 to 150 fighter aircraft at $2.34 *billion*, of 128 Leopard tanks costing $187 million plus a possible $50 million extra in foreign exchange, along with two types of missiles and a ship rebuilding program. Some further rather odd purchases include large quantities of gas masks, handcuffs, suits of body armour and 350 General Purpose Armoured Vehicles costing $175 million. The latter are used elsewhere only by the West German police as riot-control vehicles.

There has been no new White Paper, no debate on these policy reversals, no definition of Canada's foreign policy, which should determine our military requirements and, so far, no public reaction. Apparently, the public becomes interested in defence procurement only when the government wishes to publicize the magnificent 'savings' real or imagined, which it is about to pass on to the taxpayer. When it wishes to make massive expenditures, the matter is kept as quiet as possible and public debate is avoided. This is as true today as it was in 1958-59. Yet these policies and expenditures are most important. If they reflect a changing foreign policy, that should be publicized. They should not be made merely in response to internal military pressures for new equipment for its own sake, nor as an *ad hoc* reaction to external pressures to suit foreign priorities that are not necessarily the same as Canada's. If large purchases are made without full knowledge of the effectiveness of the weapons selected and of the role they will be required to perform, Canada will once again be faced with enormous expenditures for equipment which may prove to be totally ineffective — the wrong weapon systems in the wrong role, to carry out a foreign policy designed for other countries by other countries, not by Canada or for Canada, by any conscious choice.

Brigadier-General Paul Manson, head of the government's new fighter evaluation team states that the selection of the new fighter aircraft should be " based on the criterion of *flexibility* to meet any change in the military role of the Canadian Armed Forces. The emphasis ... is on the operational ability of the new airplane to meet *multi-role* requirements." He went on to say that no amount of offset (benefits) would make any plane acceptable that cannot meet these expected future roles. "It is unthinkable that industrial benefits will make an unacceptable aircraft acceptable. We want an airplane that will be adaptable, that can change one role for another. A *multi-role* aircraft will be the cornerstone of our selection if for no other reason than that the demands of the future are so unpredictable and that we need a hedge against uncertainty. If one plane cannot meet all the expected roles, a fleet of two types of aircraft, one for NATO and one for NORAD Air Defence, may be considered." He also noted that the supplementary offset proposals had already been considered.[19] The nature of these offset programs may be of little interest to the military establishment but they are nevertheless important. Not only do they affect the price of the planes we purchase, they could also, if properly bargained for, have a lasting effect on the future of Canadian technological development vis-a-vis the United States and the rest of the developed world. They therefore deserve a separate study.

The criteria as outlined by Manson indicate either that we are unable to predict the nature of the future threat, or that we are so unsure of what our purpose is in acquiring these aircraft that we are trying to cover all possible bases. As one analyst comments: "To some extent, the Canadian requirement has got to be a wish list. Because if you put everything in the airplane that the Canadian requirement calls for, there probably isn't any airplane that can take all that hardware at one time — and number two, I don't think there is anybody can afford to buy the airplane with all that hardware in it ... They have got some hard decisions to make ..." In other words, it is essential to determine our roles and our missions, and to straighten out our priorities.[20]

Six planes are in competition for the current Canadian contract. In their public advertisements, the manufacturers of all of them make claims for wide versatility, since they believe this will appeal to the Canadian purchasers. Yet as noted by Wayne Ralph in his discussion of design parameters and performance,[21] for every increase in versatility, there is a loss of performance in specific roles and, for certain roles, capacity in both can result in ineffectiveness in either role, since the optimum design requirements are incompatible. One of the crucial factors is wing design. Wide differences in required performance as, for instance, between interception and air combat, versus low level attack and ground support roles can be mitigated, but only partially, by use of a variable-geometry wing, whose characteristics can be altered in flight. Only two of the planes under consideration have a variable-geometry wing, the Grumman F-14 and the Panavian Tornado. The fact that these planes carry the highest estimated price tag indicates the cost penalty involved.

Probably the lowest-priced plane is the General Dynamics F-16, advertised as a "multi-role, high-performance, low-cost" aircraft. It has a single engine and carries a pilot only. Slightly higher in cost are the F-18L offered by Northrop and the F-18A by McDonnell-Douglas. These planes were developed from the same prototype, designed jointly by the two companies. The F-18L is more than 2,600 pounds lighter than the F-18A. According to Northrop, the F-18L can do practically everything. Developed as a single-seater, twin-engined land-based version of the F-18 Hornet, a U.S. Navy and Marine Corps tactical fighter, the U.S. version "will perform missions now requiring two aircraft, the F-4 and A-7". According to Northrop, the "same versatility enables *CF-18L* to fulfill both air defence missions in Canada and Canadian NATO obligations in Europe, replacing the CF-101, CF-104, and CF-5," all the fighters currently employed by Canada for very different roles. Northrop further describes its mission capability as "air superiority, fighter escort, combat air patrol, intercept, close support, interdiction, reconnaissance". It describes its performance characteristics as suitable for both a "fighter mission" and an "attack mission," two usually incompatible roles. Truly a marvellous plane, without even the benefit of a variable-geometry wing!

The claims made by McDonnell-Douglas for its version, the F-18A, are moderate. For its other entry, the F-15 Eagle, it claims that it is cheaper than the Grumman F-14, simple to operate, and that it is designed for flexibility, not specialization (a frank admission), with low wing loading and excess power for hard turns at low speeds. These characteristics are consistent and appear to adapt it admirably to the American scenario of open-air combat. It is twin-engined and carries a pilot only. Its price will probably be below that of either the Grumman F-14 or the Panavia Tornado. The F-15, F-16 and F-18 are all 'optimized' for the air combat role. The F-15 would be expensive for use in the European role, where attrition rates would doubtless be quite high.

The Grumman F-14 Tomcat is an already-flying, twin-engined, two-seater plane with a variable-geometry wing, so that the wing-loading and chord/thickness ratio can be varied in flight, altering its performance characteristics and somewhat increasing its versatility. Its chief claim is its ability to take on multiple targets, with its six long-range Phoenix missiles. However, the value of the greater missile range may be limited in effectiveness by visual identification problems, not yet overcome even by BVR (Beyond Visual Range) target location systems. In active combat conditions, the rate of destruction of friendly aircraft could thus be very high, as it was in the 1973 Egyptian-Israeli war.[22] It is probably the best high-level interceptor, but too sophisticated and costly to be employed in attack or strike roles.

The only non-American plane is the Panavia Tornado, produced by a European consortium. Probably about as expensive as the F-14, in terms of Canadian dollars, it is a twin-engine, two-seater plane, also with a variable-geometry wing. It is advertised as the West's "first truly multi-role, multi-mission, Mach 2-plus weapons system", with all-weather, long range, high speed, high-precision strike and reconnaissance capability, long-range air-to-air intercept ability, multi-targetting and anti-shipping capability. It offers about as broad a range of claims as the Northrop F-18L at a much higher price. But it is twin-engined, carries both a pilot and a weapons system controller and is equipped with the more versatile and expensive variable-geometry wing. According to its publicity, it will replace the CF-104 and CF-5 in their surface attack and reconnaissance roles in NATO and the CF-101 used for NORAD Air Defence — a wide role spectrum and level of capability. It appears, however, that there are two versions of the Tornado; the Interdictor Strike Version (IDS) *and* the Air Defence Version (ADV) and both would be required to fill the NATO and NORAD roles respectively. This could increase the cost over that of the basic airframe. Also, as with the Grumman Tomcat, it is a very expensive plane for use in a low-level European scenario.

No matter what plane or planes we buy, it is inevitable that there will be increased costs for modifications and equipment. According to Wayne Ralph, NORAD's minimum requirements could be met by any of the contenders, even a late, updated version of the F-101E.[23] But the Grumman Tomcat would doubtless be the best high-level interceptor, as well as the most expensive. As for NATO requirements, there is no consensus as to what the most likely requirements will be, even one year from now, and the possibilities are changing constantly, with the rapid development of new electronic equipment, ECM jamming, cluster bombing of airfields and the advent of the low-flying cruise missile. It is no wonder that Brigadier-General Manson is asking for an almost impossible versatility, as the future is so unpredictable. Brian Cuthbertson claims that our options with respect to NATO and NORAD are changing so rapidly that we now have an opportunity to re-order our priorities and achieve greater independence in our defence strategies.[24] In fact, as Ralph facetiously suggests, aircraft may even become "obsolete". But then, we were told that twenty years ago, weren't we!

None of the planes being offered has yet reached the predicted speed of the Mark 11 Arrow. In other respects, as one former Canadian flight engineer, now working for one of the competing firms, recently remarked, "They are just beginning to catch up with the Arrow, aren't they!"

1 "A Historical Perspective," *Wings*, NFA Issue,
Summer, 1978, p. 13

2 McLin, Jon, *Canada's Changing Defence Policy,
1957-1963*, Johns Hopkins, Baltimore, 1967

3 *ibid.*, pp. 164-5

4 "Intelligence Schism," *Aviation Week*, Mar. 2, 1959, p. 26

5 McLin, *op. cit.*, pp. 135, 160

6 Bain, George, "What Wings for the RCAF Abroad?",
The Globe, Feb. 14, 1959

7 *Canadian Aviation,* Nov. 1958, p. 51

8 *Wings*, Summer 1978, p. 50

9 *ibid.*, p. 14

10 McLin, *op. cit.*, p. 182

11 Godfrey, David, "Score Sheet on the Half-Century,"
Canadian Aviation, 50th Anniversary Issue, 1978, p. 48

12 *Wings*, Summer 1978, p. 13

13 *ibid.*, p. 15

14 *idem*

15 "Northrop Corporation," *Wings*, Summer 1978, p. 34

16 McLin, *op. cit.*, pp. 130-1

17 *Wings*, Summer 1978, pp. 15-16

18 Walker, John R., "Policy by Purchase," *Report on
Confederation*, July-August, 1978, pp. 19-21

19 Romain, Ken, "Flexibility Key Factor ...,"
Globe & Mail, Toronto, Sept. 29, 1978

20 Ralph, Wayne, "The NATO Scenario," *Wings*,
Summer, 1978, p. 22

21 "Myth of the Multi-Role Fighter," *ibid.*, pp. 23-7

22 "Questions Raised by New Technology," *ibid.*, p. 73

23 "Canadian Sovereignty," *ibid.*, p. 42

24 Malone, Richard S., "Canada Should be More
Self-Reliant in Defence," *Globe & Mail*, Toronto, Mar.
27, 1978

155

Chapter 8
A Matter of Economics

The decision to maintain military forces of any kind is a matter of policy. In most countries, the kind of military forces maintained is closely related to a definite foreign policy and the alliances which that country has chosen to make. The decision as to the kind of forces and equipment then depends to a certain extent on the decisions of the alliance as a whole. Once these decisions are made, the acquisition of that equipment then becomes, contrary to *Maclean's*, a matter of economics, as is any other government purchase. The government must decide what equipment will best do the job, where it can best obtain that equipment with respect to both quality and price, and the reliability of the source. As with any other products, it has to decide whether it costs less in the long run to protect an industry and employment by tariffs or subsidies — we use both — or to let the industry die and import the products and export the jobs. If we do the latter we must then earn the foreign exchange to pay for the imports by selling something else for export. If we have no distinctive products or technology for sale, we must sell our natural resources in ever - increasing amounts to pay for the increasingly sophisticated and costly products we are forced to import.

As in any purchase, a number of factors are involved if we are to get our money's worth. We want to ensure that the supplier can provide the kind of equipment we need when we need it, and that there will be a reliable source of supply, especially in an emergency. If we need a new, modern lawn mower, we don't buy from a neighbour an outdated hand mower, just because he has an extra one lying around and wants to get rid of it. We don't buy his small sports car, if we need a larger car to carry heavier loads for long distances. We don't buy his bicycle if we need a sports car with high performance, just because the bicycle is cheaper. Neither do we go next door for candles in a black-out if we know from experience that the uncle who makes them may, in an emergency, reserve the whole supply for himself. In such a case, it would be better to have someone in our own house who could make candles, especially if we know that we will continue to need them and that such emergencies may happen. Furthermore, from making candles, one can progress to making lamps, then electrical equipment and electronics.

In most modern countries, investment in and support for national industries that generate a high level of research and technological development is considered an investment for the future. Such industries do not necessarily pay their own way directly, all the time, but government support is considered essential, since they maintain a leading edge of technological development which spills over and extends its benefits throughout a wide range of industries, enabling the country to stay abreast of product development, technological breakthroughs and the creation of distinctive export products and markets. It also serves to keep within the country the best talents and to attract others, to build up a growing pool of the "people and skills" which Dr Deutsch says we lack. This is one of the usual excuses for our lack of development, but we are losing the ones we have in a constant stream, along with their expensive education, to other countries who know how to use them.

Governments in Canada do not appear to understand this. They obviously think only in terms of the lowest common denominator — a given number of jobs. We spend millions in efforts to entice U.S. corporations to set up branch plants in Canada, or to move to an area of high unemployment, whether economical or not, just to provide 'jobs'. Few of these branch plants do anything to raise the standards of Canadian skills or to improve the goods produced. U.S.

corporations in Canada are here for one of two main purposes only: to control and ensure a supply of raw materials to the American firm, in order to provide jobs and manufacture export products in their plants; or to hold the Canadian market as cheaply as possible, by turning out copies of American mass-produced products to sell to Canadians, at higher prices than if made in the U.S. on the other side of possible tariff barriers. American firms also come here at times to escape U.S. anti-combine laws or restrictions on international operations.

Our government spends millions in constructing facilities and infrastructure solely for the benefit of firms whose only interest is in extracting our raw materials. These industries provide notoriously few long-term jobs. Yet we construct for them such infrastructure as the Arvida power complex or the railway to Pine Point Mines. Foreign promoters can always get funds quite easily, especially from provincial governments. The Churchill Forest Industries promoters, Jens Moe of Gulf Garden Foods and Bathurst Marine, and the Bricklin car promoters can attest to this, wherever they are now.[1] To Canadian governments, it appears to be good business, or perhaps the easiest way out, to invite foreign firms into the country and bribe them with unlimited funds. At the same time they consider it uneconomic and a waste of funds to support Canadian firms.

These U.S. companies spend little on research or technological development. They are not interested in developing distinctive Canadian products that can compete in export markets against the flood of mass-produced American goods. Almost their only exports are the unprocessed raw materials shipped at favorable prices to their parents in the U.S. At the same time, they further distort our balance of payments by importing vast amounts from the U.S. parent. They pay large sums for imported 'management and technology' and an item called 'services', as well as importing almost all of their parts, components and supplies. Canadian secondary suppliers and parts manufacturers are left to die, as in the case of the Auto Pact. Such branch-plant imports and exports account for approximately 75 percent of our cross-border trade.* It is no wonder we have a foreign exchange crisis. The omens were there long ago with the increase in foreign equity ownership; we are now simply witnessing the inevitable reverse flow of capital. Foreign firms, after all, invest only in order to take profit out of a foreign country, not to continue putting money in. The profits are now so high that they can continue to buy us out without bringing in any foreign capital at all.

Officials of successive governments in Canada have stated over and over again that Canada does not need to 'waste' money on technological research; she can always buy the technology she needs more cheaply elsewhere. This is one of the biggest myths ever sold to Canadians. To date, we have been able to buy this (usually low-level) technology only at the cost of allowing its owners to buy out and take over control of most of our industries. They don't give it away, and we have little else to offer them of similar value in exchange. Costs of technology come high, no matter where one buys it, and long-term costs of short-term savings can be enormously more expensive in the long-run. Further, when our technology is imported through branch plants, we have no control over the quality of the technology, the use to which it can be put, nor the price paid.

Even when the government offers incentives and subsidies for research and development, as it is sometimes spurred into doing, most of such funds are taken by the branch plants, who direct it into the kind of research that will benefit the parent company: They then patent the result in the name of the parent company and export it to the U.S. Ninety-five percent of the patents taken out in Canada are in the name of foreign owners.[2] If we wish to use the new process or product, the development of which may actually have been paid for by our money, we then have to pay royalties to a foreign country. Payments for patent rights, technology and management then become part of our bill for imports.

---

* The exports are almost all in the form of unprocessed raw materials; the imports are predominantly manufactured products and services, much of them in the high-technology category. Canadian exports to the U.S. of unprocessed raw materials are admitted duty free but even a minor degree of processing almost inevitably incurs heavy tariff barriers.

By contrast, much of the almost $300 million spent on the development of the Arrow and the Iroquois engine programs and of the $100 million spent on the Astra-Sparrow programme represented high technology research and development. This was the only sector of the Canadian aeronautical industry that was doing research, design and development to any extent in Canada.

These companies were helping to build up subsidiary industries, to design and manufacture in Canada every thing from highly specialized electronics equipment to plastics, machine tools, new metals and alloys and equipment of every kind. Many of these firms were Canadian companies that had never before produced competitive, high-standard technologically-advanced products, nor heard of working to tolerances of ten - thousands of an inch. There had been no demand in Canada for such products. Trained and assisted by Avro, with access to the research and technology developed there, Canadian firms were becoming increasingly capable of handling skilled work and exacting contracts. Many of them were, for the first time, bidding on foreign contracts. One in Western Ontario had just received, as a beginning, a $300,000 contract from South America. Pathex Canada Ltd had developed the giant autoclave ordered by Avro for bonding large metal aircraft sections. In 1958, this company secured a contract from the aircraft division of Twin Coach Ltd of Buffalo to supply a similar unit, and were negotiating with U.S. companies for two other large contracts for autoclave installations which would be worth an estimated $1 million.[3] Other companies were set up by newcomers from Europe, the highly-skilled people whom we were told Canada needed. One such newcomer, a toolmaker, had spent hundreds of thousands of dollars to build and furnish a plant in Hamilton to manufacture machined equipment. With an order from Avro for a start, he planned to expand and be able to handle many other types of orders. Other firms from the U.S. set up subsidiary industries, employing Canadians not merely to sell but, for the first time, to design and develop products for a Canadian industrial market right here in Canada.*

---

* The head of one branch plant of a California-based company was fired by his head office when he began to manufacture some of their products in Canada.

Avro itself had developed many new types of tools, fabricating equipment and new techniques. Many Canadian patents had been taken out not only by shop technicians, but by the company itself. For example, a division of A.V.Roe, Canadian Applied Research, formerly Photographic Surveys Corporation, developed a special process for producing the light-weight, high-precision turbine blades required for the Iroquois engine. This became a high-value export item, which brought millions in revenue to Canada.

Few Canadians had any idea of what a change this had created in our industrial development in the short space of a decade, or of the favorable climate it was creating in Canada, to attract industry, to attract and hold our skilled immigrants, and to induce our own graduate engineers, scientists, technologists and skilled technicians to remain in Canada. For years we had been paying to educate them here, only to lose them at an appalling rate to the United States not merely for better pay, but for the opportunity to do interesting and challenging work. This export of our best-trained and most highly-qualified citizens has been a far greater loss to Canada than we could afford, in ways far beyond even the high cost of their education. In 1956, the Royal Commission *Report on Canada's Economic Prospects* stated: ' 'If Canada is to continue to grow and develop at its present rate, it is of the utmost importance that adequate numbers of trained and skilled manpower of all descriptions be available.''[4]

For a long time, Canada has suffered from an atmosphere where research and development are starved for funds, and where excellence in anything except the arts and medicine is sneered at. This not only drives away our own graduates for lack of opportunity, but fails to attract really good people from abroad. Of course, our academic community will hire anyone from anywhere else in preference to hiring a Canadian graduate and giving him the opportunity for high-level work in which to gain his reputation and prestige.

It would appear to be of unquestionable value to Canada to promote the growth of all-Canadian industries, to create a climate of expansion and growth, and to begin to turn at least some of our plentiful raw materials into finished products at home, instead of shipping them out of the country to create jobs in the U.S., Japan and Korea. Yet strangely, these developments were not welcomed in some quarters in Canada. We might be in danger of forgetting that we were "too small, too poor, too lacking in skills and technology," too unwilling to invest our own capital at home, to do anything for ourselves except sell raw materials. Too small to grow! Too poor to use our own resources, existing man-power and skilled top-notch personnel, instead of sending them all out of the country! It sounds too incredible to be believed.

In 1959, an article in *The Globe and Mail* suggested a reason for this unprecedented campaign against everything Avro was doing and developing in Canada, commenting that "the two leading exporters of capital, the U.S. and the U.K. are animated by different motives involving different methods and producing different results. The U.S. ... *seeks to create new raw material sources* for its expanding fabricating industries, and *new outlets for its own export surpluses*. Great Britain ... seeks to create a more active flow of two-way trade" (Italics added). The article points out that the United States tends to set up subsidiary firms in other countries when necessary to avoid tariff barriers, but still keeps the business, profits and know-how in the U.S. Also, it does not encourage export trade from these branch plants in other countries, since this would compete with American exports.[5]

Perhaps these comments are relevant to J.J. Brown's conclusion that .

> . . . in economic terms alone, the decision [to cancel the Avro programs] was one that was to impair our standard of living for decades to come. This is not so much because of the money lost, because we have lost four hundred million on other projects before and survived, but chiefly because the Avro design team that it had gathered with so much difficulty from all over the world was, in 1958, considered the best aircraft team in North America. These men's ideas stimulated a ferment in nearly every other Canadian industry. This would have resulted in a host of new products and techniques. But with the cancellation of the Arrow, the team dispersed almost immediately.[6]

Most of them are now good Americans, part of the teams the U.S. gathers from all over the world because it has interesting and demanding work for them to do, not merely sub-contracting of bits and pieces and assembly 'under license', which is all we seem to be able to get.

For a long time, the far East, near East and South American countries have been staked out by the big powers as sources of raw materials and markets for finished products. Any industrial development by these countries themselves was discouraged or prevented. These countries did not become prosperous; they remained backward and primitive, developed few skills, and remained second-class or third-class nations. But the countries that exploited them became fat and wealthy and developed highly-industrialized and highly-skilled economies. This old political colonialism has been almost entirely shaken off. To replace it, the power centres have developed a new method of control: economic imperialism. In some cases, the control now exerted by the more powerful country is more complete, more devastating to free development, than the colonial system of old. Consider the political results of Guatemala's attempt to distribute to poor, landless peasants some of the enormous land holdings of the U.S. United Fruit Company, or the threat to Cuba when she had the audacity to nationalize the sugar industry whose profits never left the New York banks, or the recent case of Chile, which dared to nationalize the copper industry owned by U.S. Anaconda.

Or consider merely the remarks of our former ambassador from the United States, who "gave the world to understand that people in the United States were growing restless, even a trifle resentful, over Canadian handling of American economic interests. He was referring to such matters as the Foreign Investment Review Act and the purchase of foreign-owned potash holdings by the government of Saskatchewan."[7] It would be interesting to listen to the American reaction if another country made similar comments about its sovereign right to regulate its own economy and foreign investment as it sees fit. But then, many of them "do not regard Canada as a foreign country."

Perhaps the American concept of Canada is similar to that of France towards her colonial 'departments', a whimsical concept supposed to transform all matters of colonial administration into 'purely internal affairs of France'. When the author was working in Africa, it was a rare event to hear Canada spoken of in the same terms as, say, Australia and New Zealand, which are regarded as independent countries in their own right with independent roles in world affairs. When referred to at all, Canada was usually lumped into the generic term 'North America', playing a shadowy yes-man to the United States.

So safe and stable does the U.S. consider Canada, as an economic satellite, that she has transferred most of her South American investments in minerals and petro-chemicals from South America to Canada. Most of the countries in Latin America impose strict controls on foreign corporations operating on their soil. Many of these countries use foreign capital for development, certainly; many of them have U.S. branch plants — but not the way we do. In 1958, Venezuela raised the government tax on U.S. oil company profits from 50 to 60 percent. *Barron's Financial Weekly* noted that the raise had little effect on the market. A few years before, our government had reduced the tax on dividends to foreign corporations, including oil companies, from 15 to 5 percent, so afraid were they that the U.S. would impose a quota on Canadian resource exports. Later, in 1970, the National Energy Board practically assured an American consortium that they could build a pipeline. Again, the fear was that our exports of non-renewable resources might be even slightly curtailed. Since we have little else to export, it takes little pressure to gain concessions.

In 1958, Brazil was trying to attract foreign investment, but an article in *Time* magazine noted the very stiff terms under which it must operate, to Brazil's benefit. They were having no trouble in getting the investment. But the firms were required to set up a separate Brazilian company, over 50 percent Brazilian owned; the profits they could take out of the country were severely limited, and they had a fixed time in which to train Brazilian personnel to take over a given percentage of all jobs, including technical and executive, and to arrange for at least 95 percent of the product to be manufactured in Brazil.[8]

Compare this with one of our largest 'Canadian' industries,

our 96-percent U.S.-owned automobile industry. The design and engineering is done in the U.S., a large percentage of the components are made there and come in duty-free, the profits go to the U.S., and the technical know-how stays there. Policy is decided in the U.S. and they allocate our share of the market. We do not export without their permission. Canada, of course, would never dream of imposing any restrictions; we are so afraid it might annoy the Americans. For our audacity in having dared to try to enter the big time in advanced, technological developments on our own, especially products which would be competitive with those of the U.S., we have been properly put in our place.

First the Jetliner was reduced to scrap, to allow Boeing to introduce "the only American Jetliner flying today," eight years after the Canadian Jetliner had flown. Thirty-seven supersonic Arrows have now been reduced to scrap, just in time to prevent the first Mark II from flying and bringing the world's speed record to Canada. Asked in Parliament if it could not be allowed to fly, to at least show what we had achieved, Mr Pearkes answered, with great satisfaction, that he could not grant this request, since "none of them now remain intact".

Ruling groups in other countries who sell out their countries for the benefit of foreign countries and of themselves are called 'compradors.' Canada is a very safe country for American development and profit. Our financial and political 'compradors' intend to keep it that way.

So we expanded our airports and western bases for the use of the U.S. Air Force, and re-equipped the RCAF with relatively expensive U.S. planes, to defend us against the bomber threat that we were told in 1958 no longer existed. When we found we had paid more for inferior American planes, both for Canadian defence and for our NATO squadrons, Pierre Berton did not write another column about how we had kept large corporations such as Northrop or Grumman or Boeing or McDonnel-Douglas or Lockheed in business and poured millions of taxpayers' money "down the drain" — and out of the country altogether. In 1978 we are obliged to do it again.

According to McLin, "while the possibility of scuttling an industry by consistently denying it large contracts is a very real one, the danger from any particular adverse decision tends to be exaggerated. For example, the scrapping of the Arrow was widely regarded as a crippling blow to the aircraft industry in Canada, yet this industry did approximately *the same dollar volume* of business in 1962 as in 1955." (Italics added) [9] McLin claims that the government's argument that the need for manned interceptors would disappear by the mid-60s "exceeded the bounds of legitimate disagreement," and was contrary to an overwhelming body of testimony. The real reason it was cancelled, he claims, was because it was "too expensive for Canada to buy," but to admit this required the recognition "that Canada could no longer pay the price which advancing technology exacted to remain a producer of the more sophisticated military equipment" as a "substitute" for U.S. equipment. [10] For McLin, in Alabama, any attempt to produce advanced planes in Canada represents merely a "substitute" for U.S. equipment, and the production in Canada of U.S. planes under license, as long as it provides a certain number of jobs and dollars, is a fair enough share for Canada.

When a team of Soviet scientists and aircraft designers toured the Avro plant in October, 1958, they could not understand the company's worries about the future of the program. They said: "You have an excellent plane. How is it you might not produce it?" When told it was a matter of economics, of money, they said: "But that should not be your worry. That is what your Minister of Finance is for: to find the money for what the country needs." Experts in the U.S. and Europe have also found it difficult to disguise their inability to understand how the government could have so stupidly thrown away such a large and successful investment, or how Canadians in general could have been so misinformed. British and American aviation experts while trying to be polite, could not quite conceal their sarcasm. They had been lavish in their praise of both Avro and the Arrow. Only in Canada was it called a "costly mistake."

Contrary to Blair Fraser's inaccurate article in *Maclean's*, experience with the CF-100 and the Orenda engine proved that it was less costly by far to manufacture this equipment at home than to purchase equivalents abroad. The savings are estimated to have been over $100,000 per plane, not including the revenues derived from export sales of both the plane and the engine, amounting to over $52 million. The product was better adapted to Canada's role than were any alternatives and, most important, both the plane and the best engines for it were available when needed. Foreign planes seldom are, as first-line planes. The appropriate engines are even harder to obtain elsewhere when required, as was proved in the case of both the Jetliner and the Arrow.

George Bain[5] pointed out that both the CF-100 and the F-86 Sabre, equipped with the Orenda engine, were supplied at the direct request of SHAPE, NATO's headquarters in Europe. They were requested because they were the best planes available. The CF-100s, with the RAF Javelins, made up the only all-weather component of the NATO air forces. The Canadian Air Division (C.A.D.) held the air gunnery championship with a score more than double that of its closest rival. It was the only formation that had met and maintained the serviceability requirements set up by Allied Air Forces Command in Central Europe. Both the CF-100 and the Sabre/Orenda have had lower wastage losses than were anticipated.*

The all-weather and serviceability records allowed the C.A.D. to do more flying than any comparable formation in the Command and thus to win gunnery championships. The CF-100 was designed and produced by Avro Canada; both it and the Sabre were powered by Avro Orenda engines. They were requested by NATO *after* they had proved their performance. It is most unfortunate for Canada and for NATO that the Arrow, produced by the same company and its design teams was never allowed to prove itself and to contribute its performance and serviceability to NATO, for which it was admirably suited. Jan Zurakowski, the Chief Test Pilot at Avro, in response to media 'suggestions' that it was a difficult plane to handle, replied that several pilots, including a military pilot, had flown it and that it was one of the easiest planes to handle that he had ever flown. On its first takeoff, it used only

---

* Twenty years after the last CF-100 rolled off the assembly line, there is still a squadron of 14 CF-100's flying out of North Bay. They are fitted with equipment for electronics counter-measures operations.

3,000 feet of an 11,000 foot runway. On its third flight, it exceeded 1,000 miles per hour. On its seventh flight, while still climbing, it reached just under 1,400 mph or Mach 2, at 50,000 feet.

As to costs of the Arrow, the price per aircraft delivered to the government, which Avro gave the government in October, 1958, represented one of the greatest bargains in aircraft ever offered to date and the company took considerable risk. Our government later found this out, after shopping around for other sources of supply. The costs quoted by Diefenbaker were wildly inaccurate and contradictory. They included costs never included, in any country, in computing the cost of military planes. These were not included in the costs quoted to our government for the purchase of U.S. planes, which he used for comparison. Although the company had given its written price guarantee in October, 1958, Diefenbaker continued to give to the public figures ranging from $7.8 million per plane to as high as $12.5 million per plane! No one will ever know how he arrived at this latter figure.

In other countries, research, development and test programmes, costs of special equipment and armament, such as the costs of the discontinued Astra-Sparrow programme and, least of all, costs of runway improvements are not included. They are covered under separate headings. The U.S. military procurement system is much more costly than ours, involving design studies, development and production of prototypes by several companies out of which only one is selected to be put into production. Testing is covered under the U.S. Air Force budget. The U.S. government underwrites the costs of research and development, which includes the cost of designing and producing the first prototype aircraft, usually to government specifications. For programmes thus funded, the manufacturer then repays to the U.S. government a fixed amount, called R. and D. recoupment, for every plane later sold to a third party, usually a foreign country. This cost is, of course, included in the price of planes sold to Canada, and inevitably raises the cost to us.[1]

It is interesting to compare the attitude of the government towards costs of equipment required and specified by the Air

Force with its attitude towards costs for Navy equipment, and the attitude of the Air Force compared to that of the Navy itself. *The Globe and Mail* reported on hearings in the Commons Public Accounts Committee, as to costs of Navy destroyer escorts. It was admitted that "the total costs of vessels built six years ago is not yet known." To this, the Auditor-General commented that he had "no criticism of the accounting procedures used by the Navy. The vessels cost more than originally forecast due to frequent changes in plans and specifications to improve the fighting qualities of the ships." He went on to say: "*No good naval officer is worth anything if he is money-minded. The designer of a naval vessel wants the best he can get.* The Committee should temper its criticism with this in mind." [Italics added.]

What about "a good Air Force officer?" The Air Force called for frequent changes in plans and specifications to improve the fighting qualities of the Arrow. They also wanted the best they could get. Apparently what is considered outrageous in the case of the Air Force and its aircraft is considered good and admirable practice for the Navy and its ships, and is never discussed beyond the Public Accounts Committee, where the estimates are approved with no fuss.* The Navy destroyer escorts, conventional ships only, cost $26 million each.[12] Apparently, the Navy's more experienced officers have learned how to get what they want when they want it. Our Air Force officers could learn from them; they lacked the ability or the courage to speak up in defence of *their* procurement needs. Of course, some of them had been removed from influential positions in Ottawa and replaced by officers from branches not noted for their fondness for the newest service.

The Arrow was specifically designed to fit Canada's role; the foreign planes we eventually purchased were not. The cost from then on would have been about the same as the eventual cost of the planes we purchased or built "under license."

---

* The Attorney-General, however, severely criticized the Accounting procedures respecting grants to the Canada Council university grants programme. The interest it had earned in the month it was held up before being paid to the Council was "wrongly" included in the grant when given to the Council.

Almost all of the price we paid would have stayed in Canada. Instead, in 1959, the rest of the country had to pay unusually high costs for unemployment insurance in the Toronto area. Metropolitan Toronto alone voted an additional $2.5 million for relief. We did not pay this relief to the top-notch personnel who were snatched up by U.S. companies. They left to help build up U.S. leadership and 'prestige'. We did, however, pay more for their products later than the net cost of building our own, and got very little of value in return.

In 1959, as the *Financial Post* pointed out, the Canadian government had agreed to underwrite, for Canadair, the U.S.-owned subsidiary, and for two American private airline companies, the cost of producing planes for them "under license" in Canada. This would give us nothing but would cost every Canadian $4.00 each. It would give no work to our research and design teams, in aircraft and electronics and related fields. It would give us no defence whatsoever. And we would be subsidizing, not our own defence, nor the development of our own interceptor for ourselves and the Western world, not our own research and design teams, but two private non-scheduled American airlines and an American subsidiary of the same company that owns Convair and other companies in the U.S. The plane was the CL-44D-4, backed by the government-owned Exports Credit Insurance Corporation. This was a peculiar enterprise for a Conservative government which, in order to bring down the previous Liberal government, had used as a major election issue, that government's attempt to guarantee loans for the TransCanada pipeline. The amounts involved in the case of Canadair were slightly higher; but it was not given any publicity. But then, since we are so completely dependent on our foreign-owned branch plants and on our foreign-owned resource industries, it is only reasonable that Canada should provide funding for them, if they ask for subsidies or guarantees against the hazards of the market - place. It is only Canadian firms that are told that they must learn to cope with "the harsh realities of the market-place". It is therefore little wonder that our industries are completely dominated by foreign corporations or that Canadian-owned industries continue to go bankrupt or are taken over by the hundreds by foreign corporations. From 1974 to 1978, there were 458 takeovers of Canadian firms by foreign investors. The total foreign *direct* investment in Canada increased from $1.1 billion in 1958 to $39.8 billion in 1975. We are told that this is a good thing for Canada and few Canadians are aware of the far-reaching and disastrous effects of this massive foreign ownership on Canada's foreign debt and on our rising deficit in world trade. The falling dollar is proof that the world has lost confidence in Canada's ability to manage its own economy.

---

1 Mathias, Philip, *Forced Growth*, James Lewis & Samuel, Toronto, 1971
2 Gray, Hon. Herbert, *Foreign Direct Investment in Canada*, Information Canada, Ottawa, 1972, p. 118. Of 25 countries listed, Canada is lowest in percentage of patents owned by her own nationals, and highest in percentage of those owned by foreigners.
3 *Canadian Aviation*, Nov., 1958, p. 83
4 "Highlights of Royal Commission Reports," *New Horizons*, Winter, 1956-7, p. 11
5 *Globe & Mail*, Toronto, Mar. 31, 1959
6 Brown, J.J., *Ideas in Exile*, McClelland & Stewart, Toronto, 1967, p. 312
7 Porter, Ambassador Wm.
8 *Time*, 1958
9 McLin, Jon, *Canada's Changing Defence Policy, 1957-1963*, Johns Hopkins, Baltimore, 1967, p. 171
10 *ibid.*, pp. 82-3
11 "Technical Data," *Wings*, Summer, 1978, p. 11
12 *Globe & Mail*, Toronto, April 23, 1958

Chapter 9
Defence Sharing : U.S. Style

Early in World War II, the Hyde Park declaration of April 20, 1941 recognized the "general principle that, in mobilizing the resources of this continent, each country should provide the other with the defence articles which it is best able to produce and, above all, produce quickly and that production programs should be co-ordinated to this end."[1] During the war, each country spent about $1.25 billion in the other country for military goods. Although it was agreed that co-operation should continue after 1945, nothing much came of it until the Permanent Joint Board on Defence was set up on October 12, 1949. Its purpose was "to establish a new programme for reciprocal military procurement, to augment U.S. sources of supply, to increase the dispersal of industrial facilities, to foster the industrial standardization of equipment, and to help Canada earn the foreign exchange to pay for her military purchases in the U.S."

As the American defence analyst Jon McLin points out, the collaboration was in unequal measure between the two countries. In 1951 and 1952, U.S. purchases in Canada totalled $400 million, while from April 1, 1951 to December 31, 1952, Canada spent in the United States for military procurement $850 million. According to McLin, this was not due to U.S. unwillingness to buy in Canada, but was "the result of the incipient stage of Canada's restored defense industry at this time". He continues, "during this period of rapid rearmament, the U.S. needed Canada's industrial capacity, and even such articles as advanced aircraft, which were later to be so politically sensitive, were purchased in Canada.''

By the mid-1950s, however, Canada was in a positon not only to produce most of the military equipment needed for its own forces, but also "to compete on a selective basis for U.S. orders." Canada was selling the United States at least six kinds of aircraft; only one, however, was a Canadian designed fighter, the CF-100. "Thus, one of the important preconditions for the establishment of a meaningful, comprehensive division of labour between Canada and the U.S. in defense production was fulfilled. ...only at the time when the political will necessary for such a programme was disappearing. After Korea, both governments reverted to the peacetime assumptions that domestic industry should be favoured in defense contracting. This was more pronounced and consequential in the case of the United States as was seen in its refusal to participate in the development of the Arrow, at a time when an aircraft of that type appeared to be needed by both countries and when no comparable U.S. aircraft was yet in sight." McLin contends, however, that in Canada there was "an excessive proneness to undertake projects which were not economically feasible in a country of its size."[2]

What McLin is saying, in effect, is that, to the United States defense sharing means easier access to Canadian products, but only when she needs Canadian excess capacity; standardization of all defence equipment to U. S. standards, from those of the U.K. to which Canada had been geared; but no purchases when the U.S. industry wants the market for itself, unless such purchases are needed to help Canada to pay for her purchases in the U.S. The inequality of the agreement was due, in 1951-52, to Canada's inability to produce the goods. Three or four years later, when Canada could supply these demands as well as her own, the U.S. no longer needed Canada's industrial capacity. So much for Defense Sharing agreements! From 1953 to 1958, U.S. defence purchases in Canada averaged only $35 million per year.

It would appear that there is, in the United States as well as in Canada, an "excessive proneness" to undertake projects which, in size and number, are not economically feasible. It is doubtful whether the U.S. alone would or could support the vast extent of its military projects. She is able to afford them only by pressuring all the other countries in NATO to go along with American decisions as to the military equipment they need, and inducing them to forego their own domestic purchases in favour of purchases in the United States to the greatest extent possible. The sale of military equipment, particularly grossly expensive aircraft, not only to NATO countries but to smaller countries around the world, is one of the largest export industries in the United States. U.S. pressures for "standardization" and integration of NATO and NORAD military equipment must be understood in this context.

Every NATO country has to pay its share of NATO defence, but the United States keeps almost all the business. Other nations know they can afford to build almost anything in their own countries; it is only when most of the money crosses their borders for imports that they go bankrupt. Britain and the United States know this very well. So do Sweden, Holland, France, West Germany and now China, South Korea, Taiwan and even, or especially, resource-starved Japan. All, it seems, except Canada!

As noted before, every hundred million dollars spent outside our borders is one hundred million dollars gone out of the country completely. Not one cent comes back to the government in taxes, not one cent of it helps build up Canadian industry to enable us to earn the money to pay for these costs, or to make us wealthy enough to meet our obligations to NATO and NORAD. We can only afford what we earn; yet pay we must. But all our purchases go to build up American industry, to give jobs to American scientists and engineers and skilled workmen, to produce houses, cars, refrigerators, food and clothes for Americans. It goes, above all, to pay back in taxes to the U.S. government so much of their defence costs that much less has to be financed by the rest of their economy. As the *Financial Post* estimated, 65 percent of the investment in the Arrow programme came back to the government in taxes alone. The other 35 percent was spent almost entirely in Canada. In contrast, the contract to Canadair to manufacture the F-86 in Canada "under license," accounted for a very large share of the total profits of the General Dynamics conglomerate in the U.S., which owned Canadair, during the period of the contract. General Dynamics and its other subsidiaries, of course, receive many huge contracts for defence from their own U.S. government as well, even including orders for atomic submarines.

In 1958, *Canadian Aviation* suggested that "To any mature and seasoned government, matters of defense and economics are inseparable ... Mr Diefenbaker would do well to study the attitude of the British government in this respect." The magazine observed that "the present situation in which Čanadian industry is being squeezed out of production on an advanced weapons system ... is an indication of how much participation can be expected in any future programmes."[3]

The New York *Times* reported in 1959 that British government officials were concerned over the cornering of the NATO arms market by the United States. The London dispatch continued:

> Well they may be, as Canadians know from bitter experience. Canada has had the dubious privilege of being first in learning the economic and political implications of U.S. domination in weapons. It is not a lesson we would wish for the British.

> Standardization and production sharing — much touted terms in the early days of the North Atlantic Treaty Organization — have for us been an elusive dream. With the exception of Canadian production of the Orenda equipped F-86 Sabre fighter (readily agreed to, indeed urged, by the United States during the Korean crisis), we have not produced anything of note for Allied use. Our new submarine destroyers were better than anything the Americans had, but they wouldn't buy them. We made the most powerful jet engines in the world, but who cares? Everybody in NATO, it seems, needs a good all purpose armored troop carrier, and we have developed an excellent one in the Bobcat, but nobody will buy it.

> The result is that we have no real defense but several fantastically expensive destroyers; a disappearing Canadian Air Force and aircraft industry; and a fearfully ill-equipped Army for modern conditions. And why? Because from the beginning we have not standardized; we have integrateed — which really means we

have conformed to U.S. concepts, doctrines and weapons.

In this respect, NATO has been a 10-year experiment in failure. Nuclear retaliation was the deterrent to Communist expansion before 1949, and a prime reason for forming NATO was to create the collective forces-in-being which would make this sole reliance on the nuclear weapon unnecessary. Yet today we are right back where we started, organized, deployed and committed to the Big Boom.

Whether there is to be any Canadian defense production in the future depends, apparently, on how lucky we are in getting some sub-contracts (dare we hope for a prime contract or two?) from the United States to make U.S. weapons. So we are hardly in a position to advise the British on how to compete with the United States in the European arms market. We can only hope that they fare better than we have, and perhaps they will — if they profit from our mistakes and take a strong stand.

There was general discontent among NATO countries in Europe over this situation and over their military and economic dependence on the United States. If, in 1959, even these war-impoverished countries, poorer in raw materials than Canada, were insisting that they should share the development and production as well as the cost, why not Canada? To pay for defence, there must be a return from industry, employment and taxes returned to the government. Contrary to the vociferous media, the question of where our planes and other defence equipment are produced is a matter of economics. Our media, cultural groups, folk singers and huge civil service do not produce the necessary profits. We get only a dribble by setting up assembly lines of semi-skilled workers to manufacture bits and pieces of U.S. products or "American components under license." This kind of work attracts none of the technology, skills and industrial development which make a country prosperous. Other countries realize that "prestige," solidly based on outstanding achievements, is worth a good deal to a nation in tangible terms. But we scoff at "prestige" and humbly beg the Americans to give us a few crumbs from their huge defence larder, since we have none left of our own.

Prime Minister Diefenbaker made much of the great benefits that would accrue to Canada through plans being proposed for integrated defence production within NATO countries. He claimed that this would be "cheaper for Canada, would keep our factories busy and retain our technical and design teams". Did he really believe it? The American view of "integrated defence production" was indicated in a 1959 article in *Missiles and Rockets*. The United States at the time was trying to get NATO countries to integrate their defence purchases by going together to buy — you guessed it — the American F-105. The F-105 was an American interceptor, as heavy as the Arrow, but a single-seater with only one engine, therefore with less speed, rate of climb and armament load than even the Mark I Arrow. For similar quantities it would cost about the same as the Arrow, as the Canadian government discovered. The article reported:

> It has been officially announced that the U.S. F-105 built by Republic, will soon go to the NATO-committed U.S. units stationed in England, France and Germany. And the European NATO nations *now realize* that the fighter fulfils their defensive requirements. [Italics added]

> It is understood that the first requests to the NATO Council will come either jointly or severally from Germany, the Netherlands, Belgium and Italy. England and France are aware of the plan but are uncommitted. Both have their own all-weather fighters under consideration, ... but these are years away from production and would cost as much as the F-105.*

The article proceeds to describe the U.S. concept of production sharing:

> *HOW TO SHARE* — Under the 'share' plan one of the NATO nations would be named as assembly and test manager. Another — Germany for instance —

---

* It is strange that the U.S. did not accept the same argument for buying the Arrow, since the F-108 was years away from production and would cost even more than the Arrow. Why is this logic valid only for other countries?

> could produce the guidance, another the wings or airframe, and so forth. Britain, which has three engines suitable for the F-105, *doubtless* could produce the powerplant ... [Italics added]

> It is conceded that under the proposed plan certain parts of the plane, possibly the heavy forgings, would have to be made in this country. These would be hand - led by Republic and might constitute as much as 25 percent of the cost — the U.S. contribution to the Plan. Republic would also gain by providing technical assistance throughout the life of the aircraft.

> Each of the several countries teaming in such a production 'share' plan would contribute a portion of the cost and draw planes from the final line in proportion to that contribution. While the sharing of cost is a big item, the fact that it would provide work for aircraft plants of the countries involved is another large factor in the plan ...[5]

If you have ever read anything so colossally arrogant, conceited and condescending, this writer has not. The United States which takes it for granted that she is capable of turning out hundreds of planes of all types, without any technical assistance from other countries now tells these countries, many of whom have led in aircraft development and design of their own, that the U.S. F-105 is the plane which meets their requirements; she thinks she can let each of them build a little piece of it but, of course, the United States will have to make all the difficult parts, and provide the technical assistance, as well as having provided all the design and development. One pictures a father, allowing his small children to help him, but only if they are very careful, and only under his strict supervision! It will be a big favour just to provide these countries with a few jobs, no matter how little they contribute to any skills. The Americans have apparently quickly forgotten that they got the jet engine from Britain, and that Europe has long been a leader in aircraft design and production.

But if any other country had been allowed to sell a plane to NATO, it might have spoiled the picture presented at the World Congress of Flight held at Las Vegas in the late 1950s. All the nations of the Western world were supposed to be represented. They all flew past: all the planes had been made in the United States!

When an Avro technician went down to California to work for an American aircraft company he was taken through the plant to be shown their production methods. The foreman escorting him through the plant remarked "I think you will enjoy working here. Have you worked on aircraft for long?" The Avro chap replied, "Certainly, for about ten years." The foreman said: "Oh, but it will be much more interesting here; you will have a chance to work on all-metal aircraft."[6] So much for the Lancaster, the Jetliner, the CF-100 and the Arrow. Perhaps they really do believe they are doing other countries a favour by allowing them to make bits and pieces of the F-105. This in not surprising in our case; we have a habit of reducing our planes to scrap so that no one finds out about them.

It would not be hard to conceive of a far more rational type of defence production sharing. *Canadian Aviation* in 1958 published an article that noted:

> There have been continuing talks between Canadian and American defence officials *re* integrating the defence industries of the two nations for a weapons pool common to both. At the risk of suggesting the obvious, it is assumed the Canadian representatives have drawn to the attention of their American collegues the fact that Canada has an advanced interceptor, superior to any weapons system at the same stage of development, now undergoing flight tests at Malton. The Avro Arrow and its already projected later 'Marks' would be capable of filling NORAD's advanced interceptor role *for at least the next decade*. If we are going to integrate production programs there is no better place to start than by phasing the Arrow into the common weapons pool. Unreasonable and unrealistic?...
> [Not as] unreasonable or unrealistic as the suggestion that the Canadian industry's role lies in abandoning a presently well - advanced project and tooling up from scratch to turn out components for [inferior] weapons systems already in production in the United States. And a lot more economical — which is, after all, the prime reason for either nation embarking on any scheme of production facilities. [Italics added.]

The U.S. concept of defence production sharing is wasteful and inefficient. It gives very little to any of the other countries involved, except for unskilled or semi-skilled assembly jobs; Britain or Germany might be permitted to supply the engines and electronics perhaps, under U.S. direction. All the expertise, design work, technology, research and development, the most valuable spinoffs from the industry, would remain in the U.S.

In this context we should ask the question: was there any sense, economic or otherwise, in scrapping a plane ready to go into production on existing production lines, all the research and development almost complete, the testing and data programes, worth millions to Canada and other countries, almost complete, its performance already proven, the more powerful Mark II version ready to fly? Did it make any sense to scratch it, to destroy everything and throw it down the drain, so that the United States could repeat the whole process and come up with a similar product five or ten years later, if it were successful? With normal developments during that time, the Arrow could have been constantly improved, as technology advanced, to stay ahead of anything else, at far less cost. The Mark III version was already on paper.

It would seem logical that, out of the vast pool of defence material now being produced and developed for the future, into the cost of which all NATO countries have to pay, the United States could pick certain of the largest fields, such as the Strategic Air Command and deterrent bomber forces and add to that the defence lines for protecting the SAC, viz. the DEW Line, Pine Tree Line and Bomarc bases, since they admittedly serve no other purpose. The U.S. could also completely control the development of large missiles and atomic submarines, for which she already has enormous facilities.

Out of the remaining requirements, however, it would seem logical that the other countries should each develop its own answer to at least one problem, and not leave *all* the design and development in the United States, with small handouts of bits and pieces to other countries, if and when they can get them.

The United States does not have a hundred times as many people as Canada, only ten times as many. She is turning out hundreds of types of armament, including many types of planes. One would think that allowing another country to supply one of these planes could not hurt her very much, especially when she has no such equivalent even on the drawing-boards. But export sales of both new and obsolescent fighter planes is one of the United States' most enormously profitable export businesses, along with massive quantities of hundreds of other types of military equipment. This trade is also an immensely powerful weapon to pressure Third World countries to conform to U.S. foreign policy. It can serve this purpose in Canada as well.

In 1958, Dr Norman MacKenzie, then President of the University of British Columbia warned his students that Canada was becoming "a Northern projection of the United States" and put his finger on one of the most difficult and dangerous problems facing Canada. He pointed out that in the early 1950s "it was planned that the air defence of Canada would be carried out by planes designed and built in Canada and armed with missiles likewise of Canadian origin. These included the CF-100 jet fighter and its successor the CF -105 Arrow, the Velvet Glove missile and later the Sparrow II missile. Except for the CF-100, 'welcomed' by the U.S. because at that time it had no surplus capacity, all of these developments had been cancelled by early 1959 and replaced by the Bomarc and the Lacrosse missile." The CF-100 was then replaced by the F-104 and F-5. All of them were American-designed. *The Globe and Mail*, which reported on Dr MacKenzie's talk, commented that the change in policy brings its own penalty. "We are becoming unhealthily dependent on another country for the means to defend ourselves." Dr MacKenzie spelled out some of the implications: the present trend may wind up by placing all Canadian military-scientific research in the United States' hands, forcing Canada's ablest scientists to seek employment with U.S. firms.

"In this arrangement we buy their weapons, we are trained and directed by them and we provide their forces with bases and facilities in appropriate areas across our country." *The Globe and Mail* agrees:

> That is all too true. If matters continue in this fashion, we may drift into a condition uncomfortably like that of certain Middle Eastern and Latin American

countries which draw their entire supply of modern weapons from one of the Great Powers and in consequence find themselves bound to support the policies of their armorer on pain of being suddenly left defenceless. A nation in that position may be independent in name, but it has no real independence in fact.

Actually from the standpoint of national independence and self-respect, the money value of such orders is less important than their technical nature. It is not enough that we supply the United States with, say, rifle butts while it supplies us with guided missiles. Arrangements should be worked out by which Canada—if she finds its impracticable to manufacture her own missiles — will furnish the United States, and the other members of the North Atlantic Treaty Organization, with advanced weapons and equipment of some kind in return for what we receive from them.

This is the only way in which Canada can keep together her excellent teams of scientists and engineers — such as the one which worked on the Avro Arrow — and remain abreast of scientific and industrial developments. It is also the only way in which this country can pull her weight in the alliance and be accepted as an ally and not a mere satellite.[8]

In another 1958 editorial, *The Globe and Mail* again addressed the problem:

The question comes back, not as a matter of military policy, but as one of effectiveness and efficiency in *terms of economics*. Canada has spent a great deal of money on the Avro Arrow. Certainly, some of that money was wasted; but this was not Avro's fault. [Italics added.]

What counts now is the Arrow's value in terms of alternate weapons and Canada's ability to play its part in the Western defence complex. One of the virtues of the Arrow's development has been its contribution to Canada's industrial diversification. With the Arrow (and CF - 100) expenditures, we have bought new skills, new techniques, new industrial processes and plants which otherwise would not exist, but which today range far beyond the needs of the Avro program

in their service to Canada. These gains are emphatic-
ally worth keeping.

Supposing the Arrow is not permitted to play its part?
If that is the case, there will be a wide gap, an inviting
gap, in Western defenses for the next [few] years, until
the F-108 becomes available. This is a U.S. plane, similar to the Arrow, but in one vital respect very different from it. While the Arrow is in pre-production,
the F-108 is still on the drawing board. Yet everyone
is talking about adopting it ... because of somebody's
'guesstimate' of what it will do ...

Here we have an extreme example of what has been
evident since 1945 — the determination of U.S. industry to monopolize the defence systems of the West.
This is something Canada does not have to accept.
Certainly, Canada wants to have integrated defence—
but Canada should not accept an integration that en-
tails economic subordination or impoverishment.

It used to be Washington's excuse that it could not
share defence production with Canada because Canada did not have the necessary skills and industry.
Now, after considerable cost, Canada has them. So
now, we hear other excuses. They do not hold water.
The harsh fact is that the U.S. is expecting a country
running into the red by more than a billion dollars a
year to scrap an industry which has had a large part in
that country's economic growth — and to use the saving, so-called, to buy U.S.-built weapons at whatever
price the U.S. wishes to put on them. In that way, we
would become completely subservient to the U.S., not
only in the military sense but, and to a greater degree,
in the economic one.

Now, it happens to have been shown in a good many
fields that whatever the U.S. can do, we can do as well
— and often cheaper.

[One alternative for the Canadian government is to] ...
seek a little collaboration in the United Kingdom,
where, for a good many reasons, we should be buying
and selling more. If the U.S. does not want a two-way
street on defense production, perhaps the British do.

The British are pretty well up in most of the modern
weapons. And they have suffered, as we have, from

Washington's determination to dominate the munitions picture. Perhaps we can talk business with
them. And if that antagonizes the U.S., if that makes
the U.S. think Canada is being stubborn, we can point
out that our risk is no greater than theirs.[9]

Almost twenty years later, *Wings* magazine sums it up very
well:

The decision to discontinue development work on the
delta-winged CF-105 Arrow in 1959 marked an irrevocable turning point in the fortunes of the whole
aerospace industry in this country. This was for two
major reasons: the decision took us away from advanced
domestic designs, notably military fighter aircraft,
and it was only such spheres which utilized high technology. With the loss of high technology, and the research which accompanied it, we lost our human
resource base of technicians and engineers to foreign
interests and we dropped out of manufacturing fields
relating to advanced materials — notably titanium,
steel alloys, and the composite epoxies which came
later. In short, our industry became dated and obsolescent due to the rapidly advancing nature of the
whole field.[10]

As anyone could have prophesied, Canada's share of the
defence sharing agreements fell far short of the glowing
prospects suggested by Diefenbaker. What did we get?
Nothing at all really: production of wings and ailerons for the
Bomarc — kid stuff, for Canadair, our U.S.-owned subsidiary; since Canada's order had saved the Bomarc from cancellation by the U.S., Boeing was glad to give us that; production of a few radar sets, designed in the U.S., for the DEW
line; a contract for engineering work in the States, according
to O'Hurley? Oh no, that was just Canadair shipping its men
down to Boeing to work on the Bomarc, since it had nothing
here for them to do, so hired them out. Pearkes and O'Hurley
talked of trotting all over the world, hat in hand, begging for a
little bit of work for poor Canada to do. What a joke to every
other country! They support their *own* industries. Why
should they help us out, while our own industry was literally
being cut to pieces by our own government, repudiated by its
own country not because it was a failure but because it was
successful enough to be competitive?

Our 'salesmen' got a contemptuous brush-off. They couldn't even get a $3,000 order for plastic radar domes to be used in our own Arctic. A Senator from Ohio said there was a plant in his state that could make them, although the cost was higher. They got the order. The contract Canadair had been led to believe it might get to produce a proposed 'picket plane' for the Arctic never materialized. Nor did the contract for a NATO replacement plane. An extension was granted in that case to give Boeing sufficient time to put in its bid.

It would be nice to think that our officials, our Senators, and Members of Parliament work as hard for our Canadian industries as the Americans do for theirs. In spite of Diefenbaker's emotional protestations that he was doing his best to keep Avro's team of designers and engineers in Canada, nothing came to Avro except a contract they themselves negotiated, to manufacture wings for Douglas Aircraft. In fact, the Department of Defence Production did its best to prevent the company from bidding on a contract that might have meant two year's work.

As part of the Defence Production Sharing programme, the Department of Defence Production was supposed to have placed representatives at locations in the United States to get early information on contracts or sub-contracts that might be available to Canadian firms. According to the government it was doing its best to get such contracts. In the fall of 1959, a major aircraft manufacturer in the U.S. had a subcontract to let for manufacture and production of a missile carrier and launcher. A number of U.S. firms were asked to tender, and were invited to a briefing at the contractor's plant to acquaint them with the project. At this point, the U.S. contractor itself requested the Canadian government to 'allow' Avro to tender. Belatedly, the government sent the invitation to tender, not to Avro or Orenda, but to the Canadian Car Division, which could not handle such projects, as the government well knew. By the time it reached Avro, the deadline was only two or three days away. The U.S. contractor again intervened, granting a two-week extension to allow Avro to prepare and submit a bid.

With the few top designers left at Avro, with only ten working days and without any prior knowledge of or briefing on the project, Avro entered a bid. This involved analyzing the problem, working out an acceptable solution, preparing a complete technical design and presentation, a list of manpower and qualifications to prove the firm's capacity to handle the project, a list of facilities and equipment, and a cost estimate. This had to be prepared and printed in the form of two complete brochures, to be followed by a visit of appraisal by the main contractor. After some time, Avro contacted the U.S. contractor firm. They were told that they had been one of only three companies that had not been eliminated. Among those already eliminated were a number of major American companies. Avro was told that their technical presentation, designed and prepared in ten days, from scratch, had received the highest rating of all tenders received. They had been competitive with the other tenders as to cost. It was later announced that the contract had gone to two American firms who had submitted a joint bid. They had been working on it for at least a year. Avro had ten days and that, only because of a request from the U.S. prime contractor and a time extension granted by that firm. What were the Canadian Defence Production representatives doing in the U.S. ? As noted before, Avro's reputation was very high everywhere, except in Canada. But, in spite of the high rating given to Avro's bid, the contract was awarded to an American consortium.

Commander F.H. Cunnare, director of the electronics production division of the U.S. Defense Department, after a tour of Canadian electronics plants, observed that Canadian plants were capable of producing any 'finished product' then manufactured in the U.S. But he pointed out one little difficulty—that of getting permission from Congress for a Canadian order as *American business does not like sharing its contracts with other countries*. It does expect, however, to get its share of orders from these countries. Incidentally, it was an American electronics firm that spent thousands of dollars searching for an electronics expert whom it could not find in the U.S., but found at Avro.

Diefenbaker made many references to his hope that work

could be found for A.V. Roe and that it would be possible to retain in Canada at least some of the outstanding engineering and research group who had created a centre of high technology in Canada, but the government's attitude to the Avro company in particular and to the aircraft industry as a whole did not support these speeches. With respect to Avro, the government showed a complete lack of concern, both before and after the cancellation, for alternative contracts, or for the fate of the industry or of the design teams who worked there. No effort was made to bring any contracts to Avro. NATO had requested that the CF -100 be modified to extend its usefulness until a more advanced interceptor would be available to replace it. Its request was completely ignored. The company had received an inquiry from France concerning the purchase of 300 Iroquois engines. The company so informed the government. The government did not even acknowledge the letter. Either of these potential orders would have provided an additional or alternative contract to help take up some of the slack, keep some personnel in Canada and bring revenue to Canada. And if the government had really been interested in saving money, it would have granted the request from Britain for the purchase of the already-flying Arrow aircraft, and would have finalized the contract with Curtiss-Wright in the United States for manufacture of the Iroquois engine under license. After the Arrow contracts were cancelled, all the aircraft contracts of any size were directed to Canadair, the U.S. subsidiary. They have been kept busy ever since. Nothing at all was directed to Avro by the government.

As for the aircraft industry as a whole, it appeared that the government was not particularly interested in its fate either. A brief from the Air Industries and Transport Association was presented to the government in December, 1957. It asked for information regarding government intentions toward the industry and warned that it was running into serious trouble on all fronts, due to lack of government policy, planning, or consultation. The brief was ignored. When questioned in Parliament in the winter of 1958-59, Diefenbaker pretended to know nothing about it, then said that it was "secret." Finally, someone pointed out that the brief was in the Parliamentary library. It was never even acknowledged.[11]

As far as air transport is concerned, successive Canadian governments appear to be following a policy of gradually eliminating all competitive smaller airlines, no matter how necessary a service they provide, in order to give government-owned Air Canada a monopoly of air traffic and freight. It has also recently bought out both Canadair and deHavilland aircraft companies. It apparently does not wish to leave any of these industries in private hands — except for CP Air. Canadian Pacific has, of course, many close and powerful ties with the U.S. corporate structure. It is rather odd that, while removing competitive airlines, the government has been admonishing the aircraft industry that it must become "vigorously competitive" and must sink or swim on its own, without government assistance.

U.S. branch plants in Canada have been welcomed with open arms, have been given incentives, bonuses, deferred amortization, tax rebates and financial assistance both from Canadian governments and from Canadian financial institutions and banks whose cash boxes are always open to American firms. But Diefenbaker warned *Canadian* firms not to look for help from their government. He insisted that "these companies must be vigorously competitive with U.S. industry" in going after defence orders under the Defence Sharing Agreement — in which the government was supposed to be a sponsoring partner. Competitive — in this kind of market? How much did the Department of Defence get when Pearkes and O'Hurley went begging? How much did the Department of Defence Production representatives in the U.S. dig up when tenders were being let? When Pearkes and O'Hurley and others couldn't sell the Arrow or even the Bobcat, although both were needed and were later produced elsewhere to meet the demand? When English Electric had to go to the U.S. Supreme Court and still lost its bid for just two turbines for a U.S. public power project, although its bid was 19 percent lower than the lowest U.S. bid and it had met every requirement, even those imposed by the Buy American Act?

A typical Canadian story is the history of the Canadian hydrofoil, the *Bras d'Or*. It happened since the Arrow disaster, so apparently our leaders have learned nothing. In 1919, a hydrofoil built by Casey Baldwin and Alexander Graham Bell set a world speed record on the Bras d'Or Lakes on Cape Breton Island. It was far ahead of its time. During the Second World War, Canada became the third largest naval power in the world; because of our obvious capability, we were able to retain an autonomous role in the northwestern Atlantic. Then and since, Canada has been largely responsible for the Anti-Submarine Warfare (ASW) role in this sector, with the implied responsibility for keeping the shipping lanes open in the event of a war. However, when atomic submarines were developed, they could outrun any surface vessels. In 1959, therefore, the government approved the development of a prototype hydrofoil to match the speed of the atomic subs. The contract was awarded to de Havilland; they began work in 1962, to Navy specifications. The superstructure was built by de Havilland in Toronto, the hull by Marine Industries in Sorel. Although completion was delayed by a fire during construction, the hydrofoil was launched in 1968 and tested in Halifax. It was 46 metres long, weighed 210 tons, and was researched , designed and constructed in prototype at a cost of $53 million. In 1969, it established a world speed record of 70 miles (62 knots) per hour. It was also named the *Bras d'Or*.

The Canadian intention had been to develop a naval hydrofoil fleet, especially to track nuclear submarines as part of the ASW role. However, since the U.S. had no hydrofoils of its own, the Americans did not support this proposal. In 1970, there was another of the frequent policy changes on the part of our government, a new Defence White Paper that reduced the role of the Canadian Navy largely to coastal surveillance. In its new role and without U.S. support, the Navy could find no use for the *Bras d'Or*. It was the fastest ship in the world when it was mothballed in 1971. Boeing Aircraft in the United States is now working on the design of a similar type of hydrofoil, but have so far not come up with one to equal the Canadian *Bras d'Or*. A recent article in *The Globe and Mail* reports that the government has been trying to sell the *Bras d'Or*, but that it may very well be scrapped.[12] A typical Canadian story! We develop an advanced product which is ahead of any other country and fills a definite need, then, if other countries don't support it or buy it right away, our government deliberately delays the development until the United States can catch up with its own design.

Photographic Surveys, a Canadian company,* developed a device which vastly simplified contour mapping from the air, an advanced development of great value to the United States Air Force, among others. The USAF was interested in buying the device, but even though there was nothing like it in the United States, they could not get permission to buy it if the device were manufactured in Canada. In order to market the invention Photographic Surveys was forced to sell the rights to an American company to manufacture it in the United States.[13]

After the Arrow cancellation, *Aviation Week* of New York commented on the hopes of the Canadian government to get some defence contract work in the United States:

> Canada hopes to claim an increasing share of U.S. defense production contracts to help offset the effects of its controversial decision to rely primarily upon U.S. weapon systems for its own aerial defense.

> Tentative plans to give Canadian industry access to the U.S. defense procurement program and Canada's hopes for substantial U.S. business, were made known as an aftermath of the Canadian government's decision to cancel the Mach 3 Avro CF-105 Arrow interceptor and the Orenda Iroquois turbojet engine contracts. Both contracts had been widely subcontracted to Canadian industry and provided the principal support of a large percentage of the Canadian aircraft complex, the nation's third largest industry ...

> Only concrete evidence the government could offer to back its hopes for increasing U.S. defense business was the award of a $1.7 million subcontract by Boeing to Canadair for the production of Bomarc wing and tail sections ...

*This company was later purchased by A.V.Roe and renamed Canadian Applied Research Ltd. It was responsible for much of the research and development undertaken by A.V.Roe.

Raymond O'Hurley, Canadian Minister of Defence Production, says the government's present aim is to ensure equal opportunity for Canadian firms in bidding on U.S. contracts and that, once this is achieved, "the real success of production sharing endeavours depends to a large degree upon the determination of Canadian industry vigorously to seek defense business in the U.S. as either prime or subcontractors". O'Hurley added that Canadians would have to become competitive with U.S. industry in terms of technical competence, delivery and price.

One potential hitch in Canada's plans is the Buy America Act which is still in effect in the U.S. It requires, in many instances, that foreign bids for U.S. defense business be subject to duty and also must be raised by approximately six percent when its bid is considered alongside those of U.S. firms. It has not yet been determined whether the act will apply under the present loose U.S.-Canadian arrangements initiated last September.

The government apparently believes that the principal Canadian opportunity will be subcontracting to large U.S. primes. Opinion is widespread in the Canadian industry, however, that this will not work and that a definite agreement must be reached allotting Canada a definite portion of the production for mutual defense.

Feeling behind this is that the shrinking number of contracts available to the U.S. aircraft industry and the relatively large number of unemployed in the U.S. will combine to develop too great a political pressure to permit any sizeable volume of business to leave the country ...

Political thought in Canada now seems to range from a great fear that Canada will lose its sovereignty if it does not have the technical capabilities to develop advanced weapons and does not pay completely for its own defense to beliefs at the other end of the scale that, if the U.S. will not share equitably in defense production, Canada should withdraw gradually from the North American defense picture and let the U.S. carry the burden alone.[14]

Of course we couldn't make up our mind and of course no one really cared that much, so we did neither. We are now about to spend more than ever before for both our NATO and NORAD alliance, yet we still have no clear idea of what role we should be playing, or for what reasons. We have done nothing to demand a more effective Defence Sharing Agreement as part of the price for contributing to U.S.-Canadian continental defence. And our government has as little concept as ever of what is needed to lift Canada out of its slump.

Again in 1978-79, we are about to spend vast sums on fighter aircraft. We no longer have an indigenous industry that could develop and produce these planes in Canada for Canada's needs, so our money will be spent in the United States for imports — if we can find one that comes close enough to doing the job we need it for. The value of the order is $2.34 billion. In return for placing such a large contract abroad, we should be able to get some orders of equal value in exchange. But we produce no high technology products of equivalent value, so we must settle for package deals of bits and pieces put together by the competing firms in order to sell their product. We might get something of some value if we knew what we wanted, but apparently we don't.   One spokesman claims that, for such an order, the only proper offset would be a compensating contract for our aerospace industry, from which there might be some technological spin-off. Another contends that such an order would only disturb the Canadian aerospace industry which has now reached a steady low-level survival stage. To throw the aerospace industry any such large contract would be "disruptive", since the level of activity could not be sustained. Therefore, according to this view, we should select benefits which would be distributed in bits and pieces to industry in general.

In assessing some of the proposed "offset" programmes offered by the competing firms, it should be obvious that what we definitely do *not* need is aid to our existing foreign-owned branch plants, already the recipients of considerable government incentives. In spite of these incentives they have long ignored the need to invest in research and development, in new product development, or in creation of export markets; nor have they supported Canadian supply industries. Benefits to them will merely by siphoned off to the parent companies. We do not need further 'joint ventures' which almost always result in further foreign takeovers. We do not need more foreign 'investment', since the enormous amount we already have is largely responsible for the increasing net outflow of capital from Canada and our present debt-ridden predicament. Assistance in opening foreign markets would not be something we require, were it not for the fact that Canadian industry has such a remarkably poor record of taking advantage of foreign market opportunities even when they are offered to us, let alone of going after them aggressively. This, of course, is a basic characteristic of a branch - plant economy, and such industries are unlikely to take advantage of such assistance, certainly not on any permanent basis. If they were interested, these branch plants could have done it long ago, either on their own, or with the assistance that their parent companies were quite capable of giving them.

Neither do we need more unskilled or semi-skilled jobs, of which we already have too many — jobs that are the result of 'manufacturing under license' products that have been designed, tested, advertised and marketed in the United States to suit U.S. requirements. Our governments have a fixation on this kind of job creation, a sort of numbers game in which quantity is the only concern. They advertise in U.S. magazines, offering to U.S. firms subsidies of tens of thousands of dollars for each job created, if they will come to Canada and set up a branch plant. There are no meaningful criteria as to the type of products to be manufactured, the kind of jobs created, their permanence, their stimulus of related Canadian industries, creation of export revenue, nor the long-run benefit to Canada.

For placing outside the country such an enormous contract for very high-technology imports there should be some equivalent value received that would stimulate a corresponding amount of research, technology and development at home, — if not in the aerospace industry, then at least in an industry capable of providing an equivalent leading edge in the evolution of new processes, new advanced products and high-quality distinctive exports, as well as the backward linkages that spread the benefits to related supply industries. All of these Canada lost in 1959 and now desperately needs. Band-aid measures will no longer cure the chronic illness of Canadian industrial development and trade. They may kill the patient.

So what are the five competing corporations offering in return for this major contract? The detailed proposals have so far been released only to the government's Fighter Evaluation Team, which is charged with awarding the contract. But some clues as to the kind of proposals offered as offsets can be gathered from the extensive advertisements placed by the competing firms in Canadian newspapers and magazines. The proposals fall under three general headings: sub-contract or manufacture under licence of certain components or 'packages' of the aircraft; general trade opportunities for Canadian industries, or a specific volume of purchases in Canada, and offers of export opportunities; and joint ventures and transfers of technology to Canadian firms.

Northrop offers production sharing on its complete production run of F-18Ls as well as on its Canadian orders (manufacture under licence); it claims to have placed export contracts worth $20 million with Canadian firms, ranging from stationery for African countries to construction jobs in the Middle East and electrical cable and industrial castings for the U.S.

Grumman offers contracts related to development of new aircraft and space systems, and *hydrofoil* contruction and manufacture of aircraft assemblies and avionic components. It proposes to place contracts in Canada sufficient to increase the G.N.P. by $4.5 billion and to create thousands of jobs. It also promises to undertake "joint ventures" and points to its participation in the Trigull amphibian project in British Columbia.

McDonnell-Douglas makes few claims as to the enormous benefits it will bring to Canada in the way of 'packages', export contracts or joint ventures. It merely points to the fact that, for the past decade, all the wings for the DC-9 and DC-10 sold anywhere in the world have been produced in the company's plant at Malton, Ontario, its permanent commitment to Canadian industry and procurement.

General Dynamics has conducted a very low-key advertising campaign and has had little to say in public about its offset programme.   Until recently this company wholly owned Canadair in Montreal. Perhaps its Canadian contacts are so good that it doesn't need the publicity.

Panavia is the only non-American consortium competing for the Canadian contract. It is a consortium of leading British, German and Italian aerospace companies. It offers to place orders with Canadian aerospace firms for manufacture of various packages of avionic, engine and other components, and to provide continuing maintenance capability for these firms. It also offers cooperation in future design programs. From its office in Ottawa and through its Canadian consultant firms it has contacted two thousand Canadian firms, of whom six hundred have suitable products and services to offer. Panavia promises $6 billion worth of business and industrial benefits. It also offers a trade link to the European Common Market and proposes to market the deHavilland Dash 7 in Europe.

In general, the American companies appear to offer chiefly some contracts to manufacture components under license, some contracts to be placed in Canada resulting in job creation,and some cooperative joint ventures with some transfer of technology involved. The export contracts offered by Grumman are of the kind we have already been able to negotiate on our own, especially with respect to engineering and construction jobs abroad. Its joint ventures are similar to many others entered into when Canadian firms have not been able to obtain sufficient funds in Canada to avoid bankruptcy. There is little that is new. Panavia appears to offer two important advantages, in addition to Canadian business and industrial benefits which it guarantees up to a value of $4 billion. It offers long-term production runs for the Tornado production with some technological input, long-term Canadian maintenance capability for the Canadian planes, and cooperation in future design programs. It also offers increased access to the European Common Market, which could help to diversify our foreign trade. But in general, judging by the performance of past offset programs, the impact of the above proposals may well be far less than the value of the Canadian order to the corporation that wins it.

A paper presented at a meeting of the Air Industries Association of Canada discounts the potential for real gains in research and technology benefits to be derived from offset programmes, claiming that "capacity in Canada relating to both product design and modern manufacturing technology will never come from a single, once-over program .. there must be a continuing attractive environment to hold and stimulate talented people — scientists, engineers, technicians." Because of military security, the speaker adds, advanced technology in critical areas will never be made available to Canada through offset programs. Further, as proven so often, U.S. industry tends to restrict the transfer of its technology, and this tendency is now being supported by the U.S. Congress which "is seeking to stop erosion of U.S. dominance in exports by other developed nations," by restricting such exports of technology.

Canada does not have to remain in the role of 'passive recipient'. She could take a more imaginative and innovative approach to such research and development programs than she has taken in the past. As one observer puts it, Canada "must move from being essentially a sub-contractor and supplier ... [She] must encourage the integration of domestic research and development *on a full product basis*" (Italics added) rather than on subcontracting of bits and pieces as offered by most offset programmes.

Canada has two options. We can create self-contained programs by using our research and development to create a capability to produce "self-contained products or components" for the total global market. "When offset is used in this manner, programmes in which Canada is involved will not only ensure that the immediate benefit stays in the country, but that an undeniable capability is created for the long-term". The other option is to participate in international cooperative research and development. However, to gain access to such participation, Canada must undertake large-scale independent research and development programs, otherwise our only bargaining power will continue to be large foreign purchases, which have not so far brought much benefit to Canada.[15]

In other words, Canada must pay her way back into the club. This, so far, she has been unwilling to do, and the results have been obvious.

---

1 U.S. Dept. of State, *Bulletin 1V*, April 26, 1941, p. 494
2 McLin, Jon, *Canada's Changing Defence Policy, 1957-1963*, Johns Hopkins, Baltimore, 1967, pp. 174-6
3 *Canadian Aviation*; Nov., 1958, pp. 21, 51
4 *New York Times*
5 *Missiles and Rockets*, April 27, 1959
6 From conversation with the author
7 "Production Integration Should Include Arrow," *Canadian Aviation*, Dec. 1958
8 *Globe & Mail*, Toronto, Oct. 3, 1958
9 "The Road to Serfdom," *ibid.*, Dec. 17, 1958
10 "A Historical Perspective," *Wings*, Summer, 1978, p. 12
11 Air Industries and Transport Association Brief, Dec., 1957
12 "For Sale Cheap: One Fast Bras d'Or," *Globe & Mail*, Toronto, Sept. 27, 1978; *cf.* Special Committee on Defence, *Minutes of Proceedings and Evidence*, House of Commons, Ottawa, June 27, 1963
13 *Canadian Aviation*, May, 1958, p. 84
14 Butz, J.S., Jr., "Canada Seeks U.S. Defence Contracts," *Aviation Week*, Mar. 2, 1959, pp. 25-7
15 Romain, Ken, "Little Chance for Research Noted in Offsets," *Globe & Mail*, Toronto, Sept. 30, 1978

General view of the Arrow final assembly. Major components are being assembled for subsequent release to the final assembly marry-up in the background.

From Avro News, October, 1957

Chapter 10
Economics and Technology

No modern country which wishes to remain economically healthy can afford to ignore the importance of technology, especially innovative technology that alone can produce the competitive products on which export markets depend. Canadian government officials and Ministers have excused their low level of investment in technological research and development with the contention that Canada cannot afford such investment; she can always buy it more cheaply from abroad. The results of this naive penny-pinching philosophy are painfully apparent in our present position in world trade. Our manufactured end products are not even holding their own in the domestic market; their performance in export markets has led to an increasing deficit that stands at $11.1 billion as of 1977. The relationship between our merchandise trade in end products and our level of technology is very close.

We depend for our technology on foreign branch plants, hoping that they will bring with them their high-level technology, and that they will continue, through investments in research and development, to keep abreast of leading developments in their field. But they are not interested in exporting to Canada any technology of real value, nor in training Canadians to use it; Canadians might then set up their own companies to compete and might even improve on the technology. U.S. trade monopolies are largely based on their advanced technology; its transfer to another country would threaten that monopoly. They are so keenly aware of this that the U.S. Congress is now considering regulations to prevent the export of any government supported technology.

There are two kinds of technology: one concentrates on increasing the efficiency of the production process, the other leads to the design and development of new or improved products, of better quality or higher performance. Successful industrialized countries use both. But foreign branch plants bring into Canada only the former, and any research done here is for the same purpose — more efficient production. The amount brought into Canada, even of this type, is relatively small, and declining. Seldom do they bring with them or develop in Canada a capacity for *innovative* technology, the kind of technology that is competitive and capable of producing new and better products for markets both at home and abroad. There are some exceptions that pay off well, but they are few.

It is difficult to understand why our governments, economists and financiers have such a fixation on the need for *foreign* capital. So great is this fixation and so eager is the government to sell out the country, our resources and industries, that the extent of foreign ownership in Canada far exceeds that of any other modern country in the world. The government believes that it is easier — or cheaper — to let someone else take over the country and develop it for us. Of course, it isn't — not in the long run. Foreign investors go where the profits are greatest and where governments and people are the most complacent. But why are we content to mortgage our country and its wealth and live on the short-term proceeds while the mortgagee runs it for us as it suits his purposes? Mortgages do come due, and there is a limit to how many mortgages one can take out. We have about reached that limit.

Canada's international indebtedness had reached $48.5 billion by the end of 1976. One year later it had risen to $53.5 billion. It is still rising. Foreign direct investment or ownership of Canadian industries and resources amounted to $17.4 billion in 1965, $26.4 billion in 1970, and had risen to $39.8 billion by the end of 1975, an increase of $13.4 billion or 50 percent in just five years.[1] In Ontario, for instance, net federal and provincial public spending has resulted in a public debt of $4,500 per capita. Interest alone on the federal, provincial and municipal debt amounted to $2 billion per quarter in 1977, for a total of over $9 billion per annum. In the first half of 1978, it amounted to $5.3 billion.[2] From April, 1977 to January, 1978, the federal budget deficit increased from $3.8 billion to $6.61 billion. Expenditures exceeeded revenues by almost 25 percent; this was partly, but only partly, due to new agreements with the provinces which reduced federal revenues from income tax.

We are suffering from unemployment and inflation at the same time. Foreign opinion as to Canada's ability to manage her economy is indicated by the flight of capital, the closing or transferring of plants, and by the falling value of the dollar. A country cannot spend more than it earns over a period of time without going bankrupt. It must either earn more or spend less. *Internally*, it must earn enough and create enough in profits, wages and taxes to pay for its necessary services. This means not merely jobs but products as well. Resource industries provide very few jobs in proportion to the capital expended, especially if no processing is done in the country. Service industries generate jobs but no marketable products, unless they are based on industry. In most modern countries, two-thirds of the jobs in the service industries are generated by the high-technological industrial sector and its increasing specialization, otherwise they would not exist. The largest number of non-public-service jobs per dollar invested are created in the manufacturing sector. This sector also must produce as much as possible of the goods we consume each year, otherwise such goods must be imported. All imports must be paid for in foreign exchange, which we must then earn elsewhere. We do not consume services only, and even services must have goods in order to operate.

Externally, our exports of all kinds of goods and services must equal our imports if we are to avoid a deficit on our current account. A deficit on our current account can only be made up by a surplus on the net capital flow, the other part of the balance of payments. Total deficits must equal total surpluses. If the current accounts show a deficit, then we must have a sufficient net inflow of foreign capital to cover the deficit. For a long time,we have had a large and increasing deficit on current accounts, but this deficit has been covered by the increasing inflows of foreign capital investment in Canada. But capital is now flowing out of Canada, creating a net deficit in that item also; capital inflow is no longer able to mask the increasing deficit in current accounts. Those who already own so much of Canada no longer need to bring in any foreign capital to continue to buy up more of the country. They can continue to re-invest while at the same time exporting more and more capital out of the country in interest, dividends and profits.

It has therefore been necessary for the government to borrow abroad to make up the deficit on current account. But even in 1977 our foreign debt was the highest of any developed country. Because of this huge foreign debt, our increasing deficit on current account, and the net outflow of foreign private capital, as well as the poor prospects of any improvement in our potential for growth, world confidence in Canada's capacity to manage her economy has declined. It has become harder for the government to borrow abroad, except at exorbitant interest rates or by devaluating the dollar. Each of these automatically increases the total foreign debt, to be paid in foreign currencies. The government spent, in the first three quarters of 1978, a total of $3.2 billion in U.S. funds in an attempt to support the dollar; the cost in August alone was $711 million. The government was therefore forced to borrow $3 billion in foreign funds to cover the deficit in foreign exchange. Only if we are able to create a surplus on our current account can we decrease the need for a net inflow of foreign capital, either through increased foreign investment or through an increase in the foreign debt.[3]

The balance of payments reflects the economic health of a country, of which the most important indicator is the state of the current accounts. To discover the source of the increasing deficit in our current accounts, it is necessary to study its component parts. The two major items under our current account are the merchandise trade balance and the service trade balance. In 1977, there was a slight surplus of $2.9 billion in the merchandise trade sector, but it was offset by a whopping deficit of $7.4 billion in the service trade sector, for a net current account deficit of $4.5 billion. In the service trade sector, "total service receipts from foreigners for travel, shipping, interest and dividends, etc., totalled $8 billion, but Canadian payments to foreigners for the same things [services], totalled almost $15.5 billion" for a net deficit in service trade of $7.4 billion. There was a *net outflow* of $3.5 billion in interest and dividends alone; this represents a part of the "service cost" of foreign investment in Canada. "Politicians do not mention this deficit because they do not want to do anything about it. Instead, they focus on the *travel* deficit which, at $1.6 billion last year, was only half the problem the deficit on interest and dividends was ... Even if the tourist deficit was eliminated entirely, Canada would still have a services deficit in the coming year of $8 billion or more," due to debt service costs.[4] This 'service cost' of foreign investment does not, of course, include the costs of the massive imports of goods, components and supplies imported from the United States instead of being purchased in Canada by our branch plants. That comes under 'merchandise trade'. As long as we have a branch plant economy, we can do little to decrease the flow of funds out of the country for interest, dividends, technology and management costs and the 'transfer costs' — an interesting device used to cover further transfers of capital from Canada to the parent company. The onus for balancing the huge deficit in the service trade therefore falls onto the merchandise trade sector.

The merchandise trade sector includes the sum of the surpluses or deficits incurred in several categories, of which the most important are: raw or semi-finished goods, agricultural products, and end products (fully manufactured goods). In an article in *Engineering Digest*, J.L. Orr[5] contends that the importance of our trade in fully manufactured end products has been grossly underestimated in Canada. Since it is in such bad shape, our economists tend to rationalize it rather than concern themselves and do something about it. As Orr observes

> ... it will be seen that our modest net income from merchandise trade is grossly inadequate to offset the escalating deficit in service payments. As a result, Canada has sustained massive deficits ranging between $4 and $5 billion per year in 1975, 1976 and 1977, the impact

of which is now being reflected in the falling exchange rate for the Canadian dollar ... [The] relative growth rate of exports versus imports is *adverse in every one of the major commodity categories*. Thus, over the six-year period from 1970, merchandise imports grew by 17.9 percent per annum while exports rose by only 14.6 percent per annum. This represents an adverse differential growth rate of 22.4 percent. In the end products category, which is the dominant component of our merchandise trade, imports growing at 17.6 percent per annum have far outstripped exports [which have grown] at only 14.5 percent per annum. While increased petroleum exports probably account for the high differential growth in the crude materials category, the adverse differential growth in agriculture and food products category (14.7%) is especially surprising.

In other words, we are losing ground right across the board, not only in manufactured end products but even in agriculture and food products. Orr continues:

In terms of employment, the increase of $7.2 billion in the deficit in end product trade between 1970 and 1976 implies a loss to the Canadian economy of some 360,000 jobs. Unless the present divergent growth trend of imports in this critical sector can be reversed, the future survival of our secondary manufacturing industry will be increasingly jeopardized.

Orr points out that the decline in our net balance in end products has increased steeply since 1971. He considers this the most disturbing element in our recent trade performance; it has resulted in a net deficit in this category in 1977 of $11.1 billion. "As a result, imported manufactures have now captured some 35 percent of the Canadian domestic market, a level which is not remotely approached by any other industrialized country." It is worth remembering, as noted before, that *up to 40 percent* of our total imports consists of imports by our branch plants of components, parts, supplies and services from their U.S. parent companies or other suppliers.

A devalued dollar is supposed to present an excellent opportunity to improve a country's export/import position. If we had a healthy manufacturing industry, geared to exports, it could be an advantage in the short term and would eventually correct itself. But we have not. Canadian manufacturers are notoriously poor at exploiting opportunities to expand their export markets. Therefore, instead of using the situation to our advantage, our manufacturing volume has actually declined. At the same time, our imports have greatly increased, at a time when their cost is much higher because of the devalued dollar, and the situation has worsened on both sides of the equation.

The structural defects in our economy have been apparent for a long time. The results have been inevitable. In good times, the inflow of foreign capital has served to mask the basic weaknesses, but in slack times, our vulnerability is painfully evident.

It is fashionable for economists and our government to attribute such declines to "transient fluctuations in the economy" or to "external influences over which Canada has little control". This does not explain why Canada should be so unusually vulnerable to such influences. There appears to be a paralyzing reluctance on the part of the government and of our economists to probe more deeply into the basic causes; perhaps they are afraid it might disturb the myth concerning the virtues of foreign investment — and they have no other solution.

Orr discusses some of the specific *external influences* which are so often referred to and why they have had such a relatively disastrous effect on Canada. Our automobile industry is almost 100 percent American-owned. But until 1964, the industry had a certain degree of autonomy; it was able to purchase considerable quantities of components, parts, tires and tubes from Canadian suppliers. There was a fairly large auto parts industry in Canada. In 1964, Canada signed the Auto Pact with the U.S. It was designed to give Canada a larger share in the manufacture of automotive products, in proportion to her share of automotive purchases. But, as in most bargains between unequals, Canada has been the loser, and has run a

deficit in all but three years since 1964. This deficit has occurred, not in the final assemblies of cars and trucks, but in
auto parts and the tire and tube industries. With tariff barriers
removed, the parent companies began to order these supplies
from the same U.S. supplier for both the parent and the
Canadian subsidiary.*

A correspondent to a Toronto newspaper, who had worked
for 25 years in the auto industry, clearly illustrated that the
auto firms do not support Canadian suppliers of machinery or
equipment either. He reports that:

> Canadian auto plants ... are mere assembly facilities
> where U.S. technological prowess is prominently dis-
> played for all the daily tour visitors to marvel at.
> They see American metal stampings, some as large as
> sides of beef, automatically inserted into sophisticated
> mammoth machines with American manufacturers'
> nameplates. A button is pressed and a Detroit-built
> computerized electro-hydraulic welding system fuses
> the steel parts together to form a body shell which
> then moves along on a U.S.-designed conveyor into
> the paint booth where complicated American spraying
> equipment coats the shell in any shade or color you
> want ... and, yes, you guessed it, most of the paint is
> imported, and before the body rolls off the line as a
> finished vehicle 90 percent of the trim materials came
> from Ohio, Michigan or Oshkosh, Wisconsin.
>
> I have yet to find a Canadian manufacturer's name-
> plate on any of the many millions of dollars worth of
> equipment, machines and fittings other than metal
> fasteners ...

He goes on to state that the jobs in Canada are monotonous,
tension-building and not conducive to good health:

> There are good jobs in the auto industry, to be sure,
> but they are almost all in the United States; a mind-

---

*With the deficit of almost $11.1 billion in the end products trade, with the
increasing flow of imports of auto parts, machinery and equipment, plus a net
total deficit in the auto parts trade of about $3 billion, the federal and Ontario
governments in 1978 found it "necesary" to bribe Ford to build an auto parts
plant in Ontario; it will not of course, give work to the existing Canadian-
owned auto parts firms, but it will provide jobs. Ottawa and Quebec are now
considering an $86 million "offer" to General Motors. This exceeds the $68
million offer to Ford.

> boggling number, too, in terms of engineering, desig-
> ning, stamping, experimenting, testing, marketing
> and research, etc., none of which is carried out here.
> A stamping plant alone is a half-billion-dollar-plus
> undertaking. And there are several of them spread
> around the northern states. We don't have a single
> one in Canada but we do have the machine-tool buil-
> ders in Ontario who could supply the large machines
> common to these operations, if they could ever get the
> contracts, and a large modern steel mill sits on our
> doorstep while thousands of tons of stampings are
> transported from hundreds of miles away every week ... [6]

The effects of the automotive companies' purchasing
policies became apparent in the early 1970s, in the increased
flow of imported parts and supplies from the U.S., in the
decline of Canadian auto parts production, and in the
resulting trade deficit which more than wiped out the surplus
from vehicle assembly. By 1977, the cumulative net deficit
under the Auto Pact had reached $7.5 billion. This has
represented a loss to Canada of from twenty to twenty-five
thousand Canadian jobs.[7] For anyone who considers that free
trade between Canada and the U.S. is the answer to our
problems, a look at the effects of the Auto Pact is in order.

Orr notes that this situation was aggravated by another *external influence* which hit Canada in 1971. At that time the
U.S. government introduced the DISC tax incentive scheme,
designed to encourage U.S. multinationals to repatriate to the
parent plants in the United States much of the manufacturing
being carried out in their foreign subsidiary plants, and to
transfer to the U.S. all foreign purchases, if any, of components, supplies and services. There were penalties for non-
compliance. This led to a slow-down in investment and plant
improvements abroad, and a virtual end to purchases abroad
of services and supplies. The effect on Canada was much
greater than elsewhere because of Canada's almost total
dependence on U.S. branch plants. This, along with the tariff
terms of the Auto Pact, facilitated the rapid shift of purchases
of component and material inputs from Canadian to U.S.
sources of supply.

The decrease in capital investment is also serious; Canadian
automotive plants are becoming obsolescent since little is being

expended on modernizing equipment and production methods. Although the return on investment from Canadian plants is almost twice that of global operations of the major auto producers, new plant investment in Canada "is less than half that which is warranted".[8] From 1971 to 1974, more than $300 million, or over 30 percent of net earnings, was paid by the four major Canadian auto subsidiaries to their parent companies, and this "repatriation of earnings" has accelerated. Capital expenditures in Canadian plants amounting to $1.4 billion from 1970 to 1975 have been financed out of retained earnings, in addition to the profits remitted to the parent. But since depreciation and amortization during the same period amounted to $2.5 billion, plant and equipment were not being kept up to date to the extent justified. According to Ken Romain, "new plant investment in Canada ...has not kept pace with profits earned by the Canadian subsidiaries."[9]

With respect to technology and modernization, the record is even worse. In the United States the auto firms are extensively modernizing their plants to produce the radically different cars that are now being made. Although the Canadian subsidiaries "have contributed at least $230 million annually in the past six years to the research accounts of their parent companies," the current level of research and development effort expended by them in Canada is insignificant.[10] But Judd Buchanan, when Minister of State for Science and Technology, while criticizing the auto companies, offered them further incentives in addition to existing incentives, which will provide the companies with an additional $85 million in the next five years. They will be able to deduct 50 percent of any additional research and development expenditures from taxes.[11] Apparently it did not occur to Buchanan to suggest that they use some of that $1.38 billion which was part of their Canadian profits, and which has been contributed to the research accounts alone of their parent companies during the past six years, rather than getting another hand-out of Canadian tax dollars, to do a little bit of research and development in Canada. If they continue to neglect their Canadian subsidiary plants, these plants will not be able to play any significant role in the production of the revolutionary new designs now coming onto the market. Of course, none of the intensive research and development currently under way in the U.S., into development of new types of products to meet new government requirements is being done in Canada.

The cumulative effect of these two 'external influences' has clearly revealed the extreme vulnerability of our economic structure to decisions made in the U.S. To this extent, our economic apologists are correct in blaming external events 'beyond Canada's control'. But they fail to point out why we find ourselves in a position which allows these 'external events' to have such an abnormally severe negative impact on Canada. Canada has had the same opportunity *to control the causes* of this vulnerability as has any other country. But in other countries, only a small fraction of their industrial structure has been affected; some countries, such as Japan, Mexico and Switzerland, prohibit by law any foreign control of their industries. In Canada, almost the whole structure is vulnerable; almost all of it is under foreign control. The impact of the Auto Pact and the DISC incentives was closely connected with the rapidly increasing decline in our end product trade *with the U.S.*; this deficit rose from $2.2 billion in 1970 to $8.2 billion in 1977, an almost four-fold increase in the deficit in just seven years.[15]

Interpreted roughly, several salient points are indicated from our current accounts data. First, our branch-plant manufacturing of duplicates of American-designed products is not even capable of holding the home market, let alone of creating export markets; and a large part of the huge deficit in manufactured goods is due to the failure of our branch plants, including the auto manufacturers, to purchase parts, components, technology and services from Canadian suppliers, but to import them instead in enormous quantities. It also indicates that, even in food and agriculture, our position is declining. We are importing almost as much as we export, in spite of our large wheat sales. This sector of our 'staple economy' can no longer pay for the enormous quantities of foreign goods and services we import. Indeed, it may not even be able to hold its own for long. And yet, the Ontario Minister of Agriculture sees no reason to be concerned over the destruction of the unique lands in the Niagara fruit belt by developers, since we can always import fruits and vegetables more cheaply from the U.S. Unless we have something more valuable to sell in return than we have at present, the cost may be higher than we think.

The third fact indicated by this data is that we have only our increasing exports of petroleum products to fall back on to lesson the deficit in our current accounts. It is no wonder that we are exploiting them as fast as possible although we have been repeatedly warned that they could shortly become exhausted. The estimated date varies according to the current projects for which the oil companies are lobbying; but we do not own these vital resources so we have no way of really knowing. Instead of exploiting them ourselves, we have asked foreign companies to do it for us, and have practically given them away. Few Canadians realize the extent of the give-away. Enormous profits accrue to the foreign conglomerates who own or control almost all of our oil, gas and mineral non-renewable resources. Using conservative figures, the publishers of the *Daily Oil Bulletin* of Calgary calculated that in 1970 the value of Canada's hydro-carbon potential was $1,118 billion at 1970 prices.[13] This amounts to about $55,000 for every Canadian, even at 1970 prices. But do we own it? We do not. By 1963, our petroleum industry was 74 percent foreign-controlled; it has now reached about 80 percent. Our oil refineries are 100 percent foreign-owned. The same industry has also bought up other parts of Canada. Imperial Oil alone owned at least 30 other active Canadian companies in 1970. Net after-tax earnings were $105 million for that year. They also owned about $15 billion worth of proven petroleum reserves. Standard Oil (New Jersey) owns 70 percent of Imperial.[14]

Since 1950, a number of Canadian oil companies have been taken over by foreign companies. Among them have been Canadian Oil, bought by Shell, and McColl-Frontenac, bought by Texaco Canada, owned by Texaco, Inc. The way in which these take-overs occur, and why, is particularly interesting. Banff Oil of Canada was unable to get financing in Canada, therefore, in 1964, it sold a 45 percent controlling interest of 1,400,000 shares, to Aquitaine, a French firm partly owned by the French government, for $2.50 per share. In 1965, Banff Oil brought in the Rainbow Lake oil field in northern Alberta. By that time, Banff Oil held only a 5 percent interest; Socony-Mobil held 50 percent and Aquitaine held 45 percent. By 1968, the proven petroleum resources were worth over $100 million at well-head.   Total oil reserves at well-head prices, were estimated to be worth $1.8 *billion*.   By 1969, the $2.50 shares were worth $19.75 for a capital gain of $238 million on Aquitaine's investment alone. Banff, the Canadian firm that had discovered the field and had done the drilling, was absorbed by Aquitaine. It had been unable to raise from Canadian sources the funding of only $3.5 million paid by Aquitaine, which would have kept in Canadian hands reserves worth $1.8 billion plus the immediate capital gain of $238 million on just 45 percent of the shares.

Dynamic Petroleum Products Ltd was part of a group of Western exploration companies. It fell into disfavour with the Toronto Stock Exchange establishment because it advised its shareholders that a group of eastern financial raiders was short-selling the stock. It was de-listed until the president resigned. Dynamic then acquired mineral rights to one and a half million acres in the Athabasca region but Bay Street would not finance it. Gulf Oil did. At an expenditure of only $750,000 on exploration, Dynamic uncovered an enormous uranium ore body. Gulf sold a 49 percent interest to a German concern that wanted a guaranteed supply of uranium. Although the federal government had blocked the sale of Steve Roman's Dennison property to foreigners, U.S.-owned Gulf was assured by the Canadian Minister of Energy of the day, Joe Greene, that it needed no federal approval for its sale to the German concern. The ore body was estimated to be worth over $1 billion. Gulf's investment was $750,000.

Alarmed by such large export contracts, Ontario Hydro took steps to ensure a future supply of our Canadian uranium for Ontario; for this it incurred severe public criticism in Parliament and in the media. The energy-hungry United States and the foreign-owned energy interests in Canada couldn't have done it better. Many Canadians appear to feel that U.S.-owned corporations can do no wrong, but that any Canadian-owned corporation is fair game for every kind of vicious attack from Canadians. Because Canadian *financial* institutions invest only in 'sure things', chiefly in the U.S., foreign interests now own over 80 percent of our oil and gas production and 99.9 percent of our oil refining industry, as well as increasing amounts of our uranium.[15]

The foreign corporations that control our oil and gas will not invest in exploration unless they can be assured of a high return and immediate markets — or so they say. It is a threat that always works with the Canadian government. Sales in any present year are worth much more to the oil companies than the discounted dollars of a few years from now. They are not concerned with Canada's future needs for energy or the possible advantage of leaving some of it in the ground until we need it; after all, it won't go away. Therefore, they are constantly asking for increased export permits as fast as they find the new reserves.

In 1970, these companies asked the National Energy Board for permits to export eight trillion cubic feet of natural gas. They assured the NEB that we had reserves sufficient to last for 392 years. The NEB allowed exports of six trillion cubic feet. Three years later, when they wanted support for building a gas pipeline down the Mackenzie Valley and permits to explore in the Beaufort Sea, they suddenly 'discovered' that our reserves would be exhausted by 1980. With the increased oil and gas prices allowed, they then increased their drilling activities, to bring in the low-cost southern reserve pools. By 1977, articles in the industry's magazine, *Oil Week*, were expressing fear of a glut of oil in the western U.S. and of *a possible price decline*, and were urging people to move back into larger cars again.

Because private companies own our petroleum resources, they control the data as to the real extent of reserves. During the Mackenzie Valley Pipeline hearings, the NEB had great difficulty in getting the companies to reveal any of the test data on which their estimates of reserves were based.[16] It is therefore almost impossible for the government to formulate any realistic policy concerning oil and gas exports, even if it had other sources of export revenues. It must rely on the data which the companies themselves wish to release. Under these circumstances, it is quite conceivable that we shall find our reserves exhausted far sooner than we anticipate. The oil companies will then, of course, move on to other countries.

As to other energy sources, the recent Interim Report of the Ontario Royal Commission on Electric Power Planning was a most amazing 'political' document. It recommended a cutback in construction of nuclear energy power plants, not as a matter of energy policy, but on the grounds that we don't have enough uranium in Canada to support the proposed programme "beyond the turn of the century". Their justification for this statement? They argue that, since we have left it to foreign interests to supply much of the funds for uranium exploration, we cannot deny them their right to export what they find. The fear is that if Canada tried to limit uranium exports *unreasonably* — to last into the next century perhaps — exploration money would be cut off, and, the Report implies, we might also face *political and economic retaliation* from our major trading partners! Most countries would reject such attitudes on the part of foreign exploiters of their resources as intolerable and outrageous, but our government lets it pass without protest. We must put up with this kind of blackmail threat because we have developed no alternatives.[17]

The restrictions recommended by the Report would, according to some spokesmen, threaten to put the nuclear industry in Canada out of business. If this is the result of selling out our uranium resources worth an estimated $1 billion to companies like Gulf Oil and their German partners, just to save ourselves the meagre $750,000 cost of exploration, then we are guilty of economic lunacy. When we sell out our resources and our industries, we lose all control of what is produced and when, how it is used and for what purpose, and when and to whom it is sold. But we have no bargaining position. We have no other products that can cover the deficit in our current accounts, and we are therefore forced to sell out our energy supplies for the future on whatever terms the foreign exploiters impose.

In our present state of affairs, if and when our oil and gas run out, we will have almost nothing to export and no foreign exchange with which to pay for our imports. If we then find that we can no longer pay for imports and must manufacture more of our domestic requirements at home, we will soon discover that we no longer have enough energy to run our industries, because we will also have exported all our uranium. Sun and wind may heat a few houses, but it will not operate an industrial complex. Truly, we could not find ourselves over a bigger barrel.

With respect to other possible alternatives, i.e., a decrease in our imports and particularly, an increase in our exports of end products, especially high-technology products, it is odd that the few high-level technology developments in Canada that have managed to reach the stage where they could begin to pay off the investment and to earn sales in the competitive export markets, suddenly find themselves under severe attack — from Canadians and the Canadian media. We don't wait for the Americans to do it, we do it ourselves. Or do these campaigns originate elsewhere and we unthinkingly carry them out? The Jetliner was one such case; the Arrow was another, as was the Iroquois engine. Each threatened competition to the U.S. monopoly in the high-level technology aircraft area in the export field. Even the Bobcat and the *Bras d'Or* fall into the same pattern on a smaller scale; they might have been purchased by NATO countries and would have given our technological industries a boost. The Candu reactor is becoming another.

When the first experimental reactor was built at Chalk River, its facilities were available to research groups. Many such groups from the U.S. made use of it. It had not yet begun to pay its way; it had not become commercial. Then we built a couple of highly successful commercial reactors, with unusually high productivity ratings. They cost less to operate, they created less pollution of the atmospheric layers than do thermal generators, and they did not require that we import coal from the United States. They were simpler, safer and, above all, more economical than the American reactors which the U.S. was now selling all around the world. Canadian reactors use unprocessed uranium; American reactors use enriched uranium. The process of 'enriching' consumes enormous quantities of electricity. The whole purpose of reactors is to create electricity, to replace coal or oil-fired generators, to relieve the shortages when other fuels become scarce. But the

American reactors are cannibalistic; they consume their own product merely to produce the fuel they feed on. Until recently, more electricity had been used up in the U.S. to produce enriched uranium than had been produced by the reactors the uranium was supposed to feed.

When the first Candu reactor was sold abroad, it crossed the borderline between being an interesting experiment on the part of their northern neighbours, and becoming a threat to U.S. export sales of the U.S. monopoly in high-technology reactors. Strangely enough, the earliest, most virulent (and inaccurate) attacks were led off by a Canadian engineer who at the time was doing work for Westinghouse. Westinghouse has a fairly large stake in the production and sale of American nuclear reactors! These circumstances cannot be attributed to sheer coincidence. If we were allowed to develop more Canadian-owned industries especially in high-technology fields; if we supported them and developed high-technology products competitive in export markets; if we produced more domestic products and thus reduced our huge deficits on imports, then we should not find ourselves totally dependent on ever-increasing export sales of our petroleum products and future energy reserves to which the U.S. is so determined to have access. In other words, we would no longer be so vulnerable.

Although we are exporting our energy resources at ever-increasing rates, our deficit in current accounts still runs at from $4 to $5 billion per year. Even the sale of our future resources is not enough to cover the rising cost of our imports and the decline in exports. It should be obvious that the only possible remedy is to restrict our imports and to produce a greater volume of competitive exports. However, with our present industrial structure, we are pitifully unable to do so. Any such decisions would have to be made by foreigners.

It is generally recognized that our manufacturing industry is 'chronically ill', but some of the recommended remedies would surely kill the patient. Our experts do not even attempt a realistic diagnosis of the disease, but persist in treating only the symptoms. Since an accurate diagnosis would force us to re-examine our myths and our structures, our experts fall all over themselves in prescribing headache pills for the more painful symptoms. The Opposition charges the government with creating the problem by taking over too large a share of the Gross National Products by providing too many 'services,' by interference with business, by increasing the money supply too fast — in a word, by usurping the role of the private sector and living beyond its means.

In response, the government cut back on expenditures, not by reducing the fat in government but by cutting off such research programmes as the Petawawa (Ontario) Forestry Experimental Station and the Fisheries Research Station at Halifax, small, active groups whose work was worth far more than the tiny cost. Of course, forest products and fisheries are two major Canadian resource industries which bring in considerable revenue and provide many jobs. When they are not healthy, we pour in subsidies at the other end of the process. It would seem that these two small but valuable research programmes would be essential to their continuing modernization and growth. The return per dollar expended in research programmes in End Product industry is estimated to be from two to four times the return on fixed assets in terms of productivity.

We eliminate our Fisheries Research Station but allow foreign trawlers to take over most of our eastern catch, while a European consortium proposes to take over the Newfoundland fish processing industry to market our fish under the Birdseye trade name. This process was developed in Canada, but is now trademarked in Britain. On the west coast, in five years, the Japanese have poured nearly $20 million into B.C. firms and now control, partially or totally, 12 of the 60 processing companies. Their huge purchases of debentures in these companies may result in forcing some Canadian firms out of the market. Their bidding for catches has forced up prices, as for instance, an increase from $400 to $1100 a ton for herring roe in 1978. It has been predicted that, *faced with restrictions in the United States* the Japanese will turn increasingly to British Columbia. They appear to have unlimited funds; one of the largest Japanese trading houses has invested nearly $12 million in B.C. fishing industry debentures as well as acquiring controlling interest in one of the larger processing plants.[18] The cost of operating the Petawawa Forest Research Station was only $2 million per year. The Fisheries Research Institute cost about the same. If taken over by a private plant, its work will not be available to smaller processors. In any case, its scientists will be lost to the U.S.[19]

But programmes are 'visible' and easier to cut than routine government overspending on new buildings or redundant administrative jobs. In its obsession for 'jobs' *per se*, regardless of the quality, the government is also setting up make-work programmes that remove the jobless from one government roll to another, as though *activity* were a substitute for *productivity*. It is also, of course, as a conditioned reflex, offering more incentives and subsidies to foreign-owned plants like Ford. The importance of small but growing Canadian companies, and of small, ongoing research projects in creating viable industries and jobs, completely escapes the government. It has learned nothing new; it can only continue to frantically woo more foreign investment.

A shocking case in point is the story of the development of the Trigull amphibian. Trident, a small aircraft company in Vancouver, developed a highly promising amphibian aircraft. It is a good plane and is priced right, according to aircraft experts. But, as Hugh Whittington of *Canadian Aviation* reports,[20] Trident's president, David Hazlewood, "has fought a battle against bureaucracy and politics that no Canadian in his position should have to fight. In a country with a million out of work and very little incentive to change things, guys like Hazlewood should be encouraged. Instead, they're treated as pests and kept dangling with promises" — until an American company like Grumman can come along and take them over, as part of its package of offset goodies.

Hazlewood first tried to find private Canadian financing. As he recalls, "I prowled the corridors of finance in Vancouver and Toronto. The lenders all said it was a good project, *but the lending limit was $250,000*". What happened to flexibility or the merit of a project, and who set the limit?

To date, $4 million has been spent on the project, to pay for all the design and development, to pay a staff of 26, to build and test three planes and to obtain certification. Of this, the government contributed $1.7 million in loans and grants. With certification in hand, Hazlewood went to Ottawa and met with Jean Chretien, then Minister of Industry, Trade and Commerce. Chretien liked what he saw and eventually promised "a $5 million loan guarantee if, among other conditions, Trident had 25 firm orders for the airplane and if it bought back manufacturing rights from Canadian Aircraft Products Ltd where the existing three Trigulls were built".

In September, 1977, Hazlewood wrote to Chretien. He had bought back the rights and had the orders. He never got a reply. Jack Horner had taken over at Industry, Trade and Commerce. Hazlewood had to release his staff of 26 in December. By April, he had 38 firm orders with $10,000 in deposits plus 26 additional production line reservations.

According to the new minister, there was nothing in writing and he did not feel obliged to honour an oral promise made by his predecessor. Trident scraped together money for a few months and was ready to go into production in April, 1978, with an eventual production target of 10 planes per month, but had no more funds. By refusing to honour the previous Minister's commitment merely to guarantee a loan, the new Minister in effect threw away the government's original loan/grant of $1.7 million, of which the loan would have been repaid, as well as the $4 million invested by the company, along with the future production, export sales and employment it would have engendered. Government loan guarantees, far in excess of $250,000 or even of $5 million have, of course, been readily available, time after time, to Canadair and other U.S. branch plants. Grumman Aircraft of the U.S. has now offered Trident a joint venture proposal and funding which will likely result in Trigull being manufactured as an American development, with the profits — and perhaps even the company — moved to the United States.[21]

The Conservative Party in 1978 held a conference with businessmen called "Window on Tomorrow". Various speakers proposed a series of remedies; these included reductions in income taxes to stimulate spending, and incentives to business to encourage new plant investment. But these measures would lower government revenues and increase consumer purchases, mostly of imported goods, thus increasing our current accounts deficit, our foreign borrowing and the money supply, as well as causing further inflation. We are already spending more than we earn, especially on imports; our plants already have excess capacity without any further capital investment. It is naive to expect that their parent companies, in return for further government incentives, will inject any significant dose of upgrading and technological modernization to make them more competitive. They are already decreasing such expenditures. In any case, one does not normally advise someone who is near bankruptcy to go on a spending spree, at least until he has found a way to increase his income. Sinclair Stevens, the Opposition 'economics' critic proposed, as a solution to the income problem, that we stop aspiring to be an industrialized country and rely, as we once did, solely on the income from the sale of our natural resources. This, of course, is precisely where we have been heading, and the results are all too evident.

The Senate Committee on Foreign Affairs recommends tariff reductions or, better still, a bilateral free trade agreement with the United States, trusting to a floating exchange rate to achieve a trade equilibrium. It admits that this would require some restructuring of Canadian industry but claims it would lead to an economically stronger Canada. Just as the Auto Pact did, no doubt — or the Defence Sharing Agreement!

The Economic Council of Canada and C.D. Howe Research Institute appear to have similar ideas. To listen to spokesmen for these two bodies, it is hard to tell whether Canadians or Americans are speaking.* Certainly their proposed remedies would be music to the ears of Ambassadors William Porter and Thomas Enders and their government in Washington. Mr Roy Mathews can, presumably, speak for both of these bodies since he was a research director for the C.D. Howe Institute and is now a staff member of the Economic Council of Canada. He claims in effect that, since our manufacturing industry is "chronically and gravely ill" we should let it die and concentrate on service industries. He notices the increasing deficit in our trade in fully manufactured goods, the fact that imported end products have now taken over 35 percent of

---

* For example, Mr. Carl Beigie, an American with C.D. Howe Institute, recently promoted free trade and even, possibly, political union with the U.S. — on a CBC TV programme.

our market, "a level not remotely approached by any other modern country". He also notes that capital investment in manufacturing is declining and that expenditure on research and development has been falling at an accelerating rate since 1965 and especially since 1971. But he does not relate these significant factors to the balance of payments deficits, nor suggest that *these* are the conditions to be improved. Instead, he suggests that we give up altogether. He goes on to observe that in Canada, as in the U.S. and other industrialized countries, the service sector now accounts for the greatest increase in numbers of jobs. His conclusion appears to be that Canada should therefore concentrate on service industries, not manufacturing, and enter the 'post-industrial' phase of development which he claims is now the norm. Mathews admits that many service industries such as health, education or public administration lie outside the market systems; they must be paid for out of taxes. But, he claims two-thirds of service jobs are market-oriented; in Canada, these include hotels, restaurants, finance, insurance, real estate, amusement and recreational services, and services to business management.[22] This analysis is so superficial and naive that it is highly dangerous. It sounds vaguely like the argument for scrapping the Arrow in favor of the Bomarc; the Arrow was obsolete because we were entering 'the missile age'. In each case, sophisticated 'buzzwords' are used to give a kind of ersatz credibility to the argument.

In comparing his panacea with the trend in the United States, Mathews ignores the most fundamental differences. In the U.S.,the manufacturing industry is already large and technologically advanced. There has not been, as in Canada, a precipitous drop in an already low level of research and development. The increase in the so-called 'service sector' is not the result of a decline in manufacturing, but the result of a revolution in the high-technology component of that sector. This has resulted in a new division of labour. For example, computer services, engineering consulting, management services, communications, transportation and a host of other functions have been moved out of the blue collar category and into the role of 'services to industry'. Without industry, they could not exist. Although employment in (strictly defined) 'manufacturing' may be declining relatively, production is increasing and the relative increase in service industry jobs is the result of advances in technology and production methods. Sixty percent of the service jobs in the United States are not only market-oriented, they are oriented to the increasing demands of an increasingly sophisticated manufacturing industry. As Laurent Thibault points out :

> In a highly complex modern society, it is the relationships and linkages between various activities that are most crucial. Today's industrial complex could not be operated without the sophisticated support services that provide skilled tradesmen, engineering consulting, data processing, communications, banking, insurance, transportation, etc. Without such a service base, industrial development does not take place.

This was well-proved by some of the regional make-work projects of the government under the Department of Regional Economic Expansion. Thibault notes that when such services are withdrawn, as in a strike, "there is an immediate decline in industrial production." But to enjoy these services, income must be generated from the goods-producing industries. Unless these are growing dynamic industries, "there is just no way to produce the needed income." In reply to Mathews, Thibault points out that, in Canada, it is not the manufacturing industry that is protected by government, but the banking business, protected from foreign competition by law, and agriculture, where "the various forms of subsidies, minimum prices, etc., are equivalent to a tariff of 27 percent."[23]

Mathews' prescription would not put us into a position comparable to that of the U.S., as Mathews implies, but to that of the Caribbean countries. His list of industries resembles that of Nassau or Barbados. These places also rely on the tourism and recreation industries that Mathews recommends for Canada; even with a better climate than ours, their revenues are very uncertain, the industry is foreign-owned, develops no supporting industries, purchases few supplies locally (importing them instead from the U.S.), and provides only jobs at an even lower level of skill and self-respect than do our foreign-owned branch plants. Most of these small countries still rely on support payments from the U.K. or Europe. Of course, most Canadian hotels and resorts were also built by or have been sold out to American chains. Matthews forgot to mention lotteries! We can always fall back on them as the government is doing — or on gambling, as some other small countries have tried to do.

In 1971, a Report on *Foreign Direct Investment in Canada* was submitted to the Government by the Honourable Herbert Gray, then Minister of National Revenue.[24] This Report analyzed the unusual extent of foreign ownership and control of Canadian industries and resources, and pointed out the effects it was having on our future development. The Report aroused considerable public support and finally, in 1974, the government established the Foreign Investment Review Agency (FIRA), to screen applications for takeovers of existing Canadian businesses, and for new investments by non-Canadians. According to the then Minister of Industry, Trade and Commerce Allistair Gillespie, control of foreign investment would be an important part of building a 'distinctive' Canada. "The kind of Canada we want to build must be more than a mere appendage of foreign corporate giants south of the border and resource-hungry multi-national firms of other industrialized countries". In recognition that foreign control of the Canadian economy had costs as well as benefits, the government was introducing legislation to establish a screening agency "to minimize the costs and maximize the benefits" of foreign takeovers of Canadian businesses and the establishment of new foreign businesses in Canada".[25] Takeovers of firms with gross assets below $250,000 and gross sales of less than $3 million per year were excluded from review as were investments by existing foreign firms *in related fields.* This latter, of course, represents most of the increase in foreign ownership and control, amounting to $2.6 billion or more per year in 1975 and 1976. Small, growing businesses, the kind that attract foreign takeovers, are the life-blood of a growing economy. But both of these areas were excluded from any screening process. As it turned out, it didn't really matter.

As an Ottawa newspaper put it, FIRA was a half-hearted response by the government, and its "limited mandate was laughable".[26] Nevertheless, in the U.S., both business and government reacted angrily and violently to even this mild effort to control the wholesale sellout of control of Canada's economy. U.S. ambassador William A. Porter even defied diplomatic niceties to reprimand Canada for not showing enough concern "for U.S. economic interests". As a result, FIRA, weak as it was, was watered down even further, and time required for approvals was cut. By 1978, foreign takeovers of Canadian businesses had reached their highest rate since 1974. In the year ending in March, 1978, the Cabinet approved 241 takeover bids of existing companies valued at $684 million, up from 153 takeovers in 1977, while rejecting only 11. In the same year, 300 applications for new investment were approved, up from 166 in the previous year. Only 14 were disallowed. The proportion of foreign investment which involved the takeover of *existing* Canadian controlled firms rose in one year from 38 to 50 percent.[27] This is the highest rate in the world. These takeovers involved the creation of no new businesses; many of them involved the merging of existing firms with U.S. corporations, or their eventual closing down altogether.

In April of 1959, then Minister of Finance Donald Fleming had stated that Canada needed foreign capital "and therefore we must — and this is the policy of the government — create a climate hospitable to foreign capital investment". The volume of foreign investment in Canada in 1958 was $1,112 million. Fleming stated that there would be no decrease. There hasn't been. By 1965, foreign direct investment in Canada had reached $17.4 billion; by 1970, $26.4 billion and, by the end of 1975, $39.8 billion. Since FIRA was set up in 1974, five out of every six takeover applications have been approved and nine out of every ten new foreign investment appliciations have been allowed. In four years, there have been 458 foreign takeovers of Canadian-controlled businesses and 233 new foreign-owned businesses established.[28] The government has fallen all over itself to assure American investors that FIRA is no bar whatsoever to investment. George Howarth, the Agency Commissioner, states that "he is anxious to eliminate any concern investors may have about red tape involved in gaining approval to invest in Canada ..." He rejected any suggestion that the Foreign Investment Review legislation has discouraged investors. He told the Commons Finance Committee that an Agency study had reported that FIRA has had "no measurable effect" in discouraging foreign takeover bids and new business proposals.[29] The Agency also stated, moreover, that where takeover bids had been rejected, there had been no loss of jobs. In only two cases did the Canadian business cease operations when the takeover was disallowed — a most interesting comment on the need for takeovers at all.

Those who had seen the need for controls were concerned. They claimed that FIRA was no longer functioning as a screening agency but merely as a 'funnel' for channeling foreign investment into Canada. The government did not share this concern; it was busily reassuring U.S. investors that it "intended to reduce the popular notion that it [FIRA] is a restricting rather than a consulting agency". In March, 1977, Jean Chretien outlined to a Los Angeles audience the dangers and restrictions inherent in basic decisions as to Canada's economy being "made in boardrooms outside Canada" and of its effects on Canadian initiatives and on the lack of stimulating work. However, he then vigorously denied that Canada was trying to block foreign investment through FIRA and cheerfully quoted favourable comments from the Chase Manhattan Bank. He even quoted the very cynical comment of *Barron's Financial Weekly* that "It is difficult to imagine a legitimate business venture which would be impeded by the Foreign Investment Review Act . . . (except) Murder Inc".[30] In New York, in 1978, Manitoba's Conservative Premier Sterling Lyon received a standing ovation from an audience of 350 influential U.S. businessmen, bankers and bond analysts for castigating FIRA as a "symbol of prissy economic nationalism" which Canada cannot afford.[31]

Premier Allan Blakeney of Saskatchewan is one of the rare political leaders who has attempted to diagnose the fundamental problems and to mention them out loud: "Some of our political leaders", he says, "are eagerly racing to extol the virtues of foreign control over the Canadian economy ... How often must the cost of foreign ownership and control be totalled up before we finally conclude that such a road is a dead end — a dead end not only economically but politically and culturally as well? How can we expect a Canadian identity to emerge and flourish when Canadians own so little of their own country? ... Canada must be perceived to be more than a branch plant of another country". He concludes : "I would have thought that this proposition needed only to be stated to be readily accepted. I am depressed that this has not proved to be the case."[32]

It is generally recognized that Canada's manufacturing industry is already struggling against heavy domestic odds. These include "high [unit] labour costs, a low level of investment in productivity improvements and in research and development, the branch plant system and uncertainty over government policy," according to J.J. Shepherd, Executive-Director of the Science Council of Canada. He calculates that, as a result, "10,000 jobs in manufacturing have been lost *each month* since 1976, and the annual trade deficit in manufactured goods has risen to $11.5 billion".[33]

Most Canadian experts identify a low level of productivity as a major problem. But they define the causes of low productivity as: a small domestic market which allows for no economies of scale in plant size or production run, low unit productivity of labour because of high wages and other costs, and — you guessed it — lack of skills, technology, good management and capital! The cure usually recommended is: more foreign investment, more branch plants, more imported technology and management — that is, more of the same medicine we have already had, which has brought us to this state. The 'experts' also customarily recommend fewer benefits to labour and the unemployed.

Contrary to this 'conventional wisdom', econometric studies of manufacturing in Canada and elsewhere have demonstrated that, above a relatively low threshold size, plant size has no significant influence on productivity.[34] J.L. Orr, in *Engineering Digest* points to countries such as Sweden, Switzerland and the Netherlands which, with small domestic markets, have built up technologically sophisticated and internationally competitive manufacturing industries. He notes

This giant fuel test rig simulates various flight conditions for Arrow fuel testing.

Courtesy A.V. Roe

Five complete Arrows being destroyed. Photo taken day after cabinet ministers stated completed Arrows would not be destroyed.

Photo by Herb Nott, Weekend Magazine

First centre fuselage and first inner wing in assembled position.

Courtesy A.V. Roe

Extensive use of metal bonding in the Arrow resulted in Avro acquiring this huge auto clave pressure chamber.

Courtesy A.V. Roe

that E.F. Denison of the Brookings Institute identifies five key *determinants of productivity*. These determinants and their relative inputs into productivity are: resource allocation, 9.5 percent; economies of scale, 12.7 percent; labour quality, 14.3 percent; capital employed, 25.4 percent; level of technology, 38.1 percent. The effect of technological input on productivity is over three times as great as scale of production, and two and two-thirds times as great as the quality of labour.

Orr also cites Michael Boretsky of the U.S. Department of Commerce, who illustrates "the vastly superior performance of technology-intensive industry compared to other industry from 1957 to 1973 in the U.S. In the technology-intensive industries, real output showed that, in these industries, relative growth was 45 percent higher, growth in employment was 88 percent greater, growth in productivity was 38 percent higher, exports showed a 49 percent greater growth rate, and rate of growth of price inflation was 44 percent *lower*". Dr Jacques Defay of Belgium demonstrated that, in general, the return on research and development (Rand D) investment was "typically two to four times greater than the return on fixed assets for the manufacturing industry". Orr notes that "Canada is almost totally dependent on imported technology for its product designs and manufacturing processes". This imported technology has consisted almost entirely of *production* technology, and Canadian industry "with a few notable exceptions — lacks any indigenous capability for technological innovation".

Canadian industry's investment in research and development as a percentage of Gross Domestic Product ranks fourteenth of 16 industrialized countries and is declining. Orr points out that "it is obviously impossible to establish any 'comparative advantage' using obsolete technology or second-hand product designs, or for such technology-dependent manufacturers to compete in world markets". D.C. Marrs, President of Westinghouse Canada Ltd, one of the few exceptions, states that 85 to 90 percent of their exports are products of technology developed in Canada. Orr pinpoints one of the problems: "current economic theory has been unable to embody this 'key factor of production' which has thus been largely ignored by economic analysts".[35] This is certainly true in Canada. As a major cause of low productivity, it is almost completely ignored.

Sweden is a small country of less than ten million population. She had iron ore reserves, but not as great as those of Canada. However, instead of selling the mines to her big neighbours, the Russians or the Germans, she raised the capital and developed them herself. From this, she has built up a world-wide industrial complex based on sophisticated steel products, and has become one of the wealthiest countries per capita in Europe, and a leader in high technology products.

Denmark has a population half the size of Sweden's. From a purely agricultural base, she developed distinctive high-quality products in furniture, ceramics and glassware which command high prices around the world. The government supported Denmark's industry and its research and development, and set up a patenting system to protect their designs and their manufacture.

Switzerland, a tiny country with a small population, concentrated on high-precision products of high-technology content, and the world beat a path to its door. India is a large country with a very large population; it has little industry, is not at all technologically advanced and is relatively poor. But Japan, with a large population of well over one hundred million on several small crowded islands with almost no natural resources ranks high in technology. From an ancient feudal-peasant system based on primitive agriculture she has, in a relatively short space of time, become a dominant threat to other countries in the field of manufactured goods. Buying her raw materials from countries like Canada, she shipped them back to Japan, produced copies of designs from elsewhere during a learning period and then began to innovate. Through intensive research and development, she has trained a labour force, developed many high-technology products and found markets for them around the world. But she *owns* her own industries and is free to do so. Japan's revenues are now so high and its currency so strong that its trade dominance has become an embarrassment, and it is looking all over the world, and particularly to Canada, for places to invest its surplus capital; while we who own the resources she uses can't even afford to develop them ourselves — not even our fisheries, in which Japan is investing extensively. Japan's balance of payments surplus on current account in 1977 was $15 billion. Her currency has appreciated by 40 percent in the past two years.

We import a great many finished products from Japan, from Sweden, Denmark, Switzerland, Italy and other countries that have been 'nationalistic' enough to work for their own future. But even when looking for a gift, it is difficult to find a distinctive Canadian product, except for Inuit carvings. There are no foreign-owned multinationals in Japan, and, so far as we know, none in Switzerland, Sweden, Denmark or Italy that are over 50 percent foreign controlled. They have built up their own. In Japan and Mexico, foreign ownership is *forbidden by law.* In almost every other country it is severely restricted. The U.S. trades with them, yet with respect to Canada, is outraged by even the ineffective FIRA and threatens retaliation. She can do it with impunity because we have developed no alternatives.

W.G. Deeks, Executive Vice-President of Noranda Sales Corporation Ltd of Toronto warns that "unduly restrictive or misunderstood policies" — relating to further processing of resource products in Canada — *"can invite sharp and devastating counteraction* from Canada's trading partners. Foreign countries may, in the future, only permit our access to their markets on the basis of a supply of raw materials, as well as processed and manufactured goods".[36] Such implied threats of retaliation were also contained in the Report of the Ontario Royal Commission on Electrical Power Planning. Truly, we have given the world our measure and they have accepted it. One wonders if similar threats were made to Sweden or Japan when they proposed to process their own raw materials and offer the manufactured products on world markets. If so, apparently such threats were merely laughed at. They developed their own bargaining counters before it was too late. One hesitates to push around a man who stands up on his own two feet, runs his own business and manages his own affairs. But there is often a strong impulse to kick a

'Uriah Heep' where it will do the most good, or simply to push
him aside. Seldom does he merit much respect.

---

1 *Bank of Canada Review*, 1978, p. S-137
2 Statistics Canada, *Bulletin No. 13-001*,
  Information Canada, Ottawa
3 Cheveldayoff, Wayne, "Restoring the Dollar ... ",
  Globe & Mail, Toronto, Sept. 29, 1978
4 *idem*
5 Orr, J.L., "The Crisis of Canadian Secondary
  Manufacturing," *Engineering Digest*, May, 1978
6 Lynch, Harry, "Letter," *Globe & Mail*, Toronto,
  April 14, 1978
7 Shepherd, J.J., "Auto Industry Future ...", *Journal*,
  Ottawa, Oct. 7, 1978; *cf.* McKercher, Cathy, "Direct
  Deals Urged," *Citizen*, Ottawa, June 10, 1978
8 Shepherd, *loc. cit.*
9 Romain Ken, "Federal Review of Auto Pact ...",
  Globe & Mail, Toronto, June 25, 1977
10 Anderson, R., "The Auto Pact," *Globe & Mail*,
   Toronto, June 29, 1977
11 "Minister criticizes auto industry," *Globe & Mail*,
   Toronto, Sept. 26, 1978
12 Orr, *loc. cit.*
13 *Canadian Petroleum*, May, 1970
14 Brossard, Philippe J., *Sold American!*, Peter Martin,
   Toronto, 1971, p. 65
15 *ibid.*, pp. 67-73
16 National Energy Board Hearings on Application to Build
   Mackenzie Valley Natural Gas Pipeline, 1976
17 "Report spells crisis for nuclear industry,"
   Financial Post, Toronto, Oct. 7, 1978
18 *Globe & Mail*, Toronto, Sept. 29, 1978
19 Surette, Ralph, "Snick, snick ...," *Globe & Mail*,
   Toronto, Sept. 16, 1978
20 Whittington, Hugh, "Trident: Still Hoping,"
   Canadian Aviation, June, 1978
21 Grumman advertisement, *Maclean's*, Sept. 4, 1978, p. 3.
   Grumman promised to enter into a "joint venture" with

Trident as part of the package of offset goodies Grumman would bring to Canada in return for winning the $2.34 billion contract for the new fighter aircraft. Such joint ventures have taken place for years without such a huge bribe.

22 Mathews, Roy A., "Time for a new realism: stop favouring manufacturing," *Globe & Mail*, Toronto, Aug. 3, 1978

23 Thibault, Laurent, "Manufacturing 'necessary' to quality of life," *ibid.*, Sept. 19, 1978

24 Gray, Hon. Herbert, *Foreign Direct Investment in Canada*, Information Canada, Ottawa, 1972

25 Cheveldayoff, Wayne, "Business opinions ...", *Globe & Mail*, Toronto, Oct. 3, 1978

26 *Citizen*, Ottawa, Feb. 4, 1977

27 *ibid.*, Oct. 18, 1978

28 *idem*

29 *Globe & Mail*, Toronto, Mar. 25, 1977

30 *Weekend*, Mar. 12, 1977

31 *Citizen*, Ottawa, Oct. 25, 1978

32 Webster, Norman, *Globe & Mail*, April, 1978

33 Anderson, Ronald, "While Rome Burns," *Globe & Mail*, Toronto, Feb. 24, 1978

34 Orr, *loc. cit.*

35 *idem*

36 *Globe & Mail*, Toronto, April 19, 1977

Chapter 11

Unity — Under what flag?

If the story of the Arrow represented merely the closing down of a Canadian industry, it would be of no more special interest than thousands of other closings, except to those who worked there. And in many respects it was not unique. There has been a long history of similar events on a small scale. But we should consider the proposition that the basic flaws in our political, industrial and even our cultural structure, which combined to make the Arrow debacle inevitable, are the same flaws that have reduced Canada to her present state in economic development and in world confidence. Our institutional structures, our political leadership, the attitudes and perceptions which Canadians have come to hold of our country as a nation, the continental relationships we have so carelessly allowed to develop, based on the myths we have accepted without question, — all of these played a part in the playing out of the Arrow story. Only in two respects was it extraordinary. One unusual element was the combination of personal animosities and 'personality foibles' of the powerful protagonists, which introduced an element of the bizarre and obscene into the final act. The second unusual factor was the extent of the massive disruption which was caused by the cancellation, especially in those firms across Canada that were breaking into the field of high technology, and even more importantly, the long-term effects on Canada's reputation and potential in the industrial and trading world. This was particularly accentuated by the tremendous and partisan publicity which was used to manipulate public opinion but which spread far beyond Canada's borders.   In other words, when we reduced to scrap not only the Jetliner but, later, the Arrow and its Iroquois engine and, in effect, the company and the teams who had produced them, we gave the world our measure of ourselves. It is small wonder that they have accepted it.

Canada has been an enormously wealthy country, more so than most countries in the world. It offered space and opportunity for hard-working and enterprising people, who have settled the country and have been proud to build it. But, except for occasional surges, its energy and initiative have been slowly eroding; it has been losing its people, its capital and the industries its people had been building. In fact, it has cheerfully been giving them away. True, we still have some minerals, although their foreign owners have rapidly depleted them and left ghost towns in their wake. We still have some oil and gas, although we do not own it, and do not control the rate of depletion. We still have fresh water although detailed plans have for a long time been in existence in the United States for its massive diversion to the midwestern states. We still have prairie wheat, although the arable land is declining, and more and more of it is owned by foreign corporations.

We have expensive educational systems, colleges and universities, perhaps placing insufficient emphasis on science, engineering and business administration, but we have many more graduates, even in these fields, than we can find a use for, since over one-third of them must leave the country to find jobs and we are left 'empty of skills'. We have experience in mechanics and technology, and have produced a long series of 'firsts,' of real breakthroughs in technological innovation, but few of them have been put into production in Canada to bring us a return on our investment. Many innovations, new products, processes and developments have been designed by Canadians, often well in advance of other countries and at less cost, but few of the patents for these inventions are held in Canada; ninety-five percent of the patents registered in Canada, even when developed with Canadian funds, are registered in the name of foreign firms or individuals.

We have a history of entrepreneurs who, from scratch, have

built small businesses into large, successful enterprises and who have even captured a share of the export market, but few of them are today owned by Canadians. We have markets in Canada, sufficiently large to support a wide variety of industries; markets demanding all kinds of goods, from food and clothing to highly sophisticated equipment like cars, appliances and space satellites; but we import almost all of our requirements, even our processed foods, from abroad. We have many highly competent engineering firms, but we almost always hire an American firm for any major project in Canada. These Canadian firms say that they can win major contracts abroad but find them hard to get in Canada.

Our large and tightly-knit financial institutions gather from all over Canada vast amounts of capital, from Canadian pension funds, savings and profits, which is more than sufficient to finance the development of our resource industries, our new businesses and venture projects, those projects on which an expanding economy depends for new life and direction. But our resource industries are almost completely foreign-owned and Canadian enterprises are starved for lack of capital and forced to sell out to foreign corporations.* Our government, repeating that hoary incantation "We must have foreign investment," pours billions of dollars into incentives, grants, tax rebates and other inducements to foreign-owned corporations, and into make-work projects, but refuses to make available to promising Canadian enterprises sufficient funding for long enough to begin to bring in a return on the investment. What little they get is *ad hoc*, short-term and unpredictable, therefore they fail and the investment as well as the potential enterprise is lost.

Our children are educated from foreign text-books since we are too 'poor' to publish our own; we read more foreign magazines versus national magazines than any other country in the world, and few of our own have survived. Some of our

---

* A.P. Newey of Charter Consolidated was quoted in the *Globe and Mail* Business Section (Oct. 7, 1978) as saying that "High on the list of major influences on growth must also be included the availability and cost of finance ... it is not always clear whether developed capital market institutions are indispensable or are serious impediments to business investment." The fact that a corporation official actually poses this question in Canada is worthy of our economists' notice.

university departments, even in sociology, are staffed predominantly by foreigners, whose background in political and social conditions is completely different from ours and does not relate to the Canadian situation. But our own graduates cannot find jobs, unless they go south.

We have no foreign policy of our own. Our politicians check to see which way the wind is blowing from Washington before making any decision. We have no defence policy; *That* depends on knowing what one's foreign policy is and why. We have no industrial policy. Almost all decisions as to what we produce, where we produce it, where we sell it and to whom, what we charge for it, whether we expand an industry or close it down and move it and its jobs elsewhere are made in another country. We depend for our technology on foreign branch plants, and are satisfied with the truncated and obsolescent technology we receive, little of which is made available for the use of new and expanding Canadian industries. We have reached a state of such total dependency on another country whose only interest is us is in the profit they can gain from our resources and our markets that we have almost completely lost any freedom of action, even internally. The government and the Economic Council of Canada are evidently happy with this situation.

This dependency affects not only our economic position, but our cultural life as well. In the U.S., hundreds of foundations support local cultural groups, art galleries, museums, orchestras and writers. But in Canada, when Peter Swann sent out three hundred letters to the largest Canadian corporations, asking for financial donations for the Royal Ontario Museum which badly needed funds, he received only two replies — and no funds. At a development conference in the Interlake region of Manitoba a couple of years ago, when the question of funding sources arose, the Canadians present could suggest only government-sponsored programmes such as DREE, and Arda and similar programmes. They were asked: "What about your corporations, your foundations?" The Canadians had to explain that our large corporations were not interested in development programmes in the mid-Canadian shield, unless they involved minerals, and that the foundations these large 'Canadian' firms supported were in the U.S., not in Canada. A few years ago, when a Canadian film industry was beginning to develop, the Hollywood producers were able to get the Canadian government to sell out its support of its own industry in return for occasional 'mentions' of Canada in Hollywood films. It is not a picture of a healthy, developing country, proud of what it is doing and proud to support its developing industries and cultural programs, proud to be Canadians.

Perhaps our most devastating weakness, amounting to a national paranoia, is the apparent Canadian reluctance to invest in any long-term benefit with future potential. Canadian financial houses and governments have taught our entrepreneurs not to bother in Canada; the dice are loaded against them — so why not give up or sell out to an American firm and let them take over? *They* can always raise the funds in Canada. So Canadians will spend money wildly on personal goods and on imported products as long as we have a credit card, even if this helps send the country down the drain. We will gamble on Lotto Canada, Lotto Ontario, Lotto Quebec, Lotto anything, in the hope of earning a fast buck. But if asked to invest in developing the wealth or the future of Canada and to leave it invested long enough to begin earning a solid return, we are no longer listening. We are quite happy to have foreigners come in and take them over. If the government attempts to retain some Canadian control by purchase of vital resources, for instance, it is attacked at once by the private sector, which is largely foreign-owned, and Canadians themselves join in the attack.

According to a recent survey, Members of Parliament whose backgrounds are in law or business have the lowest scores in comprehension of the problems and scope of Canadian scientific research.[1] Perhaps this is why, when the government does invest in research and technology, or provide short-term backing to a Canadian development, its members begin to get restless if the enterprise doesn't begin to pay off immediately. They are afraid someone will raise it in Parliament, the media will pick it up, or the Opposition will see a chance to score a point and the government will be 'caught out' again. So, on the rare occasion when the government does support a promising new development that could not find funding in the private sector, it holds its breath, tiptoes very carefully, with one eye on the Opposition and the other on the media, and hopes the investment will pay off fast before anyone finds out about it. If it doesn't — and few really lasting ventures pay off that fast — then, snick! — it is cut off. More money has gone down the drain in Canada, not because such projects have been supported, but because they were not supported long enough to mature or because not enough capital was provided to really succeed. Canadian history is littered with this type of *'saving money.'* When you add to this the incredible inefficiency of our bureaucracy which is now so large that it is almost impossible for a problem to get from the bottom to the top and down again to whoever is really responsible (if anyone really is) you get a case like that of Trident and the Trigull.

The list of Canadian inventors and entrepreneurs who have had to sell out their inventions or their innovative products, or move to the U.S. to find financial backing, continues to grow. John Appelt recently developed a grass-hopper harvester in Saskatchewan. He tried to have it developed in Canada but the federal Department of Agriculture refused to recognize it as a legitimate machine since, he believes, "his invention would use mechanical means, not chemical sprays, to control the Prairie pests". He said: "I solidly believe that Agriculture Canada is bought and sold by the chemical companies. The grass-hopper harvester goes against the idea of chemicals."
He had to give up planned tests on a pasture; the federal government sprayed it before he could begin. The chemical companies are, of course, largely American-owned, and government departments are easily pressured by them. The federal Ministry of State for Science and Technology even lost the forms he submitted, requesting some financial aid. He was advised to take his invention south. A Montana firm replied to his inquiry within two weeks; most Canadian organizations did not even reply. He said: "I've always been a fighter. I don't give up easily, but this country has got me beat."[2] A country "empty of technology and skills"? No wonder. We not only don't help inventors, we drive them out, not merely due to lack of support, but from sheer frustration.

Philip Coulter is "still seeking support for establishment of a Canadian manufacturing plant for aerogenerators ... [but] he's not waiting for fresh air to blow through the conservative corridors of government and banking in Canada. His wind energy systems company, Winflo (Canada) Ltd., has obtained government assistance in the United States and is opening a plant that, he says, will be shipping wind-generator components back to Canada before the year's over." This entrepreneur and engineering consultant has "harsh words for private business in Canada as well as for government ... he talks bitterly about the conservatism of Canadian investors and about a lack of attention for new technology in Canada". He has obtained $240,000 in long-term, low-interest support through the New York State Business Development Corporation. "We got unbelievable co-operation from every level of government and industry down there."[3] At the same time that it is stifling entrepreneurs such as these, the government is proposing to subsidize research into energy conservation studies — under government control, of course. No wonder there is so little return for the massive funds spent by the government to artificially stimulate the very thing that they are, with the other hand, driving out of the country.

Dr Frank Maine, a chemist, was director of research at Fiberglas Canada until recently. A new kind of plastic was invented and developed by researchers at the University of Toronto and Fiberglas Canada Ltd. "But Fiberglas Canada terminated the project for what the company said were technical reasons. Mr Maine says it was scrapped because the Canadian researchers had been 'kindly invited' to stay out of the essential and lucrative U.S. market...Development of the plastic continued down south and now the U.S. companies will not export samples of this material into Canada... He was frustrated and furious that Canadians would not benefit from a Canadian invention and that a successful Canadian research and development effort ... would lose out once again to the United States. The problem, he felt, was a political one and he was 'pretty annoyed' with the country's science policy." He believes that the plastic developed in Canada "is about to hit the big time in the U.S., particularly in new-model automobiles. He quit the Fiberglas Company and ran for the Federal Parliament.[4] So, once again, our research and development, the funds invested, our patents, our innovative products and the profits they might have brought to Canada in export sales, are taken south. They make the profit and we have nothing to show. This is not unusual; it is standard practice — one further cost of our branch-plant economy.

Joseph Kates of the Science Council of Canada told the International Federation of Operational Research Societies that, if Canada fails to implement a national industrial strategy, its growing dependence on foreign technology may force the country into economic slavery within ten years. "Ten years from now, our area of choice, our capacity for self-determination and our will to resolve the problem will be further, and perhaps irretrievably, vitiated." Government and business leaders have succumbed to a "political paralysis". In the early 1970s, the government reduced expenditures on research and development and "industry, for its part, reacted to market uncertainties and to curtailment of government support by cutting back its own research and development spending." He suggests that the real problem lies in Canada's tariff policy, which has created a "fragmentation of manufacturing plants and inhibited the growth of Canadian companies." Extractive industries and branch-plant operations have proliferated, but technology-based manufacturing industries have not been encouraged. Canadian manufacturing suffers from "a lack of unique or original products to sell in world markets". He contends that until this dependence on foreign technology is overcome, it will be impossible for us even to compete in domestic markets, let alone abroad. Canada spends much less than most developed countries on research and development, and the result is a growing trade deficit in manufactured goods and increasing unemployment. "Such research and development as we do perform is carried out to a larger degree in government laboratories than is the case in many other countries, and to that extent it is effectively isolated from market exploitation ... If our policy paralysis and incremental tendencies persist, even in the near term, we will witness what has been described as the demise of secondary manufacturing in Canada and the rapid evolution from a branch-plant to a warehouse economy''. He also notes that countries like the U.S. are now proposing to ban the export of any technology financed by the government, and warns that the implications could be serious for Canada since about 80 percent of the technology we utilize in Canada flows from or through the United States.[5]

One could list indefinitely, promising ventures in Canada which died because they could find no private funding, either because the Toronto Stock Exchange would not list their share offers and no other venture capital was available, or because they got no government support or so little that the project had to close down just before it could begin to pay off. Instead of supporting our innovative entrepreneurs and producers, instead of buying and using their products, providing a showcase for them and then promoting their sale as other governments do, our government and our financiers have dropped them and disclaimed any further interest, as if they were ashamed of having dreamed of supporting them in the first place, if they even did that. At the same time, our industries are dying through lack of modern innovative technology, but our government is satisfied to buy obsolete, truncated technology from abroad through foreign-owned branch plants that are not remotely interested in building a healthy developing Canadian industrial growth or export trade. The patents and technology they hold are used by some American firms to gain a degree of control over Canadian companies by offering them the right to use them 'under license.' The technology thus purchased abroad frequently comes in a package, which may include items of no use to the Canadian firms; or restrictions on the use of the technology or on the sale of the goods produced; they may require the purchase of U.S. products or components in return for their use. All of these needless costs are, of course, added to the cost of the goods produced in Canada and sold to Canadians. In a few cases, we have gotten good value for what we paid; in many others we have not. It has been a high price to pay for a small amount of usually low-level and non-transferable technology. It would have been cheaper and more profitable for Canada to develop her own.

A few Canadian establishments and even a few foreign-controlled corporations have demonstrated what should have been the pattern of development in Canada. The National Research Council, certainly without any vast quantities of government funding for research and development, has made a number of important breakthroughs and has developed products which the U.S. had failed to develop even at far higher expenditures. But the government has seldom supported their production in Canada, therefore most of them have simple been dropped or are now being manufactured abroad — like the aerial mapping device or the first commercially successful fast freezing process for fisheries — both of which were developed in Canada.

We are often told that, if we attempted to buy back our country, it would result in a greatly lowered standard of living. In the first place, we are obviously heading in that direction precisely because we have *not* brought our major industries under our own control. The evidence as to the direction in which we are heading and as to the causes of this decline is overwhelming. Furthermore, it is not necessarily true in any case. One has only to look at the enormous profits, interest and dividends and retained earnings of our major corporations to realize the extent of the wealth that is produced in this country. It is so great that these corporations can continue to buy up more of Canadian resources and industry at an ever increasing rate, without bringing in any foreign capital at all.

Or, one could look at a successful Canadian corporation which is wholly Canadian-owned and has built up profits and exports by intensive use of its research and development facilities. Polymer Corporation was set up during the war to manufacture synthetic rubber, as no private corporation could be found in Canada that would take the risk. It built up an outstanding research capability. Following the war, it developed a wide range of diversified products both for the domestic and the export market. The value of its export sales amounted to several millions of dollars per year, before it was sold by the government in 1972 to the Canadian Development Corporation. Set up in 1942, by 1944 Polymer had already achieved a position where all subsequent growth could be financed by internal profits and commercial borrowings. It had also paid back all cash advances, paid dividends, debenture retirement, income taxes and interest, for a total of almost four times the original government investment. Its net income in 1972 was over $7 million; its net sales totalled $201 million and its retained income by the end of that year had reached $94 million.[6] It was financed, set up, staffed and operated by Canadians; Canadians developed the new technologies and products. The profits stayed in Canada and repaid the investment many times over.*

Northern Electric, now Telecom, which manufactures high-technology equipment for Bell Telephone, was formerly jointly owned by Bell and American Telephone and Telegraph of the United States. Then U.S. anti-trust action forced A.T. and T. to divest itself of its ownership. Northern Electric was cut off from the technology it received second-hand from its U.S. parent, and was forced to develop its own. As a Canadian company, owned 90 percent by Bell Canada, Northern has built up its own research and development capability and has developed many distinctive products, some of them aimed specifically at our export market, and at bringing foreign exchange revenues into Canada.[7] Canadian ownership and control is obviously profitable.

Wherever seed capital has been made available, there have been many success stories. These have returned the original investment many times over. However, when support capital has not been available, the story has been quite different. Gerald Bull was a young scientist working for the Canadian Army Research and Development Establishment (CARDE) in the 1950s; he was Chief Aerodynamicist on the 'Velvet Glove' missile project, later cancelled. On his own, he developed a hypervelocity gun which could be used for the aero-dynamic testing of missiles. Unable to get any support at CARDE — Diefenbaker, when questioned, publicly denied that any such

---

* The Canadian Development Corporation was set up by the government primarily as a means by which the government could divest itself of Polymer, in response to pressures from the business and financial community. Shares of the C.D.C. may now be bought on the market.

But Anthony Hampson, head of the CDC, has recently stated, as did Sinclair Stevens, Conservative financial critic, that Canada should continue to rely mainly on resource industries. Since its takeover by CDC, Polymer, now renamed Polysar, has not been doing very well. In view of Hampson's recent statements, it will be interesting to see what happens to Polymer's excellent RandD division. Perhaps it also threatened the U.S. owned export industry.

work was being done — Bull left for McGill. NASA in the United States had been sufficiently interested to offer him a contract. McGill then put up $200,000 to set up a firing range in the Barbados, using a U.S.-donated Navy gun. With it, Bull has been firing probes into the upper atmosphere for a very low cost compared to the normal cost per shot of $5 million, using the Explorer vehicle. Gun firings are not only cheaper, they are more accurate than multi-stage rockets. In the U.S., half a billion dollars a year is spent on this type of research. But Canadian military and civilian scientists took no interest in Bull's revolutionary idea until NASA became involved, not even to the extent of a few hundred thousand.

There has obviously been no lack of technological ability in Canada. When funds have been made available, they have paid off handsomely for Canada. When put into production by a Canadian firm as in the case of Polymer, the initial investment was paid back fourfold within two years. This indicates the magnitude of the profits that are available to U.S. branch plants. If these firms were Canadian-owned and the research and development directed by Canadians, to Canadian requirements and Canadian export markets, the flow of funds out of the country could be reversed. New plastic products developed jointly by a private company and the University of Toronto using funds generated in Canada would be put into production here and not shipped south to be produced by Fiberglas' U.S. parent, while we were "kindly invited" to stay out of this lucrative market. Not only would there be revenue earned from exports, but products now imported could be produced in Canada. By acting on our balance of payments through both imports and exports, as well as providing more high-level jobs, taxes and profits at home, we could work ourselves out of the red. We could eventually buy back our industries out of the retained earnings and profits alone. With the balance of payments deficits eliminated, it would no longer be necessary to sell off our non-renewable resources as fast as possible, as we now do, to cover the cost of our imports and foreign service costs. Furthermore, as A.V. Roe illustrated, it is possible to extend the benefits of an industry across the country to hundreds of supply industries by placing orders for the components, parts and supplies and services in Canada.

That alone could cut out imports bill by a large part of that 40 percent.

American branch plants cannot buy made-in-Canada components and services because of the policies of their parent companies. But Avro could build up Canadian suppliers from coast to coast. Our automobile industry is full of huge equipment, machines, computers, metal stampings and forgings, all with U.S. nameplates on them. The content of end products made in Canada by U.S. branch plants is largely U.S. content; but in the short space of eight years, the content of the Avro CF-100 and Orenda engine changed from 90 percent or more of foreign components to 90-to-95 percent Canadian components.

Our branch-plant economy spends only 0.35 percent of its Gross Domestic Product on research and development, and little of that is innovative or of high-technology content. Patents are registered in the name of the U.S. parent, and are not available to Canada except at a high cost. But Avro by 1958 was accounting for 70 percent of all the research and development being done in Canada; its multitude of patents for processes, design and new products were registered in Canada and were available across Canada. Many of the products developed by A.V. Roe and its member company, Canadian Applied Research Ltd., such as the process for producing special light-weight high-precision turbine blades, brought export sales and profits to Canada.

U.S. corporations don't like to share their technology, even through their branch plants, for fear it would erode their monopoly position in high technology exports, and are considering laws to prevent export of their technology. They seldom train Canadians in their more advanced methods and processes. Avro, on the contrary, helped to set up or to update companies across Canada and shared with them their precision training, methods and technology. As J. J. Brown pointed out, this stimulated "a ferment in nearly every other Canadian industry."[8] There is no ferment emanating from Canada's branch - plant manufacturing industry to - day. As Wayne Ralph and others have shown, when we scrapped the Arrow so brutally and publicly, we told the world that we were turning our

243

Less than 3 months after this annual dinner, the total Arrow Programme was cancelled.

Courtesy A.V. Roe

Orenda Iroquois Engine, Ottawa, January, 1977.

Courtesy Ken Jay

back on high technology, the research that accompanies it, our human resource base of technicians and engineers, and the scientists whom we have lost to foreign interests. We made a decision that was to impair our standard of living for decades to come, because we lost the design teams whose ideas would have resulted in a host of new products and new techniques. At Avro, their research ideas, developments, processes, new products and patents had not been restricted by a foreign parent company, nor sent out of the country to be exploited in the U.S.; they had been available to everyone in Canada who could use them. According to Jan Zurakowski, not only the Arrow and everything connected with it were reduced to scrap, but millions of dollars worth of research equipment and the accumulated data was destroyed.* But this is of no importance in Canada, or to Canadian governments. We can always buy technology, or its costly products, from the United States — at a price![9]

Our government has spent millions in trying to promote national unity. In their travels across the country, special commissions have been amazed to find that people everywhere were more concerned about the state of the economy, and the lack of Canadian leadership. The government apparently fails to realize that national unity requires a common purpose, and a common loyalty. It also requires a degree of confidence in the leadership of a country and a concern on the part of those leaders to make that country worth caring about. But, regardless of the party in power, the establishment, with which all governments are willing to collaborate, is less concerned about the future of Canada as a country than about the security of their investments and their positions of power. If these can best be served by strengthening their American contacts and letting them take over the country, so be it. To listen to the advice emanating from the C.D. Howe Institute, the Economic Council of Canada, our economists, most of them followers of economist Harry Johnson of Chicago, academics and government spokesmen, one could almost believe that there is a well-organized and persistent public relations campaign to persuade Canadians to give up and sell out to the United States. As a matter of fact, we have already done so in many areas of our national life.

---

*As he says, for a cost of one or two percent of the money already spent on research, the accumulated knowledge could have been properly compiled and documented for useful future work.

When Thomas Symons, as Chairman of the Commission on Canadian studies, crossed the country in 1972, he found that "the first task of the Commission was to suggest that it was important for a reasonable amount of attention to be devoted to their own country by Canadians." He later said: "I would have thought it should be reasonably clear that a society, like an individual, needs to know itself and its place in the context of the world. [But] we found there was a tremendous doubt as to whether it was *academically appropriate,* or *worthwhile* or *legitimate* or *dignified* for scholars or teachers to pay attention to Canadian questions. [Italics added] [10]

How can we "know ourselves and our place in the context of the world," when to know it is to realize that we are not a free and independent country in charge of its own destiny, with leaders who are interested in promoting its growth and independence, but a satellite whose leaders are content to sell out the country as fast as they can and who are content to abdicate their responsibility and capacity for independent leadership in return for a half-dozen directorships on the boards of foreign-owned corporations when they retire?

Do our Canadian academics denigrate Canadian history because they wish to appear more 'sophisticated' in the company of their American friends, or are they contemptuous of everything Canadian because so many of them are non-Canadian, because our text books, even for Grade I, are written and published by foreigners? Or is it due to some perverted inferiority complex?

Our so-called elite, including many of our academics, tell us that 'nationalism' is a childish and naive luxury that we should outgrow. But all strong nations base their cosmopolitanism on a deep pride in their own history and achievements. We are told by our economists that "ownership isn't important" as long as we are given jobs. But James Conrad of the Committee for an Independent Canada calls that the "grateful servant syndrome"; we are grateful if anyone merely provides us with a job, "even if it's just as a servant — even when it's in our own house." "It's as if we had 100 acres and every spring we sold an acre and called it income" until it was all gone. [11]

When we first read George Grant's *Lament for a Nation,* [12] we were appalled by his pessimism, but now we are not so sure. Perhaps Allan Blakeney should not have been 'depressed' that no one listened to what he thought was "a self-evident proposition." He should have remembered what happened to Herb Gray, Eric Kierans, Walter Gordon and the many others who have really cared about our country and where it is going. Canada is already the weakest federation in the world. But with no strong leadership or direction at the centre, the provinces have been steadily eroding more and more of the powers which should be exercised by the federal government. As a result, the central government can no longer control the economy, the money supply, or foreign takeovers, even if it would. It has abdicated both its powers and its responsibility to use them in Canada's interest. And almost all the provinces, from Alberta to Ontario and Quebec and even the Maritimes, would sell out even faster than the federal government would if that were possible. In concentrating on the constitution in its search for national unity, the government has missed the point. National unity? Under what flag?

As Jan Zurakowski, the award-winning test pilot who first flew the Arrow, recalls the destruction of everything connected with that great plane, he implies that other interests were also involved. "There was a common impression at the time," he says, "that politicians wanted all tangible evidence rubbed out to prevent it returning to haunt them in later years ...Canada, by creating its own industry, could have satisfied most defense requirements — but not the American industrialists who wanted the market ... Diefenbaker and Defense Minister Pearkes were blinded by the salesmanship of people whose vested interests lay in seeing Canada's aircraft industry die."[13] And so it did, except for small transport aircraft, and aircraft manufactured under license or merely modified from U.S. designs. But the Americans alone could not have done it; it had to be done by Canadians.

1 Dotto, Lydia, *Globe & Mail*, Toronto, Feb. 20, 1978
2 *Globe & Mail*, Toronto, Oct. 25, 1978
3 Marshall, John, *ibid.*, Sept. 26, 1978
4 *Globe & Mail*, Toronto, April 18, 1977
5 Stevens, Robert, *ibid.*, June 21, 1978
6 Polysar Ltd., *Annual Report*, 1972
7 Carruthers, Jeff, "The Innovation Issue,"
   Report on Confederation, May, 1978, pp. 27-9
8 Brown, J.J., *Ideas in Exile*, McClelland & Stewart, Toronto, 1967, p. 312
9 *Leader*, Eganville, Ont., Aug. 30, 1978
10 Symons, T.H.B., *To Know Ourselves*, Report of the Commission on Canadian Studies, Association of Universities and Colleges of Canada, Ottawa, 1976
11 Webster, Norman, "A House with Soft Master," *Globe & Mail*, Toronto, April 7, 1978
12 Grant, George, *Lament For a Nation,* Toronto, MacMillan, 1970
13 *Leader,* Eganville, Ont. *loc. cit.*

Jan Zurakowski the experimental test pilot for Avro Arrow.

Courtesy Jan Zurakowski

APPENDICES

APPENDIX I

OTTAWA ONT FEB 20/59 1148AME

Orenda Engines Ltd*

Attn. E K Brownbridge, Vice-President & Genl Manager take notice that your contracts bearing the reference numbers set out below including all amendments thereto are hereby terminated as regards all supplies and services which have not been completed and shipped or performed thereunder prior to the receipt by *you of this notice stop you shall cease all work immediately, terminate subcontracts and orders, place no further subcontracts or orders and instruct all your subcontractors and suppliers to take similar action stop* you are requested to submit to the Department of Defence Production, Ottawa, Ontario for consideration, any claim which you may have as a result of this termination stop such claim and those of your subcontractors and suppliers, if any, are to be submitted on the prescribed departmental termination claim forms stop on receipt of this notice, you should make application in writing to the chief settlement officer, Department of Defence Production, Ottawa, for the requisite set of forms stop your claim and all correspondence concerning it should be addressed to Mr. D.B. Wallace, Chief Settlement Officer, Department of Defence Production stop reference numbers of terminated contracts: BD69-12-88 SERIAL 2-B-4-717; BD69-12-88/2 SERIAL 2-B-5-846; BD 18-36-75 SERIAL 2-B-5-585, BD18-26-74 SERIAL 2-B-5-263; BD 18-26-74/2 SERIAL 2-1B-7-1484; BD18-36-74/A6 SERIAL 2-B-7-1015; 4-7-02/2 SERIAL 1-B-6-12; 4-7-02-1/2 SERIAL 1-B-6-23; 4-7-02/2/2 SERIAL 1-B-6-13 stop ends. (Emphasis added)

D B Thompson Dept. Defence Production

CNT TN004 91/74 RX

DP TLX OTTAWA ONT FEB 20/59 1148 AME

Orenda Engines Ltd.

Attn E K Brownridge, Vice-president & Genl. Manager you are hereby authorized to cease immediately all purchasing or other acquisition and installation of the capital equipment listed in schedule. "A" to the PS-13 capital equipment agreement dated July 31, 1955, as amended, bearing reference B.69-12-88; CD DR2/AIR/DEV/109 stop take notice that the cost of any capital equipment purchased subsequent to the receipt by you of this notice shall not be subject to reimbursement under section 4 of the said agreement stop ends.

D L Thompson Dept. Defence Production.

"A" PS-13 31, 1955 P.69-12-88 of DRB/AIR/DEV/109 4 last ends RPT ends 1220 PME.

---

* A similar telegram was simultaneously delivered to Avro Aircraft, Attn. J.L. Plant. The reference numbers of the terminated contracts covered the pre-production contracts for 37 aircraft and the development and test programmes.

APPENDIX II

Canadian Aviation, November 1958, had an article entitled 'Shelving the Arrow is bad military, economic medicine — West's most advanced interceptor may be last token of Canadian political and technological independence'. In this article it gives further comparisons of the capabilities of the Arrow as compared to other (American) defence weapons. (Note that all the weapons mentioned are effective only against the 'manned bomber', precisely the same threat which Mr. Diefenbaker and Mr. Pearkes said no longer existed to justify the Arrow. Yet these were the weapons we were then buying or considering.)

"Ceiling — Bomarc —up to 100,000 ft. (some figures quote 75,000 ft.)

 — "Arrow — well above 60,000 ft. plus the height of missiles fired from the plane at this height" (new ones will have a range of 6 miles). "It thereby matches the Bomarc's kill altitude." The Arrow, in addition, carries up 6 to 8 missles on each flight and can bring them back if not used.

"Speed — Bomarc — about 2,000 miles an hour". It cannot however, be launched until the target has been identified, course plotted, and decision taken to destroy the target, Once fired, this cannot be altered, new factors allowed for, or the Bomarc recalled. Its gear can be jammed by enemy counter-measures.

 — "Arrow —without operational engines, has already climbed at 1000 miles per hour" (it actually climbed at just under 1400 m.p.h. and was not full out). "With Iroquois engines, it is expected to reach 2,000 m.p.h. It has proven capable of achieving more speed than any other airframe design for any comparable amount of power available".

Further, it can take off at once, can receive course plottings while climbing, can identify, make decisions, change course, and think its own battle. It can then fire its missles, or bring them home along with itself. The Bomarc does not come back.

Another important factor, seldom mentioned, is the 'rate of climb'. That of the Arrow is very high, compared to other planes — i.e. it can get up there faster. This was also true of the CF100, even though a much heavier plane than similar American planes.

"Range — Bomarc — most advanced version — about 400 miles". (Others, about 250).

— "Arrow —conservatively estimated at about 1500 miles" As with all aircraft, even the F108, these figures, as well as maximum speed, vary greatly with the type of mission being flown. Other sources have put the Arrow range at more nearly 1000 miles, the same figure which has been given for the F108's expected range. In any case, it far exceeds the figures given by Mr. Diefenbaker to Parliament, which were ridiculous. "It can, moreover, attack more than one target on each flight. Each of its 6 to 8 missiles is capable of killing an intruder. In the North American defence concept, margin of range is critical".

The Arrow has been designed to operate either 'with or without Sage (ground control radar). It can operate quite independently of it. It can also be phased into it if required. Mr. Pearkes has been well-informed of this, but continues to state the opposite.

Canadian aviation went on to say:

"The most critical phase of our type of defence in the current cold war, (i.e.) denying the enemy the advantage of surprise, is a constant watch as to whether an attack is actually taking place. *Radar systems and missiles cannot tell us this.* The most critical phase of the watching must be carried out by manned aircraft with the ability to intercept the unknowns and make positive identification. Until the interception and identification have been completed, missiles and bombers must remain in tactical and strategic reserve."

As to other fighters —

"The CF105 has been widely recognized as the most advanced interceptor in the free world at its present stage of development. The belief that the U.S. has an aircraft with the performance capabilities of the CF105 presently in production, *is erroneous.* The F106, the latest of the American Century series now in production, has been singled out in a number of reports and commentaries following the Prime Minister's speech, as comparable to the CF105, and available to Canada. *This is not the case."*

"The F106 is a single-seater, single-engine plane, therefore lacking the twin-engined CF105's margin of safety for long patrols over isolated areas which are the everyday duty of Air Defence Command squadrons."

"The CF105 with the same amount of armament as the F106, is far above the range of the F106. Operating at the same range, it can carry much greater fire-power. It has a much greater itercept and kill capacity. With two more powerful engines than the F106's one, *it is much superior.* The F106 *was not* designed for and *cannot* fill Norad's requirements for a long-range interceptor."

"That Norad's chiefs and defence planners *are still seeking a plane similar* to the CF105 is proved by the development work now begun in the U.S. on the F108, a twin-engine, two-man interceptor. It is still in design and engineering stage, therefore three or four years away from production, and *several more years away from operational service.* The CF105 would be available for squadron service in 1960."

APPENDIX III

COMPARATIVE STATISTICS: The Arrow and planes purchased by the Canadian Government since 1959.

Statistics provided to Mr. Greig Stewart by the RCAF, courtesy of Captain T. Kennedy, Information Officer, CFB, Downsview and made available to the author.

	ARROW CF-105	CANUCK CF-100	ORENDA SABRE CF-86	STAR-FIGHTER CF-104	VOODOO CF-101-B	FREEDOM FIGHTER CF-5
Length	77' 9"	54' 2"	37' 5"	58' 3"	71' 1"	47' 2"
Span	50' 0"	57' 5"	37' 1"	21' 11"	39' 8"	25' 8"
Height	14' 6" (canopy)	10' 3"	14' 7"	13' 6"	18' 0"	13' 2"
Weight	30 tons maximum	20 tons	8 tons	13.5 tons	25 tons	10 tons
Speed mph	1600 + (est) 1200 mph cruise	575 max. 450 cruise	671 max.	1500 max.	1200 max. 525 cruise	1100 max.
Power	Twin Iroquois 22,000 lbs. thrust ea.	Twin Orendas (7,200 lbs. thrust ea.)	1 Orenda 7,200 lbs. thrust	1 J-79 15,000 lbs. thrust	Two P & W J-57 16,000 lbs. thrust ea.	Two J-85 4,300 lbs. thrust ea.
Armament	Rockets	Cannons Rockets	Cannons or Machine-guns	Cannons Bombs	Cannons (X) Rockets Bombs (X)	Cannons Rockets Bombs
Range	1500 mi. plus	1200 mi. (plus)	1000 mi.	1200 mi.	1200 mi.	1000 mi.
Ceiling	75,000'	45,000'	40,000'	55,000'	50,000'	45,000'
Cost	$3.5m (100) $2.6m (200)	$550,000	$1 million	$1.5 million (plus)	$1.5 million	$1.2 million (to $2m)

Some of the above data, especially as to armament, range and cost, is at variance with other sources. It does, however, provide a fair basis for comparison.

"Intelligence Schism." from *Aviation Week,* March 2, 1959. p. 26.

OTTAWA — Variance in Canadian government's interpretation of intelligence on the Soviet bomber potential and that of the U.S. government, apparently from the same information, became apparent during House of Commons debate on the cancellation of Mach 3 CF-105 interceptor. Minister of National Defense G.R. Pearkes said:

> All of the information we can get from the sources available to the government indicates that the threat of the manned bomber against this country is diminishing.

At another point, Pearkes told Commons that "the indication has been that the Russians are not continuing the production of any type of bomber more advanced than that known by the code names of the Bear and the Bison, and that the number of Bear and Bison aircraft in the Russian inventory is extremely limited and, furthermore, that these are the only two types of Soviet bomber which could reach this country and return again."

The Defense Minister also challenged a statement by an opposition Member of Parliament that military observers recently said that the Russians in the mid-1960s would still have an inventory of 1,000 to 2,000 bombers capable of striking Canada in addition to its inventory of intercontinental ballistic missiles.

Pearkes replied that the statement "must not be taken as indicating that these 2,000 bombers could reach this continent or that more than a small fraction of that number could even make the return flight even if they were unopposed."

U.S. military intelligence has reported that the Russians now have under development a supersonic bomber code-named the Bounder. While USAF in 1957 revised downward its estimates of Soviet production of the Bison jet bomber after it became evident to the Russians that the aircraft would have difficulty in performing an intercontinental mission, there has been little serious suggestion that the manned bomber threat has diminished. Development of the Bounder apparently was designed to provide an effective replacement for the Bison.

Details and initial test flights of a prototype of a Soviet

nuclear powered aircraft were first reported by *Aviation Week* in an exclusive story last Dec. 1. (p. 27).

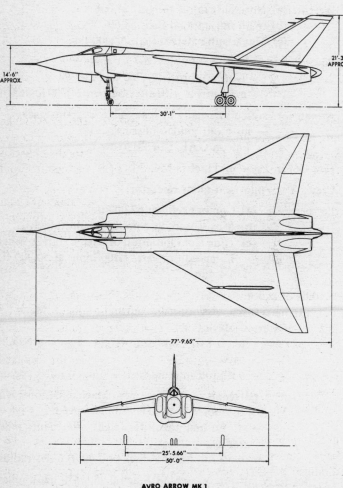

14'-6"
APPROX.

21'-3"
APPROX.

30'-1"

77'-9.65"

25'-5.66"
50'-0"

AVRO ARROW MK 1

ARROW Mark I: Design and performance data.

Sources: various published articles, models, personal contacts
   and experience.

Size: Span: 50' 0"
   Length: 77' 10" approx.
   Height: 14' 6" approx. at canopy; 21' 3" approx. at tail.

Weight: (a) Normal take-off weight: 51,048 lbs.
   (b) With full internal fuel: 58,600 lbs.
   (c) Max., with external fuel: 62,400 lbs.

Power plant: 2 Pratt & Whitney J67 jet engines.
   — Normal thrust: 11,700 lbs. each.
   — max. thrust with after-burner: 21,500 lbs. each.

Armament: stored internally in removable weapons pack;
   — air-to-air guided missiles:
      Falcon GAR 1 or Sparrow 2.

Fire Control system: Hughes MG-3

Crew: Two, pilot and radar operator.

Performance: (a) Combat ceiling: 62,000 ft.
   (b) Max. speed, at combat weight: Mach 2.
   (c) Time from initiation of engine start to Mach
      1.5 speed (approx. 1,100 mph) at 50,000 ft.:
      4.4 min.

Radius of action:
   (a) max. speed mission: cruise out and combat at Mach 1.5,
      return at Mach 0.95:
         — at normal take-off weight: 200 naut. miles
            radius;
         — with full internal fuel: 430 naut. miles radius.

   (b) max. range mission: cruise out at Mach 0.95, combat at
      Mach 1.5, return at max. endurance speed:
         — at normal take-off weight: 300 naut. miles
            radius;
         — with full internal fuel: 650 naut. miles radius.

   (c) ferry mission: cruises at Mach 0.95: 1870 naut. miles.

Turn-around time (on the ground): to refuel, change armament
  pack and replenish oxygen: 10 min.

Notes: (a) 1 naut. mile = 1.1516 statute miles, i.e., the radius of
  action for the max. speed mission with full internal
  fuel = 430 naut. miles or 495 **Statute miles.**

  (b) Mach number represents speed relative to the speed
  of sound. Mach 1 is the speed of sound in air, which is
  approx. 767 mph at 59°F at sea level. Therefore max.
  speed of the Arrow Mark 1 was estimated to be 1,500
  to 1,600 mph (statute miles), true ground speed.

  (c) Performance given above relates to the Mark I Arrow
  equipped with the interim U.S. Pratt & Whitney J-67
  engines.
  The Mark II Arrow, equipped with the Avro Iroquois engine was expected to reach a speed of 2,000
  mph, or Mach 3.

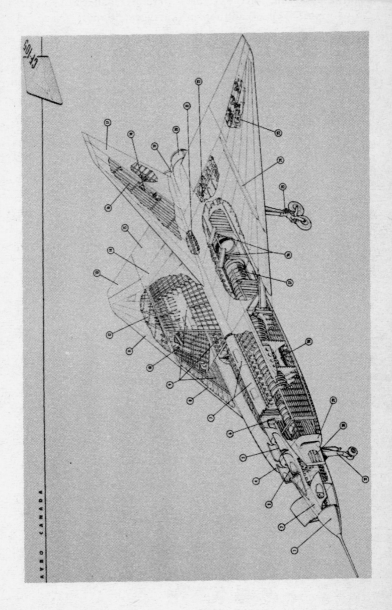

LEGEND

(1) Radome and Probe.

(2) Nose Electronics Compartment.

(3) Pilot's Cockpit.

(4) R. H. Engine Intake.

(5) Radar Operator's Cockpit.

(6) Air Conditioning Equipment.

(7) Fuselage Fuel Tanks.

(8) Inner Wing Leading Edge.

(9) Wing Fuel Tanks.

(10) Main Landing Gear Bay.

(11) Outer Wing Leading Edge.

(12) Outer Wing Section.

(13) R. H. Aileron.

(14) Inner Wing Trailing Edge.

(15) R. H. Elevator.

(16) Fin.

(17) Rudder.

(18) Rudder Operating Hydraulic Jack and Control Linkage.

(19) Landing Parachute Stowage.

(20) Engine Afterburner Nozzles.

(21) Fin/Wing Lap Joint.

(22) L. H. Elevator Control Linkage.

(23) L. H. Aileron Hydraulic Jack and Control Linkage.

(24) Inner/Outer Wing Joint Fairing.

(25) Main Landing Gear.

(26) Fuselage Frame/Wing Pin Joints.

(27) L. H. Engine Intake Duct.

(28) Armament Bay.

(29) L. H. Engine Intake.

(30) L. H. Engine Intake Ramp.

(31) Nose Landing Gear.

Index